Lecture Notes in Artificial Intelligence   9002

Subseries of Lecture Notes in Computer Science

More information about this series at http://www.springer.com/series/1244

Francisco Grimaldo · Emma Norling (Eds.)

Multi-Agent-Based Simulation XV

International Workshop, MABS 2014
Paris, France, May 5–6, 2014
Revised Selected Papers

 Springer

Editors
Francisco Grimaldo
Universitat de València
Burjassot-València
Spain

Emma Norling
Manchester Metropolitan University
Manchester
UK

ISSN 0302-9743   ISSN 1611-3349 (electronic)
Lecture Notes in Artificial Intelligence
ISBN 978-3-319-14626-3   ISBN 978-3-319-14627-0 (eBook)
DOI 10.1007/978-3-319-14627-0

Library of Congress Control Number: 2014959825

LNCS Sublibrary: SL7 – Artificial Intelligence

Springer Cham Heidelberg New York Dordrecht London

Printed on acid-free paper

Springer International Publishing AG Switzerland is part of Springer Science+Business Media
(www.springer.com)

Preface

The long-standing goal of the MABS workshop series has been to bring together researchers from multi-agent systems engineering and the social, economic, and organizational sciences, and this volume represents the 15th in this series. It is based on papers accepted for the 15th International Workshop on Multi-Agent-Based Simulation (MABS 2014), which was held in conjunction with the Autonomous Agents and Multi-Agent Systems conference (AAMAS) in Paris, May 2014. The papers presented at the workshop were extended, revised, and re-reviewed, incorporating points from the discussions held at the workshop with their original ideas.

Forty-four papers were submitted to the workshop, of which 18 were accepted for presentation, an acceptance rate of approximately 40 %. The authors of these papers work in institutions around the world, from 19 different countries. In addition to the paper presentations, this year for the first time, the workshop incorporated a tutorial session. This session was co-presented by Rob Axtell and Scott Moss, and provided food for thought both for newcomers to the field and for experienced researchers in this area. This tutorial generated much discussion, allowed airing of different perspectives, and, we believe, helped to stimulate the discussions around the papers that were presented later in the workshop. As in previous years, the workshop attracted a large number of participants above and beyond those who presented papers, and indeed the room that was originally allocated to the workshop proved to be too small. We apologize to anyone who tried to attend the first session of the workshop but was unable to get into the room.

The workshop could not have taken place without the contributions of many people. We would like to express our gratitude to Rob Axtell and Scott Moss for the stimulating tutorial, and to all the members of the Program Committee, who reviewed papers before the workshop, and then again for these post-proceedings. Thanks are also due to Rafael Bordini and José M. Vidal (AAMAS 2014 workshop chairs), to Ana Bazzan and Michael Huhns (AAMAS 2014 General Chairs), to Alessio Lomuscio and Paul Scerri (AAMAS 2014 Program Chairs), and to Amal El Fallah Seghrouchni (AAMAS 2014 Local Arrangements Chair).

September 2014

Francisco Grimaldo
Emma Norling

Organization

General and Program Chairs

Francisco Grimaldo	Universitat de València, Spain
Emma Norling	Manchester Metropolitan University, UK

MABS Steering Committee

Frédéric Amblard	University of Toulouse, France
Luis Antunes	University of Lisbon, Portugal
Rosaria Conte	ISTC-National Research Council, Italy
Paul Davidsson	Malm University, Sweden
Nigel Gilbert	University of Surrey, UK
Scott Moss	University of Koblenz-Landau, Germany
Keith Sawyer	University of North Carolina, USA
Jaime Simão Sichman	University of São Paulo, Brazil
Keiki Takadama	University of Electro-Communications, Japan

Program Committee

Shah Jamal Alam	University of Edinburgh, UK
Frédéric Amblard	University of Toulouse, France
Luis Antunes	University of Lisbon, Portugal
Joao Balsa	University of Lisbon, Portugal
Melania Borit	University of Tromsø, Norway
Tibor Bosse	Vrije Universiteit Amsterdam, The Netherlands
Cristiano Castelfranchi	ISTC-National Research Council, Italy
Shu-Heng Chen	National Chengchi University, Taiwan
Sung-Bae Cho	Yonsei University, South Korea
Helder Coelho	University of Lisbon, Portugal
Gennaro Di Tosto	Utrecht University, The Netherlands
Frank Dignum	Utrecht University, The Netherlands
Virginia Dignum	TU Delft, The Netherlands
Alexis Drogoul	IRD, Vietnam
Bruce Edmonds	Manchester Metropolitan University, UK
Andreas Ernst	University of Kassel, Germany
Jos Manuel Galn	University of Burgos, Spain
Francesca Giardini	ISTC-National Research Council, Italy
Nigel Gilbert	University of Surrey, UK
Nick Gotts	James Hutton Institute, UK
William Griffin	Arizona State University, USA

Francisco Grimaldo   Universitat de València, Spain
Alejandro Guerra-Hernndez   Universidad Veracruzana, Mexico
Laszlo Gulyas   AITIA International, Inc., Hungary
Rainer Hegselmann   University of Bayreuth, Germany
Marco Janssen   Arizona State University, USA
Bill Kennedy   George Mason University, USA
Satoshi Kurihara   Osaka University, Japan
Ulf Lotzmann   University of Koblenz-Landau, Germany
Ruth Meyer   Manchester Metropolitan University, UK
John Murphy   Argonne National Laboratory, USA
Emma Norling   Manchester Metropolitan University, UK
Michael North   Argonne National Laboratory, USA
Paulo Novais   University of Minho, Portugal
Nardine Osman   IIIA-National Research Council, Spain
Mario Paolucci   ISTC-National Research Council, Italy
H. Van Dyke Parunak   Soar Technology, USA
Juan Pavn   Universidad Complutense de Madrid, Spain
William Rand   University of Maryland, USA
Jaime Simo Sichman   University of São Paulo, Brazil
Liz Sonenberg   Melbourne University, Australia
Flaminio Squazzoni   University of Brescia, Italy
Keiki Takadama   Tokyo Institute of Technology, Japan
Takao Terano   Tokyo Institute of Technology, Japan
Klaus G. Troitzsch   University of Koblenz-Landau, Germany
Arlette Van Wissen   Utrecht University, The Netherlands

Additional Reviewers

Jeroen de Man   Vrije Universiteit Amsterdam, The Netherlands
Efrén Mendoza-Montes   Universidad Veracruzana, Mexico
Stefano Picascia   Manchester Metropolitan University, UK

Contents

Applications

Simulation Methodologies

Event-Driven Multi-agent Simulation

Ruth Meyer$^{(\boxtimes)}$

Centre for Policy Modelling, Manchester Metropolitan University, Oxford Road,
Manchester M15 6BH, UK
r.meyer@mmu.ac.uk

Abstract. Most agent-based models today apply a time-driven approach, i.e. simulation time is advanced in equidistant steps. This time advance method is considerably easier to implement than the more flexible and efficient event-driven approach.

Applying the event-driven approach requires that (a) the durations for agent and environment actions are determined before they terminate, (b) each agent is able to instantly react to changes in its environment, and (c) the update of the state of the environment can be kept efficient despite updating agents asynchronously.

The simulation toolkit FAMOS fulfils these requirements, extending an existing discrete-event simulator. The toolkit also supports a flexible representation of space and the movement of agents in that space. These are areas where existing toolkits for agent-based modelling show shortcomings, despite the fact that a majority of multi-agent models explicitly model space and allow for mobile agents.

Keywords: Event-driven time advance · Discrete event simulation · Agent-based simulation · Spatially explicit agent-based model

1 Introduction

The last ten years have seen a surge in agent-based simulation models. Several disciplines have since adopted the multi-agent approach as a new paradigm for undertaking research; amongst them the social sciences [11], economics [36], geography [15] and ecology [14]. Across disciplines, agent-based models are applied to investigate complex systems [10]. One of the main reasons for this expansion is the availability of software toolkits, which support agent-based modelling and simulation well enough to make the approach attractive for domain experts in a variety of application areas [33].

Agent-based simulation views the system to be modelled as a multi-agent system, i.e. as consisting of autonomous agents interacting in and with an environment. To build an agent-based model a modeller has to specify both the structure of the model and its dynamic behaviour over time. Simulation toolkits therefore need to provide constructs to implement a set of agents, their relationships, which influence their interactions, and their joint environment, which may be spatially explicit and contain dynamic processes in addition to the agents.

© Springer International Publishing Switzerland 2015
F. Grimaldo and E. Norling (Eds.): MABS 2014, LNAI 9002, pp. 3–16, 2015.
DOI: 10.1007/978-3-319-14627-0_1

For the description of the dynamic behaviour the actions of agents and, if necessary, the environment have to be related to simulation time. There are several ways to do this. Most widely used is the time-driven approach [26], which divides simulation time into regular intervals (time steps) and updates all agents synchronously at every time step. The modeller needs to identify the agents' actions and specify the order in which they are to be executed at each time step (see e.g. [14], p. 111). Another approach is the event-driven time advance, which combines irregular time intervals with an asynchronous update of agents (see Sect. 2).

The predominance of the time-driven approach can be explained from both its ease of implementation with regard to the simulation infrastructure – no dedicated scheduler and event list are necessary – and its simplification of modelling the agents' behaviour, since all actions implicitly obtain a duration ($\leq \Delta t$, the length of the fixed time step) and a modeller only has to specify the order of actions occurring during the same time step. Tutorials for existing software toolkits and introductory textbooks consolidate the use of the time-driven approach in their example models (see e.g. [13, 23, 25, 27, 28]).

Moreover, an analysis of existing toolkits for agent-based simulation shows that toolkits that allow for an event-driven time advance like Repast [29], Swarm [27] or James II [16] offer little or no support for the implementation of agents and environment, whereas toolkits with such functionality like NetLogo [41], SeSam [18] or Jason [7] tend to constrain model execution to the time-driven approach. This indicates that "there is a gap in the current design space for a toolkit which both provides/prescribes some structure for implementing agents but also provides a full Discrete Event scheduling implementation for the model's execution" ([37], p. 85).

Thus, agent-based models using an event-driven approach are still rare (examples are [38] and [22]), even though this approach has been tried and tested for decades in traditional discrete-event simulation (see e.g. [2, 21]).

In the following, we first discuss the advantages of an event-driven time advance (Sect. 2) before introducing a toolkit for multi-agent simulation that applies this approach (Sect. 3). Two example models, a re-implementation of Schelling's famous segregation model (Sect. 4) and the model of a city courier service (Sect. 5), demonstrate key features of this toolkit. The paper finishes with a discussion (Sect. 6) and conclusion (Sect. 7).

2   The Case for Event-Driven Time Advance

In the event-driven approach simulation time advances from one event to the next. Each event models a change in the system, e.g. an agent receiving a message or arriving at a particular location in space. The intervals between events can be of any length as they are determined by the processes occurring in the system. The state of the system is assumed constant between events.

There are several reasons to adopt an event-driven time advance in agent-based models. Firstly, this approach is more efficient than the time-driven approach, since it regards only those points in time when changes actually occur and skips inactive phases of the system. In addition, only entities affected by the current event have to be updated. Secondly, it is more accurate as it allows events to occur at the correct time whereas the time-driven approach "collects" all events occurring within one time step and treats them as if they are happening at the same time, i.e. the end of the fixed time interval. Thirdly, this leads to it being more flexible, since it can accommodate a heterogeneous discretisation of time (e.g. periods of time with many events happening close together interspersed with periods where only a few events occur) as well as agents operating on different time scales.

While for many systems a time-driven simulation is well suited or at least adequate, other systems require a correct mapping of events to points in simulation time. Examples can be found in different application domains, from competition over particular habitats in ecology (e.g. [14], p. 112) to chemical reactions ([3], p. 26ff) to financial markets ([6,8,17]). A time-driven approach would either falsify results due to treating consecutive events as happening simultaneously if the fixed time interval Δt is too big, or would be very inefficient because Δt has to be chosen as the smallest interval between two events. The latter introduces the additional problem that this interval is often not known beforehand so that several simulation runs are required to determine it. Since a time-driven approach can easily be mapped to an event-driven approach, the event-driven time advance allows for the simulation of a more comprehensive class of models.

In addition, it can be argued that the fixed clock rate and synchronous agent update of the time-driven approach defies the concept of autonomy that underlies the definition of agents in multi-agent systems: "Forcing all agents of the MAS to act in lock step does not fit with autonomy of agents" ([40], p. 177). An event-driven approach is more suitable as it does not a priori impose synchronisation on agents ([4], p. 269). Social processes in particular are rarely synchronous, which is why it is equally rarely appropriate to model them by updating agents synchronously once per time step ([1], p. 41).

3   A Framework for Event-Driven Multi-agent Simulations

The Framework for Agent-oriented Modelling and Simulation (FAMOS[1]) combines multi-agent simulation with an event-driven time advance and an explicit representation of space. A comparison with existing agent-based simulation toolkits poses the question how necessary a new toolkit could be. Several ABMS toolkits contain a discrete-event scheduler within their features; the most widely used are Swarm [27], Mason [24] and Repast [29] or Repast Simphony [28]. Using the event-driven approach in agent-based models is therefore possible. We would like to argue though, that it is not sufficient to provide the necessary simulation infrastructure. Its use also has to be adequately supported and here current simulation toolkits are lacking.

On the one hand, their documentation focusses on how to implement time-driven models (see e.g. [27], p. 3; [23], p. 16f; [28], p. 18ff). On the other hand,

---

[1] Available at http://famos.sourceforge.net.

the constructs they provide to model agent behaviour, environment including space, and interactions between agents and environment have not been adapted to the requirements of an event-driven time advance. These requirements include

1. determining the duration of actions so that the respective termination event can be scheduled in time;
2. enabling each agent to instantly react to changes in its environment, even though it is technically passive during time-consuming phases;
3. ensuring an efficient update of the environment state (which may include the current positions of mobile agents) despite updating agents asynchronously.

The toolkit FAMOS presented in this paper addresses these requirements. It supports event-driven multi-agent simulation appropriately by not only providing the necessary simulation infrastructure but also dedicated constructs for modelling agent behaviour and spatially explicit environments that have been adapted for use with an event-driven time advance.

3.1 Modelling Time

To avoid re-inventing the wheel, FAMOS builds on an existing discrete-event simulation framework and extends it with multi-agent simulation features. DESMO-J[2] ([31], ch. 10) is an open-source software development framework for discrete-event simulation and supports two of the classical world views: event scheduling and process interaction. In addition to directly re-using DESMO-J's simulation infrastructure (scheduler, event list, simulation clock), agent-based models in FAMOS can use entities and event routines or simulation processes to model any dynamic behaviour of the environment that is not related to agents, e.g. renewable resources.

The requirements imposed by the event-driven time advance are addressed as follows:

1. The durations of model-independent actions like sensing the environment, manipulation of objects in the environment, sending messages or moving in space, which FAMOS provides, are determined automatically. In the current version of the framework, all actions are assumed to be instantaneous except for movement. The duration of a move is calculated from the current speed of the agent and the distance covered, which in turn is calculated by the space model. For model-specific actions that are not provided by FAMOS a modeller may use the stochastic distributions of the underlying simulation framework DESMO-J to determine durations.
2. To guarantee that each agent can instantly react to changes in its environment FAMOS lets the environment send all agents that are affected by the change a special notification signal, i.e. those agents in whose area of perception (defined by an agent-specific sensor range) the change occurred. This signal causes an agent to automatically be scheduled for re-activation so that it can interrupt its current, simulation-time consuming action and decide itself if and how it wants to react to the change.

---

[2] Available at http://desmoj.sourceforge.net.

3. Discrete-event simulation links all state changes to instantaneous events with no changes happening between events. Time-consuming actions have to be mapped to a series of events (at least start and end); their effect usually happens at the end event. In FAMOS this only poses a problem for the movement of agents as the current positions of mobile agents may become too inexact when they are updated at the end of a longer movement process. To be able to keep positions of mobile agents exact enough while avoiding an update of the environment every time before an agent might access it, longer movements across several cells or nodes are divided into small steps that are regarded as atomic transactions. An atomic step is defined as the movement between adjacent cells in a grid or adjacent nodes in a graph. The change of position is visible in the environment whenever an agent has crossed the border between two grid cells or has passed the first half of the edge between two nodes. Its event time is calculated automatically. The moving agent is re-activated after each step by receiving a notification from the environment, which enables it to review its situation and adapt its movement accordingly if need be.

This adaptation of movement to the requirements of the event-driven approach is encapsulated in a particular `Movement` component. Its method `move()` provides agents with the ability to move in space by automatically calculating the duration of the move and scheduling a respective re-activation event. The component can be adapted to model-specific needs by choosing or implementing a particular movement strategy, which is in charge of determining the next position to move to. Pre-defined strategies are walking randomly (`RandomWalk`), following a gradient (`GradientTrace`), moving in a given direction (`MoveInDirection`) and following a planned route (`MoveAlongPath`).

This support of an agent's movement exceeds the functionality of comparable simulation toolkits, where a modeller has to combine primitive commands (delete at current position, add at new position, update agent coordinates) to achieve a change of position ([32], p. 614).

3.2 Modelling Space

The flexible, discrete space representation is another of FAMOS's fortes. It combines the prevalent grids of agent-based models with directed graphs by using the fact that each tessellation possesses a dual graph. This relation between tessellations and graphs may be self-evident but is rarely used explicitly.[3] An exception are Voronoi diagrams, whose dual graphs are known as Delaunay Triangulations (see e.g. [5]). While the former can be used to solve nearest neighbour problems, the latter are applied e.g. in Geographic Information Systems as digital elevation models.

FAMOS's space representation regards space as made up of discrete space elements connected by neighbourhood relationships. These neighbourhood links influence an agent's perception and movement by determining which elements

---

[3] Another example is David O'Sullivan's combination of graphs with irregular cellular automata to model spatial processes in cities [30].

are accessible from the agent's current position. A directed graph is used to store the spatial structure by mapping space elements to nodes and neighbourhood relationships to directed edges. This mapping can be done automatically so that there is no additional effort required for the modeller. In the current version of FAMOS this is implemented for regular grids with square/rectangular cells (RectangularGrid) or hexagonal cells (HexagonalGrid) and irregular grids, which are defined as a set of points. From these, both the Voronoi diagram (IrregularGrid2D) and the dual graph are calculated.

Access to the space model is routed solely through the environment, which acts as a façade (according to the design pattern of the same name [12]) providing agents with an interface not only to the space but also to the communication infrastructure and organisational groups.

3.3   Modelling Agents

FAMOS abstracts from a particular agent architecture and adopts a modular approach. An agent possesses a number of abilities (communication, access to the environment, movement), which may be extended as needed, and an interchangeable behaviour component. In adaptation to the event-driven time advance, each agent has its own internal "event" list, which stores external signals (notifications from the environment, messages from other agents) and internal signals (generated by the agent itself) in chronological order. The agent automatically schedules itself for re-activation for the time of the most imminent next signal. On re-activation all imminent signals are passed to the behaviour component for processing.

At the moment four such components are implemented, offering different methods to model an agent's behaviour. The simplest is a variant of event-oriented modelling (SimpleBehaviour), in which the agent's reaction to signals can be specified by implementing the process() method. Proactive behaviour can be achieved by scheduling internal signals for certain points in time with the agent-internal methods scheduleIn() or scheduleAt(). This component is ideally suited to model large populations of reactive agents and is used in the example model described in the next section. The component implementing a variant of the process interaction world view (ProcessBehaviour) is particularly suited to model proactive behaviour, which is only occasionally interrupted by events. The rule-based component (RuleEngine) integrates the rule engine Jess[4] to allow for declarative behaviour modelling. The most comprehensive component (StateMachine) facilitates the use of state diagrams to model an agent's behaviour. These can be specified using a graphical editor and then automatically parsed into executable code.

4   Example 1: Schelling's Segregation Model

To test and demonstrate some of FAMOS's key features the well-known segregation model described by Thomas Schelling [34] was chosen to be re-implemented.

---

[4] http://www.jessrules.com/jess.

Though simple, this agent-based model nevertheless allows us to showcase both the advantages of the event-driven approach and the flexible space model.

In the model two types of agents live on a square grid neighbourhood. Each agent is content with its position if at least 3 of its 8 neighbours are of the same type (tolerance threshold 0.375). If this is not the case, it will move to a free position on the grid. While Schelling originally defined the new position to be the closest free cell where the agent would be content, in computer implementations of the model this is usually replaced by choosing a random free cell.

The version implemented in FAMOS follows this approach. Since the agents solely react on the state of their local environment their behaviour can easily be modelled with FAMOS's simplest behaviour component, the event-oriented `SimpleBehaviour`. Here, the modeller has to specify an agent's reaction to incoming signals (events). In the case of the segregation model, these are notifications from the environment whenever a change occurred within the agent's sensor range, i.e. another agent moved in or out of the neighbourhood, or the agent itself arrived at a new position. An agent's reaction consists of checking if it is still content with its position and – if that is not the case – moving to a randomly chosen new position.

The action of choosing a position and moving there is delegated to framework classes. FAMOS provides several movement strategies (see Sect. 3.2) that can either be used as is or extended by a modeller to adapt to their purposes. To enable agents to pick a random new position anywhere on the grid instead of just in their direct neighbourhood the existing `RandomWalk` strategy was sub-classed to include all free cells into the selection process. This new `SegregationStrategy` class was then plugged into one of the standard movement components of FAMOS. Since the model abstracts from the duration of the actual movement in that a move to a neighbouring cell is treated the same as a "jump" to the other end of the grid, the `ConstantTimeMovement` provides the right functionality here. Inside the behaviour specification, the modeller now just needs to call the `move()` method to make an agent select and then move to a new position.

Figure 1 shows the results of simulation runs with each of the three different grid spaces FAMOS provides. The left column pictures the situation at the start of a run, with the agents randomly scattered across the space, whereas the right column contains the situation at the end of the respective run. The runs differ only in the chosen representation of space, the other parameters have been kept the same across all runs. Each grid consists of 400 cells and is populated with 140 blue and 140 green agents, whose tolerance threshold is set to the original value of 0.375. The duration for a move to a new position is set to 1.0 units of simulation time.

5 Example 2: City Courier Service Model

A more complex example, which demonstrates FAMOS's comprehensive support for the movement of agents in space and its adaptation to the event-driven time

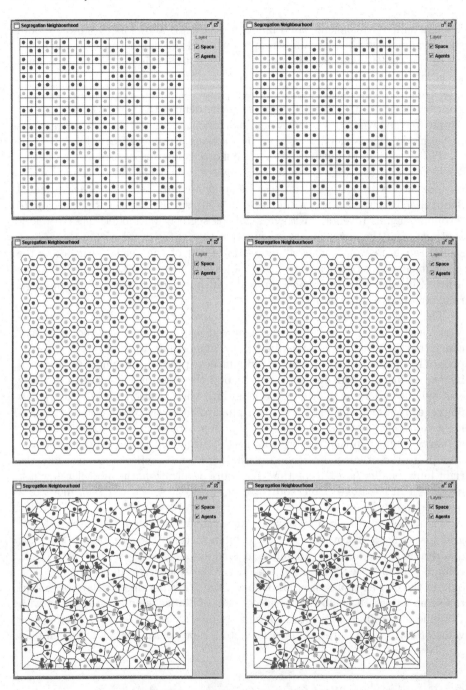

Fig. 1. Screenshots of the segregation model in FAMOS from simulation runs with the three different grids RectangularGrid (top), HexagonalGrid and IrregularGrid2D (bottom). The left column shows the situation at the start, the right column at the end of a simulation run.

advance, is the model of a city courier service [19,20]. The courier service in question consists of a fleet of bike and car couriers, who deliver orders throughout the city. They decide themselves which orders to take and plan their own route. A central office receives orders from clients and passes them on to the couriers via radio using a variant of the contract net protocol [35], which gives idle couriers priority and allows for special requests of clients.

The courier service system is naturally driven by events: Arrival, placement, pick up and delivery of orders as well as start and end of work of couriers. A model needs to map the occurrence of these events in real time correctly to simulated time to avoid falsifying results. The model also needs an explicit representation of space since the current positions of the couriers influence their decision making and thus the system dynamics.

Using FAMOS such a model can be implemented with relatively little effort. The main task for a modeller is to specify the behaviour of the agents (office and couriers), while the agents' environment (space, communication and organisation structures) can be realised with the predefined components of FAMOS. Since FAMOS uses a directed graph as the underlying space model, the detailed road network of the city of Hamburg, consisting of more than 17,000 nodes and 48,000 edges, can be represented without problems (see Fig. 2). Edge attributes modelling road types influence speed and route choice of couriers in relation to their vehicle (bike or car). FAMOS's movement component is parameterised with a model-specific rating function, which determines the duration of a move along an edge depending on the courier's vehicle and the edge's attributes. This is the only model-specific adaptation of the framework's black box classes necessary for the courier model.

The behaviour of office and couriers is complex enough to warrant modelling on a higher level than the simple reactive or proactive components Simple Behaviour and ProcessBehaviour provide. The fact that both individual behaviour and interaction of office and couriers are mainly controlled by events like arrival or delivery of an order suggests the use of the StateMachine component. The implementation of executable state diagrams in FAMOS is compliant with the UML semantics and supports hierarchical states, orthogonal regions, inter-level transitions and internal transitions, i.e. reactions to events that do not involve a state change. This makes it possible to model the part of a courier's behaviour regarding communication with the office as independent from the aspect of order processing. Only the deliberative aspects of courier behaviour (deciding which orders to take on and in which order to process them) are not yet supported by components in FAMOS and have to be implemented directly in the underlying programming language Java.

Figure 2 shows the screenshot of a simulation run with the courier service model, using empirical data from existing courier service companies amounting to 200 couriers and 2200 orders per day.

6   Discussion

The segregation model shows typical features of a discrete event system and is therefore well suited for the event-driven multi-agent simulation that this paper

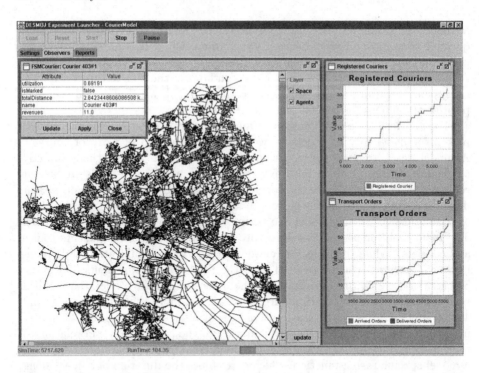

Fig. 2. Screenshot of the courier service model in FAMOS. Courier agents are coloured according to vehicle (red: car, green: bike) and current load (light: idle, dark: at least one order) (Color figure online).

proposes. After the initialisation phase, where all agents have to check if they are satisfied with their position, another check is only required if the local state of the environment has changed. All changes in this model are due to either an agent moving away from a position or an agent arriving at a new position. With a constant duration for each move this results in a quasi-time-driven simulation – but without the need to synchronously update all agents at each time "step".

Since FAMOS has agents receive a signal whenever a change occurs within their area of perception or they arrive at a new position, an event-driven control can be consistently implemented for the segregation model. A modeller just has to specify the appropriate reaction to this signal – checking if the agent is still content and possibly moving to a new position – in the agent's behaviour description.

The flexible space model allows to simulate the segregation model with different grids without having to adapt the description of the agent's behaviour. This is due to the explicit representation of locations as `Position` objects, which results in providing a layer of abstraction between the agents and the space model. In addition, using a directed graph as the underlying space representation allows for the uniform application of all movement strategies to different space models. Thus, the agents' access to their spatial environment is independent of a particular space model.

The courier service model is an example of a much more complex system that is also driven by events: The arrival of an order at the central office triggers the allocation process whose successful termination – awarding of an order to a courier – in turn triggers the pick-up and delivery process. Event-driven multi-agent simulation as proposed in this paper allows for a natural modelling of this system.

The empirical data available for the courier service model includes exact times for external events, i.e. those events that affect the system boundaries: arrival of orders and start and end of work of couriers. Depending on these events, the times of all other events arise from the simulation of the system. An event-driven time advance makes it possible to maintain the accuracy set by the empirical data – given that the duration of all relevant activities can be determined exactly enough. The courier service model applies the assumption that uniform, state-independent activities like the order-related actions of the office (receiving an order, announcing an order via radio, awarding an order to a courier) on average always take the same time; thus they are assigned a constant duration.

In contrast, the travel times of couriers and their response time to order announcements depend on the current state of the system and therefore have to be determined during the simulation. While the calculation of travel times can simply be delegated to the framework FAMOS due to its high-level support of movement in space, the determination of how quickly a courier responds to an order announcement via radio has to be done without framework support. In the model, it is approximated by a courier's interest in the order, which is calculated from the potential profit and the courier's current workload. The interest is assumed to be inversely proportional to the courier's reaction time, i.e. the higher the interest, the sooner the courier will offer to take the order.

7   Conclusion and Outlook

Systems that are inherently driven by events can be found in such diverse application domains as ecology (e.g. [14], p. 112), chemistry (e.g. [3], p. 26ff), financial markets (e.g. [6]) and the courier service described in Sect. 5. If correct timing of events is important for a system's behaviour event-driven time advance is necessary to adequately model such systems. The toolkit FAMOS and its application in the segregation model and the courier service model demonstrate that event-driven multi-agent simulation is feasible when appropriately supported. This means that not only are the technical requirements met by providing a suitable simulation infrastructure, but also that support is offered at the level of the agents and the environment. Particular focus lay on developing a flexible representation of space and comprehensively supporting movement in space because the majority of agent-based models use an explicit space model with mobile agents [9] and the movement needs to be adapted to the event-driven approach.

Many aspects of FAMOS have so far been implemented only provisionally. This pertains in particular to the support of data analysis and validation, for which only the minimum requirements like recording simulation output data and providing visualisations during a simulation run are met. Further components to specify cognitive or deliberate agent behaviour are desirable. In addition, combining several, task-specific behaviour components, which could be exchanged at run-time, would allow for adaptive agents.

References

1. Axtell, R.: Effects of interaction topology and activation regime in several multi-agent systems. In: Moss, S., Davidsson, P. (eds.) MABS 2000. LNCS (LNAI), vol. 1979, pp. 33–48. Springer, Heidelberg (2001)
2. Banks, J., Carson, J.S., Nelson, B.L., Nicol, D.: Discrete-Event System Simulation, 3rd edn. Prentice Hall, Upper Saddle River (2000)
3. Barnes, D.J., Chu, D.: Introduction to Modeling for Biosciences. Springer, London (2010)
4. Baveco, J.M., Lingeman, R.: An object-oriented tool for individual-oriented simulation: host-parasitoid system application. Ecol. Model. **61**, 267–286 (1992)
5. de Berg, M., van Kreveld, M., Overmars, M., Schwarzkopf, O.: Computational Geometry: Algorithms and Applications. Springer, Heidelberg (1997)
6. Boer, K., Kaymak, U., Spiering, J.: From discrete-time models to continuous-time, asynchronous models of financial markets. Comput. Intell. **23**(2), 142–161 (2007)
7. Bordini, R.H., Hübner, J.F.: Agent-based simulation using BDI programming in Jason. In: Uhrmacher and Weyns [39], pp. 451–476
8. Daniel, G.: Asynchronous Simulations of a Limit Order Book. Dissertation, University of Manchester, Faculty of Science and Engineering (2006)
9. Davidsson, P., Holmgren, J., Kyhlbäck, H., Mengistu, D., Persson, M.: Applications of agent based simulation. In: Antunes, L., Takadama, K. (eds.) MABS 2006. LNCS (LNAI), vol. 4442, pp. 15–27. Springer, Heidelberg (2007)
10. Edmonds, B., Meyer, R. (eds.): Simulating Social Complexity: A Handbook. Understanding Complex Systems. Springer, Berlin (2013)
11. Epstein, J.M.: Generative Social Science: Studies in Agent-Based Computational Modeling. Princeton University Press, Princeton (2007)
12. Gamma, E., Helm, R., Johnson, R.E., Vlissides, J.M.: Design Patterns - Elements of Reusable Object-Oriented Software. Addison-Wesley, Reading (1994)
13. Gilbert, N., Troitzsch, K.G.: Simulation for the Social Scientist, 2nd edn. Open University Press, Maidenhead (2005)
14. Grimm, V., Railsback, S.F.: Individual-Based Modeling and Ecology. Princeton series in theoretical and computational biology. Princeton University Press, Princeton (2005)
15. Heppenstall, A.J., Crooks, A.T., See, L.M., Batty, M. (eds.): Agent-Based Models of Geographical Systems. Springer, Dordrecht (2012)
16. Himmelspach, J., Uhrmacher, A.M.: Plug'n simulate. In: Proceedings of the 40th Annual Simulation Symposium (ANSS-40 2007), Norfolk, VA, 26–28 March 2007, pp. 137–143. IEEE Computer Society (2007)
17. Jacobs, B.I., Levy, K.N., Markovitz, H.M.: Financial market simulation in the 21st century. J. Portfolio Manage. (30th Anniversary Issue) **30**, 142–151 (2004)

18. Klügl, F., Herrler, R., Fehler, M.: Sesam: implementation of agent-based simulation using visual programming. In: Nakashima, H., Wellman, M.P., Weiss, G., Stone, P. (eds.) Proceedings of the 5th International Joint Conference on Autonomous Agents and Multiagent Systems (AAMAS 2006), Hakodate, Japan, 8–12 May 2006, pp. 1439–1440. ACM (2006)
19. Knaak, N., Meyer, R., Page, B.: Agent-based simulation of sustainable logistic strategies for large city courier services. In: Proceedings of EnviroInfo 2003, 17th International Conference Informatics for Environmental Protection, Cottbus, pp. 318–325, September 2003
20. Knaak, N., Meyer, R., Page, B.: Logistic strategies for sustainable city courier services - an agent-based simulation approach. In: Proceedings of HMS 2004, 8th International Workshop on Harbour, Maritime & Multimodal Logistics Modelling and Simulation, Rio de Janeiro, September 2004
21. Law, A.M., Kelton, W.D.: Simulation Modeling and Analysis, 3rd edn. McGraw-Hill, Boston (2000)
22. Lawson, B.G., Park, S.: Asynchronous time evolution in an artificial society model. J. Artif. Soc. Soc. Simul. 3(1) (2000). http://jasss.soc.surrey.ac.uk/3/1/2.html
23. Luke, S.: Multiagent simulation and the MASON library. Manual version 17, Department of Computer Science, George Mason University, Fairfax, VA, May 2013, http://cs.gmu.edu/~eclab/projects/mason/manual.pdf
24. Luke, S., Cioffi-Revilla, C., Panait, L., Sullivan, K., Balan, G.: MASON: a multi-agent simulation environment. Simulation 82(7), 517–527 (2005)
25. Macal, C.M., North, M.J.: Agent-based modeling and simulation: Abms examples. In: Mason, S.J., Hill, R.R., Mönch, L., Rose, O., Jefferson, T., Fowler, J.W. (eds.) Proceedings of the 2008 Winter Simulation Conference, pp. 101–112 (2008)
26. Michel, F., Ferber, J., Drogoul, A.: Multi-agent systems and simulation: a survey from the agents community's perspective. In: Uhrmacher and Weyns [39], pp. 3–52
27. Minar, N., Burkhart, R., Langton, C.G., Askenazi, M.: The swarm simulation system: a toolkit for building multi-agent simulations. Working Paper 96-06-042, Santa Fe Institute (1996), http://www.santafe.edu/media/workingpapers/96-06-042.pdf
28. North, M.J., Collier, N.T., Ozik, J., Tatara, E.R., Macal, C.M., Bragen, M., Sydelko, P.: Complex adaptive systems modeling with Repast Simphony. Complex Adapt. Syst. Model. 1, 3 (2013). http://www.casmodeling.com/content/1/1/3
29. North, M.J., Collier, N.T., Vos, J.R.: Experiences creating three implementations of the Repast agent modeling toolkit. ACM Trans. Model. Comput. Simul. 16(1), 1–25 (2006)
30. O'Sullivan, D.: Graph-based Cellular Automaton Models of Urban Spatial Processes. Dissertation, Centre of Advanced Spatial Analysis, University of London (2000)
31. Page, B., Kreutzer, W.: The Java Simulation Handbook: Simulating Discrete Event Systems with UML and Java. Shaker, Aachen (2005)
32. Railsback, S.F., Lytinen, S.L., Jackson, S.K.: Agent-based simulation platforms: review and development recommendations. Simulation 82(9), 609–623 (2006)
33. Samuelson, D.A., Macal, C.M.: Agent-based simulation comes of age. Oper. Res./Manage. Sci. Today 33(4), 34 (2006)
34. Schelling, T.C.: Micromotives and Macrobehavior. Norton, New York (1978)
35. Smith, R.G.: The contract net protocol: high level communication and control in a distributed problem solver. IEEE Trans. Comput. C–29(12), 1104–1113 (1980)
36. Tesfatsion, L.: Agent-based computational economics: growing economies from the bottom up. Artif. Life 8(1), 55–82 (2002)

37. Theodoropoulos, G., Minson, R., Ewald, R., Lees, M.: Simulation engines for multi-agent systems. In: Uhrmacher and Weyns [39], pp. 77–108
38. Troitzsch, K.: A multi-agent model of bilingualism in a small population. In: Coelho, H., Espinasse, B. (eds.) 5th Workshop on Agent-Based Simulation, pp. 38–43. SCS Publishing House, Erlangen (2004)
39. Uhrmacher, A.M., Weyns, D. (eds.): Multi-Agent Systems: Simulation and Applications. CRC Press/Taylor and Francis, Boca Raton (2009)
40. Weyns, D., Holvoet, T.: Model for situated multi-agent-systems with regional synchronization. In: Jardim-Goncalves, R., Cha, J., Steiger-Garcao, A. (eds.) Enhanced Interoperable Systems: Proceedings of the 10th International Conference on Concurrent Engineering (ISPE CE 2003), Madeira, Portugal, 26–30 July, pp. 177–188 (2003)
41. Wilensky, U.: Netlogo. Center for Connected Learning and Computer-Based Modeling, Northwestern University, Evanston (1999). http://ccl.northwestern.edu/netlogo/

RatKit: Repeatable Automated Testing Toolkit for Agent-Based Modeling and Simulation

İbrahim Çakırlar[1(✉)], Önder Gürcan[1,2], Oğuz Dikenelli[1],
and Şebnem Bora[1]

[1] Department of Computer Engineering, Ege University,
35100 İzmir, Turkey
icakirlar@gmail.com, {onder.gurcan,
oguz.dikenelli,sebnem.bora}@ege.edu.tr
[2] LIST, Laboratory of Model Driven Engineering for Embedded Systems, CEA,
Point Courrier 174, 91191 Gif-sur-Yvette, France
onder.gurcan@cea.fr

Abstract. Agent-based modeling and simulation (ABMS) became an attractive and efficient way to model large-scale complex systems. The use of models always raises the question whether the model is correctly encoded (verification) and accurately represents the real system (validation). However, achieving a sufficiently credible agent-based simulation (ABS) model is still difficult due to weak verification, validation and testing (VV&T) techniques. Moreover, there is no comprehensive and integrated toolkit for VV&T of ABS models that demonstrates that inaccuracies exist and/or which reveals the existing errors in the model. Based on this observation, we designed and developed RatKit: a toolkit for ABS models to conduct VV&T. RatKit facilitates the VV&T process of ABMS by providing an integrated environment that allows repeatable and automated execution of ABS tests. This paper presents RatKit in detail and demonstrates its effectiveness by showing its applicability on a simple well-known case study: predator - prey.

Keywords: Agent-based modeling and simulation · Model testing · Verification and validation

1 Introduction

Agent-based modeling and Simulation (ABMS) is a very multidisciplinary complex system modeling and simulation technique, which is has been used increasingly during the last decade. The multidisciplinary scope of ABMS ranges from the life sciences (e.g. Biological Networks [6], Ecology [7], social Sciences [8], Scientometrics [9] to Large-scale Complex Adaptive COmmunicatiOn Networks and environmentS (CACOONS) [10] such as Wireless Sensor Networks and the Internet of Things (IoT)). While in some domains, ABMS is used for understanding complex phenomena, in other domains it is used for designing complex systems. However, whatever the objective is, in all of these domains large sets of agents interacting locally give rise to bottom-up collective behaviors. The collective behaviors of agents, whether emergent or not [11], depend on the local competences, the local perceptions and the partial

© Springer International Publishing Switzerland 2015
F. Grimaldo and E. Norling (Eds.): MABS 2014, LNAI 9002, pp. 17–27, 2015.
DOI: 10.1007/978-3-319-14627-0_2

knowledge of agents as well as the global parameter values of the simulation run. A slight difference in any of these properties (whether intentional or not) may result in totally different collective behaviors. Such a consequence leads either to a misunderstanding of the system of interest or a bad system design.

Besides, despite all ABMS platforms are developed by computer scientists, the users of these platforms (i.e. The developers of ABMS models) are more heterogeneous. Depending on the application domains, they can be (1) computer scientists that are building ABS models for their domains, (2) non-computer scientists that are building models for their domains or (3) computer scientists that are working closely with non-computer scientists. On the one hand, non-computer scientist modelers are experts in their domains (i.e. Domain experts) and are said to be capable of building the right models. However, translating these models into their corresponding software models (i.e. ABS models) can sometimes be problematic and open to mistakes. Moreover, since they have less expertise concerning software development, it is a big mystery as to whether they are building the models right or not. On the other hand, computer scientist modelers are better at building models correctly, but they usually lack the expertise to build the right models.

In this sense, correct design and implementation of ABS simulation models are becoming highly important to increase reliability and to improve confidence. The use of models always raises the question whether the model is correctly encoded (verification) and accurately represents the real system (validation). Model verification deals with "*building the model right*" while model validation deals with "*building the right model*", as stated in [1]. Model verification is the process of determining that a model is meeting specified model requirements and reflecting the system of interest accurately. Also, model validation is the process of determining the degree to which a model is an accurate representation of the system of interest from the perspective of the intended modeling objectives. Both verification and validation are processes that gather evidence of a model's reliability or accuracy; thus, verification and validation (V&V) cannot prove that a model is definitely correct and accurate for all possible scenarios, but, rather, it can provide evidence that the model is sufficiently accurate for its intended use [27].

In the literature, there are two main focuses for building accurate ABS models: model fitting and model testing [28]. For both of these focuses the ultimate goal is to have an ABS model that appropriately mimics the real system, however each focus has different ways to achieve this. Model testing demonstrates that inaccuracies exist in the model and reveals the existing errors in the model. In model testing, test data or test cases are subject to the model to see if it functions properly [2]. Model testing focuses on observable behaviors of the real system according to the experimental or real data. On the other hand, model fitting focuses on achieving non-observable behaviors of the real system that are not gathered with scientific or experimental methods. Even though these focuses are at opposite ends of the spectrum, and certainly hybrids of these focuses offers the solution of aforementioned V&V requirements of ABS models.

Model testing and model fitting, are general techniques that can be conducted to perform verification and/or validation of ABS models. In this study, we extend the model testing scope with the requirements of model fitting. We aimed to enrich model testing methods with test scenario visualization, visual tests and logging support in order to support model fitting, especially for domain experts and non-computer scientists. As [12] points out traditional testing techniques for VV&T cannot be transferred easily to ABS. There are some efforts [13–17], but these studies do not directly deal with model testing processes and focus on late validation and verification. As well, there are few proposed model testing frameworks to conduct validation and verification throughout the model testing process [15, 18, 19]. Among them, [18] proposed an integrated testing framework, but unfortunately this framework not easy to use for non-computer scientists.

Based on the above observations, our desire is to develop an automated and integrated testing framework for ABSs in order to facilitate the model testing process for all types of model developers. Towards this objective, we took the generic testing framework proposed by Gürcan et al. [18] and improved it one step further by taking into account the requirements of testing frameworks for ABMS. Previously, testing requirements for ABMS are defined and testing levels of ABMS that can be subject of the model testing process are clarified in our previous studies [18, 22]. We also revise our multi-level testing categorization by keeping in sight the requirements of ABS testing frameworks.

2 Requirements of Agent Based Simulation Testing Frameworks

VV&T leads the simulation model development to increase understanding of the potential of models and to decide when to believe a model, and when not to, and to interpret and to use the model's results [29]. However, it should be noted that VV&T is not a silver bullet. VV&T also has some limitations and constraints. Apparently, one intending to design a testing framework should take into consideration the requirements below.

- **Integrity:** Testing of the model is not separate from the model development (especially since it covers the verification). Rather, these tasks are tightly coupled, since a testing framework for ABMS should be integrated or pluggable to the simulation environment in order to behave like a simulation engine, to interpret the model outputs and to execute the testing criteria corresponding to the evaluation rules. Thus, applying VV&T in the early steps in model development can be easily achieved.
- *Multilevel Testing:* Multilevel testing involves testing the model elements at different levels of organization; micro-, meso- and macro-levels. Due to the multilevel nature of ABMS [25] and experiences reported in the literature [26], obviously a testing framework dedicated to ABMS should support multilevel testing as discussed in other studies [18, 22, 24]. Corresponding to the multilevel testing, model components tested at lower levels can be used in upper levels. So, multilevel testing does not distinguish testing requirements. Rather, it presents a systematic way to test simulation models iteratively.
- *Automated Testing:* Automatic testing is the capability of executing model tests together and individually. Multilevel tests are not independent from each other. Moreover, each level is a prerequisite of the upper-level for proper testing. Testing

model with the model development in a multilevel manner systematically organizes the model to achieve intended reliability and accuracy. Therefore, automated testing is the essential requirement for the complementarity of the testing levels. Thus, the impact of the new model components or behaviors added to the model can be easily understood without any extra effort.

- *Monitoring:* Monitoring the simulation models, the behaviors of agents, or occurrence of special or unexpected cases are the main expectations for testing. Monitoring an agent in micro-level, a group of agent in meso-level or the whole model in macro-level testing is the main requirement to evaluate models. Such a testing framework should provide evidence to the modelers in order to assess about the model behaviors or outputs. However, monitoring should be conducted without any intervention to the model behavior if we want reliable information about the model. Most of the existing monitoring efforts [15, 18] prefer to intervene in the scheduling of agents, agent behaviors or the simulated environment. In this case, observations gathered may be different from the real outputs of the model.

- *Parameter Tuning:* Simulation parameters are the key values for the model and affect the simulation behaviors. A dedicated testing framework should provide parameter tuning capability [5] to the modeler to find appropriate parameter values, showing the domino effect between parameters, testing the variety of parameter values, drawing the boundaries for the parameter value set, testing the parameter sensitivity, etc. To perform parameter tuning modelers choose to run the model multiple times with different initial values in order to find the appropriate values. But instead of such a testing framework supports parametric test scenario definition can handle this issue.

- **Presenting Model Observation**: Evaluation of the model observations against the real data is the subject of testing [2]. Model observations are not only final outputs, but also the data that are captured at any time during the model execution. An observation value can be the value of an agent attribute, state, parameter, environment parameter or resource. Presenting observations to the modeler contributes to evaluate the potential of the model.

- **Visualization Support**: VV&T of ABMS do not only focus on quantitative methods [15]. Especially for non-computer scientists, a testing framework should present visual outputs to support model fitting[]. However, visualization is not only to visualize the simulation execution, but also to present or to summarize observations. Drawing a graphical representation of observation history should help modelers to review simulation execution or the behaviors of the agents. In this sense, modelers can monitor the behaviors of agents or a group of agents with different conditions without any extra effort. To perform VV&T based on classical quantitative techniques narrows the VV&T perspective. However, a testing framework that is enriched with the support of visualization provides a broader perspective in order to evaluate the potential of the model.

- **Logging:** Logging [15] is presenting a history of the model execution to the modeler. Some of the situations not considered in a test scenario can be determined with the help of logs. Especially in meso- and macro- testing levels, when the number of agents in the model under test increases, the impact of logging during assessment can be easily achieved. Reviewing logs help modelers to monitor the model behaviors easily. Logging should be optional and should support logging levels in order to avoid confusion.

- **Ease-of-Use:** Testing proposals [13–17] for ABS is hard-to-use and requires extra effort. VV&T is difficult enough for modelers because of its nature. Therefore, it should be identical to the model development to address all modelers, especially non-computer scientists. Thus, modelers do not need to any extra effort to perform model VV&T.

It's inevitable that such a testing framework for ABMS should support these requirements. Towards this objective, we designed and developed RatKit for ABMS to facilitate the model testing process taking into consideration ABMS audience requirements and expectations.

3   Related Work

There has been little work that specifically addresses testing of ABSs and also simulation models.

MASTER is proposed by Wright et al. [19], is a simulation model testing framework for ABSs and compatible with the MASON. MASTER is an external testing tool that provides defining acceptance tests for simulation models. MASTER aims to detect suspicious simulation runs corresponding to the user defined assertions. The modeler defines normal situations, facts, constraints and abnormal situations for the model under test; the framework monitors the simulation runs and evaluates deviations from the normal situations. MASTER is a semi-automatic testing tool and only focuses on prepared simulation models. Rather than developing credible simulation models, it focuses on final VV&T process.

VOMAS, proposed by Niazi et al. [15], is one tool for VV&T of ABMS. They propose using a group of specialized agents; agents specialized in monitoring and testing, over an overlay network to conduct the VV&T process. The agents of the overlay use defined constraints in order to detect unusual behaviors, and report violations if they occur. However, it is not clear how the constraints for the overlay agents are derived and how observations are evaluated. And also, monitoring of the model agents is not clarified. Intervention into the simulation agents breaks the normal simulation run and VV&T gets further away from its main objective.

4   RatKit: A Repeatable Automated Testing Toolkit for ABMS

RatKit (Repeatable Automated Testing toolKIT) is a testing toolkit to facilitate model testing. Testing requires the execution of the model under test as stated in [18]. In this context, each specific model designed for testing is called Test Scenario. Each Test Scenario is defined for specific purpose(s) and includes the required test cases, activities, sequences, and observations. Observations are collected by the Test Environment during the execution of the test scenario. The Test Agent is responsible for evaluating these assertions according to the collected observations in order to check if these testable elements [18] behave as expected or not.

4.1   RatKit Architecture

The UML model of the RatKit is given in Fig. 1. RatKit uses Junit[1] testing infrastructure for all testing purposes like assertions, test runners, etc. RatKitRunner is the main class for the architecture and the Junit test runner for simulation tests. When a test class is annotated by the annotation @RunWith (RatKitRunner.class) all test methods of the test class are evaluated by the TestAgent. RatKit toolkit is implemented for the Repast simulation environment [23] (RatKit4Repast[2]).

RatKitRunner first initializes the given test scenario for each test method and creates test scenario elements using RatKitScenarioLoader. RatKitScenarioLoader creates the necessary test scenario files corresponding to the defined test method parameters. RatKit provides test developers to define parametric, periodic and repeatable test executions with the @RatKitTest annotation. RatKitScenarioLoader evaluates the defined parameters for the test scenario and decides the type of test execution. Each RatKitParameter definition corresponds to a simulation model parameter. RatKitParameter values can be constant, number, value iterations like 0 to 100, or a list of values. RatKitParameterSweeper evaluates these parameter definitions and triggers the RatKitRunner for parametric/periodic test scenario executions.

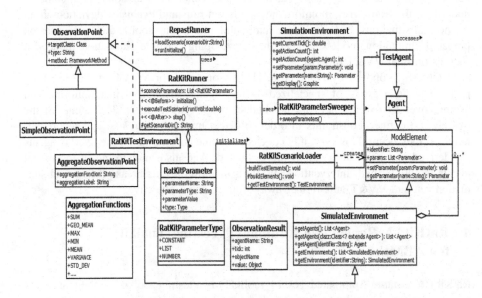

Fig. 1. RatKit architecture (UML class model)

[1] JUnit. http://www.junit.org (Accessed: July 2014).

[2] RatKit4Repast http://code.google.com/p/ratkit (Accessed: September 2014).

The test scenario is a sub-model of the model in order to achieve expected behaviors. For simulation tests, each test, corresponding to the testing levels, should have at least one observation point definition. TestAgent executes the assertions corresponding to the observation results. There are two types of observation definitions: SimpleObservationPoint (SP) and AggregateObservationPoint (AOP). SP definitions provide gathering model element properties; a property of an agent or an environment variable. AOP definitions provide summarized results for the model under test using aggregate functions (count, max, min etc.). Each observation point definition is handled by the RatKitRunner and presents it to the TestAgent during the execution of the test cases as an ObservationResult. Each observation result is time stamped, when it's observed and by whom (agent identifier) if required. RatKitTestEnvironment holds the current observation history, a map of the observation results gathered during the execution, and presents to the TestAgent. According to the test execution behavior of the developer, TestAgent executes evaluations (assertions) corresponding to the observations.

5 Case Study: Predator Prey

In this section, we demonstrate the effectiveness of RatKit and its applicability on a well-known case study: Predator Prey. We use a model of wolf-sheep predation [4] of the Repast Simphony [23] that is intentionally simple as an introductory tutorial. While the example is not intended to show real VV&T phenomenon, the model's complexity is high enough to illustrate developing ABMS tests.

This model represents a simple variation of predator prey behavior using three agent types: wolf, sheep, and grass. Both the wolves and sheep move randomly on a grid, and lose energy. The wolves and sheep need to feed in order to replenish their energy, and they will die once their energy level reaches zero. Wolves prey on sheep and may eat them if the two are located in the same spatial position. Sheep may similarly eat grass if the sheep is located on a patch that contains living grass.

In the case study, all of the possible test scenarios are implemented corresponding to our testing levels. It's ready for download in the Ratkit website. Because of page limits we only present a meso-level test: wolf agent prey on a sheep agent. The definition of the test scenario is shown in the Fig. 2. WolfSheepInteractionScenario-Builder class defines the test scenario. In the scenario, there are two fake agents [18]: FakeSheep, FakeWolf. These agent classes are extended from original agent classes to prevent random movement of the real agent classes. The real purpose of the test scenario is to test the interaction between wolf and sheep agent in the same spatial position. Therefore, both of the scenario agents are located in the same (20, 30) position. We expect at the first tick of the test execution the wolf agent will prey on the sheep agent in the same spatial position.

The test method of the test scenario is shown in Fig. 3. Case study test cases are defined by the wolfEatSheep method which is annotated by the @RatKitTest annotation. The test method annotation includes the definitions of test scenario, execution parameters, simulation model parameters and observation points. In our test scenario, sheepgainfromfood, wolfgainfromfood, wolfreproduce, sheepreproduce are model

```
public class WolfSheepScenarioBuilder extends Preda-
torPreyScenarioBuilder {
  @Override
protected void createAgents() {
Wolf wolf =getEnvironment().fakeWolf("wolf1");
Sheep sheep = getEnvironment().fakeSheep("sheep1");
getContext (). add (wolf);
getContext().add(sheep);
Grid grid = getContext().getProjection("grid");
grid.moveTo (sheep, 20, 30);
grid.moveTo (wolf,  20, 30);
  }
}
```

Fig. 2. Test scenario definition

parameters. These are required parameters for the initialization of agent instances and also parameter values which affect agent's behaviors in the simulated environment. Sheepgainfromfood, wolfreproduce, sheepreproduce are constant type parameters. And wolfgainfromfood parameter type is defined as the number (type = NUMBER). In the execution of simulation tests, the parameter value will be increased from 5 to 10 by the RatKit infrastructure.

In this scenario, we intend to test the wolf agent to see whether it gains energy and the sheep agent dies. Firstly, we need to monitor the energy value of the wolf agent. For this reason, we define a simple observation target SimpleAgent class instance (we want to monitor all wolves in the simulated environment) by collecting the values of the "getEnergy" method with the identifier "getLabel" value. Observation results are presented to the developers with an identifier and a time value (in which tick observation result is gathered).

In test cases, we need to separate which result belongs to which agent. In the definition of test scenarios, we define the identifiers of the agents like "wolf1" and "sheep1".

Another purpose of the test case to test whether the sheep agent has died (removed from the simulated environment). For this reason, we define an aggregate observation point for counting the sheep agent instances in the environment for each tick of the simulation run. The aggregate observation point targets the Sheep agents by using the "count" aggregate function which is named as "sheep_count".

In that test method body firstly an instance of the RatKitTestEnvironment class is initialized. This class is responsible for presenting observation results to the developers. To test whether the wolf agent gains energy from the eating behavior that is executed in the first tick (tick value is 1.0), we need to get observation results of the "getEnergy" observation results of the initial and final ticks. The wolf agent is created with an initial energy; its energy is decreased by one for each simulation tick and in the first tick the

```
@RatKitTest(runUntil=1, scenarioBuilderClass=
WolfSheepScenarioBuilder.class,parameters =
{@RatKitParameter(parameterName="sheepgainfromfood",
parameterValue="5",parameterType = DOUBLE),
@RatKitParameter(parameterName="wolfgainfromfood",
from="5",to="10",step="1",parameterType =DOUBLE,
type= NUMBER),
@RatKitParameter(parameterName="wolfreproduce",param
eterValue="0",parameterType =DOUBLE),
@RatKitParameter(parameterName="sheepreproduce", pa-
rameterValue = "0",parameterType=DOUBLE)},
observationPoints =
{@ObservationPoint(targetClass=SimpleAgent.class,
method="getEnergy",label = "getLabel"),
@ObservationPoint(targetClass = Sheep.class, func-
tion=COUNT,type=AGGREGATE, label = "sheep_count")})
public void wolfEatSheep(){
RatKitTestEnvironment
env=RatKitTestEnvironment.getInstance();
double initialEnergy= env.getSimple( "wolf1",
0.0,"getEnergy");
double energy = env.getSimpleObservation("wolf1",
1.0,"getEnergy");
assertTrue(energy > initialEnergy);
double gain= getParam-
ters().getValue("wolfgainfromfood");
assertEquals(initialEnergy - 1 + gain, energy);
int initialCount=env.getAggregate(0,"sheep_count");
Assert.assertEquals(1, initialCount);
int finalCount= env.getAggregate(1,"sheep_count");
assertEquals(0, finalCount);
}
```

Fig. 3. Test method definition

wolf agent gains energy by eating the sheep agent. These values are evaluated based on the model parameter "wolfgainfood" value.

Another purpose of the test method is comparing the initial and the final sheep count in the environment. For this reason, we get the "sheep_count" observation results of the initial and the final tick value. And we expect here that there are no sheep in the final tick.

6 Future Works and Conclusions

This paper has introduced RatKit and its VV&T approach against ABMS. A tool supporting all needs and aforementioned requirements for VV&T targeting ABMS is an important lack. Our main motivation is filling this gap by the development of RatKit.

Currently using RatKit, users can define simulation tests according to their VV&T purposes. All of the tests are implemented by the users. However, for future work we intend to support automated test case generation from the test scenarios. Most of the testing requirements for the models except domain specific ones have some common points. So, automatic generation of common test cases will be supported by RatKit next versions. In this study, we defined the requirements of ABMS testing frameworks.

Besides, as we mentioned before, a testing framework leading to right design and implementation of ABS models are highly important in order to be able to increase their reliability. For another future work, we intend to define a test driven development methodology for ABMS. Trying to verify, validate and test the ABS models after model building makes ABS development more complex. Such a test driven development methodology that is supported by a testing framework is another gap in the ABMS literature.

References

1. Balci, O.: Validation, verification, and testing techniques throughout the life cycle of a simulation study. In: WSC 1994, pp. 215–220 (1994)
2. Balci, O.: Principles and techniques of simulation validation, verification, and testing. In: WSC 1995, pp. 147–154. IEEE Computer Society (1995)
3. Love, G., Back, G.: Model verification and validation for rapidly developed simulation models: balancing cost and theory. In: Proceedings of the 18th International Conference of the System Dynamics Society (2000)
4. Wilensky, U.: NetLogo Wolf Sheep Predation model. Center for Connected Learning and Computer-Based Modeling (1997)
5. Calvez, B., Hutzler, G.: Automatic tuning of agent-based models using genetic algorithms. In: Sichman, J.S., Antunes, L. (eds.) MABS 2005. LNCS (LNAI), vol. 3891, pp. 41–57. Springer, Heidelberg (2006)
6. Gürcan, O., Türker, K.S., Mano, J., Bernon, C., Dikenelli, O., Glize, P.: Mimicking human neuronal pathways in silico: an emergent model on the effective connectivity. J. Comput. Neurosci. **36**, 235–257 (2013)
7. Grimm, V., Revilla, E., Berger, U., Jeltsch, W.M., Railsback, S.: Pattern-oriented modeling of agent-based complex systems: lessons from ecology. Science **310**, 987–991 (2005)
8. Epstein, J.M.: Agent-based computational models and generative social science. In: Generative Social Science Studies in Agent-Based Computational Modeling. Princeton University Press, Princeton (2007)
9. Niazi, M.A., Hussain, A.: Agent-based computing from multi-agent systems to agent-based models: a visual survey. Scientometrics **89**, 479–499 (2011). Springer
10. Niazi, M.A., Hussain, A.: A novel agent-based simulation framework for sensing in complex adaptive environments. IEEE Sens. J. **11**(2), 404–412 (2011)

11. De Wolf, T., Holvoet, T.: Emergence versus self-organisation: different concepts but promising when combined. In: Brueckner, S.A., Di Marzo Serugendo, G., Karageorgos, A., Nagpal, R. (eds.) ESOA 2005. LNCS (LNAI), vol. 3464, pp. 1–15. Springer, Heidelberg (2005)

12. Sargent, R.G.: Verification and validation of simulation models. In: WSC 2005, pp. 130–143 (2005)

13. Terano, T.: Exploring the vast parameter space of multi-agent based simulation. In: Antunes, L., Takadama, K. (eds.) MABS 2006. LNCS (LNAI), vol. 4442, pp. 1–14. Springer, Heidelberg (2007)

14. Klügl, F.: A validation methodology for agent-based simulations. In: Proceedings of the 2008 ACM Symposium on Applied Computing, SAC 2008, pp. 39–43. ACM (2008)

15. Niazi, M.A., Hussain, A., Kolberg, M.: Verification and validation of agent-based simulation using the VOMAS approach. In: MAS&S at Multi-Agent Logics, Languages, and Organisations Federated Workshops (MALLOW), vol. 494 (2009)

16. Xing, P., Lees, M., Nan, H., Viswanthatn, T.V.: Validation of agent-based simulation through human computation: an example of crowd simulation. In: Villatoro, D., Sabater-Mir, J., Sichman, J.S. (eds.) MABS 2011. LNCS, vol. 7124, pp. 90–102. Springer, Heidelberg (2012)

17. Railsback, S.F., Grimm, V.: Agent-Based and Individual-Based Modeling: A Practical Introduction. Princeton University Press, Princeton (2011)

18. Gürcan, O., Dikenelli, O., Bernon, C.: A generic testing framework for agent-based simulation models. J. Simul. **7**, 183–201 (2013)

19. Wright, C.J., McMinn, P., Gallardo, J.: Testing Multi-Agent Based Simulations using MASTER (2012)

20. Balci, O.: Golden rules of verification, validation, testing, and certification of modeling and simulation applications. SCS M&S Magazine (2010)

21. Beck, K.: Test-Driven Development by Example. Addison Wesley, Vaseem (2003)

22. Gürcan, O., Dikenelli, O., Bernon, C.: Towards a generic testing framework for agent-based simulation models. In: MAS&S 2011, pp. 637–644 (2011)

23. North, M.J., T.R. Howe, N.T. Collier, Vos, R.J.: The Repast Simphony Runtime System, Argonne National Laboratory (2005)

24. Soyez, J.-B., Morvan, G., Dupont, D., Merzouki, R.: A methodology to engineer and validate dynamic multi-level multi-agent based simulations. In: Giardini, F., Amblard, F. (eds.) MABS 2012. LNCS, vol. 7838, pp. 130–142. Springer, Heidelberg (2013)

25. Drogoul, A., Amouroux, E., Caillou, P., Gaudou, B., Grignard, A., Marilleau, N., Taillandier, P., Vavasseur, M., Vo, D.-A., Zucker, J.-D.: GAMA: a spatially explicit, multi-level, agent-based modeling and simulation platform. In: Demazeau, Y., Ishida, T., Corchado, J.M., Bajo, J. (eds.) PAAMS 2013. LNCS, vol. 7879, pp. 271–274. Springer, Heidelberg (2013)

26. Burstein, I.: Practical Software Testing. Springer, New York (2003)

27. Thacker, B.H., Doebling, S. W., Hemez, F.M., Anderson, M.C., Pepin, J.E., Rodriguez, E. A.: Concepts of model verification and validation. Technical report, Los Alamos National Lab., Los Alamos, NM, US (2004)

28. Stasser, G.: Computer simulation as a research tool: the DISCUSS model of group decision making. J. Exp. Soc. Psychol. **24**(5), 393–422 (1988). ISSN 0022-1031. http://dx.doi.org/10.1016/0022-1031(88)90028-5

29. Carley, K.M.: Validating computational models (1996)

Man on Earth – The Challenge of Discovering Viable Ecological Survival Strategies

Bruce Edmonds[✉]

Centre for Policy Modelling,
Manchester Metropolitan University, Manchester, UK
bruce@edmonds.name

Abstract. Many previous societies have killed themselves off and, in the process, devastated their environments. Perhaps the most famous of these is that of "Easter Island". This suggests a grand challenge: that of helping discover what kinds of rationality and/or coordination mechanisms might allow humans and the greatest possible variety of other species to coexist. As their contribution towards this, the agent community could investigate these questions within simulations to suggest hypotheses as to how this could be done. The particular problem for our community is that of designing and releasing a society of plausible agents into a simulated ecology and assessing: (a) whether the agents survive and (b) if they do survive, what impact they have upon the diversity of other species in the simulation. No other community is currently in a position to explore this problem *as a whole*. The simulated ecology needs to implement a suitably dynamic, complex and reactive environment for the test to be meaningful. In such a simulation, agents (as any other entity) would have to eat other entities to survive, but if they destroy the species they depend upon they are likely to die off themselves. Up to now there has been a lack of simulations that combine a complex model of the ecology with a multi-agent model of society – there have been complex models of society but with simple ecological representations and complex ecological models but with little of human social complexity in them. In order for progress to be made with humanity's challenge, we will have to move beyond simple ideas and solutions and embrace the complexity of the socio-ecological complex as a whole. A suitable dynamic ecological model and simple tests with agents are described to illustrate this challenge, as the first steps towards a meaningful test bed to under pin the implied research programme.

1 The Dangers of Ecological Damage and Societal Collapse

The evidence is overwhelming that, many times, humans have destroyed the ecologies they inhabited to their own and other species detriment – sometimes causing whole settlements or civilizations to disappear. Examples include: the inhabitants of Easter Island who built its famous stone statues in a race for status and killed all trees on the island in the process [13], or the Mayan civilization where a combination of increasing

---

Man on Earth—The title comes from John Reader's book of the same name.

© Springer International Publishing Switzerland 2015
F. Grimaldo and E. Norling (Eds.): MABS 2014, LNAI 9002, pp. 28–40, 2015.
DOI: 10.1007/978-3-319-14627-0_3

climatic aridity, demands of agriculture and societal conflicts lead to an abandonment of their impressive step temples in the jungle [15]. However you look at it, humans have a profound effect upon the ecosystems they come into contact with, even to the extent that (as some have argued) we are in the middle of the sixth great extinction event – the Holocene [11].

However, how humans will effect a particular ecosystem is not always clear – sometimes it seems that a balance between humans and the rest of the ecosystem is established, but at other times, the arrival of humans can only be described as catastrophic [8]. The "Social Intelligence Hypothesis" [12] suggests that the main adaptive advantage that our brains give us is our ability to socially organize. In this view our brains provide us with social intelligence first (for example abilities to: recognize other individuals, to develop a personal identity relative to a group, to be able to communicate, to be sensitive to status, to imitate, to train our offspring for a long time, and to adsorb a whole culture when experienced over a long time); any "general" intelligence we have as individuals is a by-product of these social abilities.

Due to these social abilities, groups of humans can inhabit a variety of ecological niches. They do this by adapting to a niche in terms of developing a body of knowledge, including words, ideas, techniques, social norms, systems of value and ways of organizing, that enables the group to survive there [14]. Once established, this body of knowledge can be passed down to new members of the group so that the group can retain its ability to survive in that niche over time. Broadly, this set of knowledge can be associated with the culture of the group. Thus, the abilities of groups of humans can change far more rapidly than that of most animals that have to rely on genetic evolution. Humans are thus at a distinct advantage in terms of any adaptive "arms race" with other species. Their social intelligence has equipped them to survive in a hostile and unpredictable world, ensuring their own immediate survival as their priority (as with other species).

However, they do not necessarily plan for the long-term and can cause such a degree of environmental damage to the niches they inhabit that they endanger the survival of their own group [8]. In this way, the arrival of humans within a system of ecosystems can have a profound impact – not merely changing the extent of extinction but also the whole way that the dynamics of that ecosystem works. The abilities of humans are over-tuned towards immediate survival, with the contrary result that, in the longer-term, they grab resources to themselves in a way that can jeopardize their own group survival. Now that humans, using their technology, can inhabit almost any ecological niche on earth, any ecological disaster that we cause might well not be limited to a particular niche but may affect us globally.

The wider challenge for humanity is to find a way of living on our planet, however that is, in order to ensure our own long-term survival along with the survival of the greatest possible diversity of other species. This may involve the development of new coordination mechanisms that might allow a planet of people to agree to binding, mutual plans of action. It may involve educating people in certain ways of thinking that will change how we look at and plan for the future. It may require the construction of new ways of communication or new incentive schemes to encourage and spread more sustainable lifestyles. However it is almost impossible to see how any of these innovations would actually work without trying them, and we do not have time to try all of them before significant ecological disaster is upon us. Thus it is that agent-based modellers might have a particular part to play in solving this.

2   The Particular Challenge for the Multi-agent Community

What that multi-agent based simulation could do towards solving this project is to help pre-select which strategies are worth trying. This would involve building up a test-bed that is realistic enough that human survival strategies could be tried out and some of the complex consequences understood. In this was MABS could contribute to the development of viable ways of living, and hence make a real contribution to the survival of our and other species on this planet. This challenge can be seen as an amplification of that implicitly posed in [2] or else a contribution to that of [7].

There have been many agent-based simulations addressing the interaction of man with the environment, going back (at least) to 1994 [1] (see [3] for a review). Individual-based ecological models go back even further (see [9] for a review). However to fully address this challenge we need to have a multi-agent model concerning human decision making and social interaction combined with an individual-based model of an ecology that more fully reflects the dynamism and complexity of real ecologies. Up to now, models of humans interacting with their environment have had either a relatively simple model of human interaction or a simple model of the ecosystem they are embedded in (such as a systems dynamic model). As it said in [6] in 2012:

> *"...The more serious shortcomings of existing modelling techniques, however, are of a structural nature: the failure to adequately capture nonlinear feedbacks within resource and environmental systems and between human societies and these systems."* (p. 523)

In other words, to fully address this challenge we need to start to understand how the complexity of human cognition, the complexity of human society and the complexity of dynamic ecologies might interact. Otherwise, we might miss some of the complications that might affect our and other species survival. Merely playing with abstract ideas or hypotheses, however attractive and plausible they are to us, is unlikely to be sufficient – the combined socio-ecological complexity is simply too great, and any assumptions to the contrary likely to be wishful thinking [9]. Thus, to really contribute something beyond computational analogies to the debate we need to move to simulations that capture more of the observed complexity of the problem. This paper represents a step in this direction – towards the construction of a test-bed that will allow different survival strategies to be experimentally evaluated in a model that is realistic enough to reveal some of the otherwise unpredictable consequences.

The Socio-Ecological Test-Bed. To ensure that the environment in which the agents representing humans and their society is sufficiently challenging, we require a model where:

(a) The environment needs to include space, so that there can be a differentiation in terms of niches and allow for some spatial migration between locations
(b) The environment needs to include niches with different characteristics, for example deserts (which can not sustain life) and natural barriers to migration

(c) Complex food webs of species need to be able to develop within each niche either extracting resources from the environment or other individuals (predation)

(d) New species need to be able to evolve in response to the pressure of the environment, other species and humans

(e) Agents representing humans need to be embedded within these niches, needing to use/eat other species to enable their own survival

Once such a test bed is established, the challenge would be implemented in several phases:

1. *Bed in the ecology.* Run the ecological model for a while to allow a rich and dynamic ecology to evolve.
2. *Inject the human agents.* Then place a small society of agents with given cognitive and social abilities into the ecological simulation.
3. *Assess the result.* After a suitable period of simulation time assess the outcome.

The assessment of the final state of the simulation could be done in a variety of ways, including:

- Measuring the diversity of the ecology, for example the average genetic difference between individuals, as in [5] (excluding humans).
- The species-number distribution – how many species are there with a population of at least 2^n, where n varies (the "Species Abundance Distribution" of [10].
- The number of trophic layers that have survived for a period of time since the injection of human agents, shown by the distribution of trophic layers.
- The health of the society of agents, in terms of the number of surviving humans and its variability over time.

Measures such as these can be brought together to assess the sustainability/health of the socio-ecological system as a whole.

Thus this challenge can be encapsulated as follows:

To design plausible cognitive and social abilities that, when implemented in agents and assessed in the above way, reliably result in a sustainable and healthy socio-ecological system.

3   Towards a Socio-Ecological Test-Bed

To illustrate such a test-bed, I describe a simulation test-bed that meets the stated criteria, has been tested with simple agents representing humans, and assessed in some of the above ways.

The Basic Set-Up. In this, entities, plants, herbivores and predators, are represented as individual objects. They inhabit one of a number of patches arranged in a 2D grid that makes up the world. Each patch is well mixed so that interactions within that patch are random, but there is a probability that each individual can migrate to one of the four neighbouring patches each tick. Each patch and individual has a binary bit-string that represents its characteristics. There is a basic energy economy; so that energy is 'rained' down into the world (each tick), divided equally between patches, and which ultimately drives the whole ecology. These bit-strings and a fixed random interaction matrix, described below, determine whether an individual can extract energy from a patch or predate upon another. The bit-string of any individual is passed to any progeny but there is a probability that one of the significant bits of their characteristic is flipped at birth.

Species Abilities and the Energy Extraction/Predation they Allow. Key to this understanding this simulation is how it is determined whether individuals can extract energy from a patch or predate upon another. This method is adapted from that in [4]. A random interaction matrix with the dimensions of the length of individuals' bit-strings is generated at the start of a simulation. It is filled with normally distributed random floating-point numbers (mean 0, SD 1/3). This interaction matrix determines which entity can eat another entity as follows: (1) the non-zero bits of the predator select the columns of the matrix, the non-zero bits of the potential prey select the rows; (2) the intersection of the selected rows and columns determine a set of numbers, (3) these are summed; (4) if the sum is greater than zero the predator can eat the prey, in which case the prey dies and the predator gains a percentage of its energy value (the rest is lost). This calculation is illustrated in Fig. 1.

Essentially the same process is used to determine which entities can extract energy directly from the environment, except that the part of the prey is taken by the patch with its bit string (padded with zeros to reach the appropriate length). In this case only those with scores greater than zero get any of the patch's energy. The patch's energy is divided between all qualifying individuals in proportion to their score against the patch. This scheme has the consequence that no individuals can extract energy from a patch with a bit-string of all zeros (a 'desert').

This interaction scheme allows complex food webs to be evolved, for example via a genetic "arms-race" between predator species and prey species, since it allows for

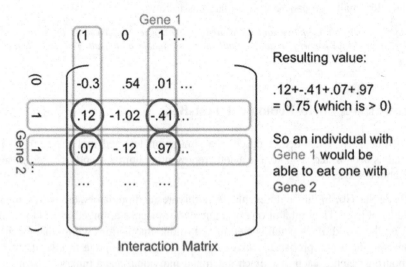

Fig. 1. The use of the interaction matrix to determine predation as well as energy extraction from a patch to give its relative fitness

adaption with respect to another specific species. It also allows for competitive adaption to particular kinds of patches. In other words fitness is not an absolute number but relative to the environment and the other existing species, if it extracts energy from this, or another species. Reference [4] showed that this kind of scheme can be used to evolve complex ecologies with plausible characteristics including food webs with similar network characteristics to those of observed food-webs (however this was for a single patch).

Simulation Execution. At the start of the simulation, the random interaction matrix is generated. Each patch is allocated a random bit-string with the given number of bits, padded out with zeros to make it the same length as individuals' bit-strings. The "environmental complexity" is the number of significant characteristics that patches can have – the number of bits in their bit-string. Bit strings of length 2 allow for 4 types of patch, of length 3 for 8 types etc.

The simulation starts with no individuals. Each tick:

- *Energy Distribution.* A fixed amount of energy is added to the model, equally divided between all the patches.
- *Death.* A life tax is subtracted from all individuals, if their total energy is less than zero it is removed.
- *Initial seeding.* (In the initial phase), until a viable population is established, a single random individual is introduced with a given probability each tick.
- *Energy extraction from patch.* The energy stored in a patch is divided among the individuals on that patch that have a positive score when its bit-string is evaluated against the patch's bit-string (in the above manner) in proportion to its relative fitness, at the simulation's efficiency rate.
- *Predation.* In a random order, each individual is randomly paired with a given number of others on the patch. If it has a positive dominance score against the other, the other is removed and the individual gains a fixed proportion of its energy, given by the "efficiency" parameter.
- *Maximum Store.* Individuals can only retain so much energy, so any above the maximum level set is discarded.
- *Birth.* If an entity has a level of energy > the "reproduce-level", it gives birth to a new entity with the same bit-string as itself, with a probability of mutation. The new entity has an energy of 1, subtracted from the energy of the parent.
- *Migration.* With a probability determined by the "migration" parameter, the individual is moved to one of the neighbouring 4 patches.

4   Typical Behaviour of the Basic Simulation

There are four different ecological kinds of outcome observed in this model: (1) a non-viable outcome where nothing thrives or reproduces, defined as being fewer than 10 individuals in the whole space, (2) a situation where one, or two, plant species dominate, (3) a plant ecology, not case 1 or 2, with no herbivores or higher predators and, (4) a mixed ecology like case 3 but with herbivores and higher predators. In practice if there are fewer than 10 individuals there are usually one or no individuals within a few simulation ticks, and if there are either one or two species or many. Thus although the division is somewhat arbitrary, it very clearly distinguishes four cases between observed simulation trajectories. Furthermore these four kinds tend to persist for many simulation ticks so that each can be meaningfully identified. These are each described with outcomes from a typical run below. Some of the later results will be in terms of the occurrences of each of these four types.

Each description is accompanied with three figures (left) is a visualisation of the patches and individuals, the colours of the background patches indicates its bit-string, plants are indicated by a small star, individuals higher up the food-chain are indicated by a circle whose size is related to how many other individuals they have eaten; (centre) is a graph of the number of species over time; and (right) is a graph showing the number of individuals of each trophic level on a shifted log scale.

Non-Viable Ecology. Here species do not manage to extract any energy from the environment, so any introduced species quickly starve with no reproduction. There is only ever one individual since when this one dies a new random one is introduced (Fig. 2).

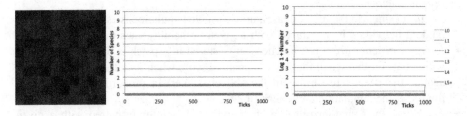

Fig. 2. Typical Non-Viable Ecology (left) the world state (middle) Number of Species (right) Log, 1 + Number of Individuals at each trophic level

Dominant Species Ecology. Here one, or a few, species dominate. The dominant species is both a plant and a predator, eating any new other species that appear. Thus, occasionally individuals are classified as belonging to a higher order trophic level, although no other species manages to achieve a long-term survival. Very occasionally two or three dominant species occur, each destroying the others that wander into the patches they dominate (Fig. 3).

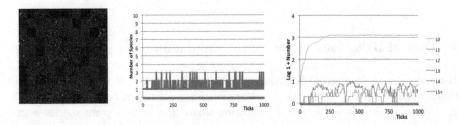

Fig. 3. Typical Dominant Species Ecology (left) the world state (middle) Number of Species (right) Log, 1 + Number of Individuals at each trophic level

Rich Plant Ecology. In this case a rich plant ecology develops where many different species compete as to their efficiency in extracting energy from the different kinds of patch, and are resistant to potential herbivores who, if introduced, simply starve. In terms of the number of individuals this state often produces the greatest number of species and the highest population (in terms of number of individuals). Species only gradually replace older ones as they marginally out-compete them in terms of energy extraction (Fig. 4).

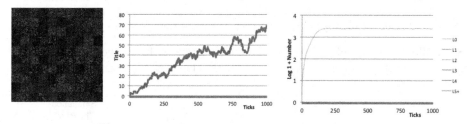

Fig. 4. Typical Herbivore Ecology (left) the world state (middle) Number of Species (right) Log, 1 + Number of Individuals at each trophic level

Mixed Ecology. In the last case, successful herbivores and higher predators evolve to produce a highly dynamic ecology. There is a continual "arms race" both in terms of bit-string evolution as well as over the space of patches. There are typically far fewer species than in the rich plant ecologies since many plant species are wiped out. This typically results in a power law in numbers of individuals at each trophic level with an order of magnitude between the prevalence of each layer. Here you get a more constant replacement of older species as found in [8] (Fig. 5).

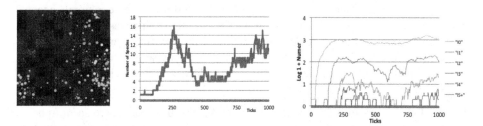

Fig. 5. Typical Mixed Ecology. (left) the world state (middle) Number of Species (right) Log, 1 + Number of Individuals at each trophic level

The 'Human' Agents. Broadly speaking, the agents representing humans should be processed in manner similar to any other individual with only a few differences. The most important difference is in the acquisition and passing on of techniques among their own group. Thus their "bit string" that determines their ability to predate upon (or resist being predated upon) is not determined genetically but can be learned socially by imitation from parents and/or peers. Whether an agent predates upon another individual and when it moves to a neighbouring patch could be part of what is determined by the agent's decision processes. One might well set the required minimum energy that humans need to give birth as much higher than for other individuals and allow them to store more energy. They might have a complex social structure with food passing between themselves according to its rules (e.g. an internal economy). They may have a tribal structure that allows each individual to recognise others from their own tribe and those who are outsiders, which may affect their behaviour. Many other extensions are possible to reflect other human attributes, e.g. warfare between groups, deliberate planting of crops or hoarding.

Some Illustrative Results. Figure 1 shows the a graph of the number of species in a typical initial stage of the model, showing the development of plants, then herbivores

Fig. 6. A typical run of the model during the "Bedding In" phase, making the state of the simulation suitable for the injection of agents representing humans

and finally predators, providing a suitably complex and dynamic environment, with a range of trophic levels, ready for the injection of agents representing humans.

To give a simple flavour of some of the possible results, some very simple agents were injected at the point indicated in Fig. 6. Then the simulation was run for a further 1000 simulation ticks with different migration rates (the probability any entity or agent would move to a nearby patch in the 2D grid). 25 otherwise independent runs were performed both with and without 'human' agents added, and the final mean ecological diversity measured.

Typical Behaviours in a Run with "Human" Agents Injected. There seem to be a variety of different kinds of trajectory possible once the agents have been introduced into the model.

One possibility is that they do not manage to predate upon any existing organisms and rapidly die out. In this case they have little impact upon the ecology. Another is that they predate only upon a thin top layer of 'herbivores'/'predators' and then die out after they have eliminated any of those around themselves. This has the effect of a temporary depression in the numbers of these, which recover as soon as the agents have gone. These are not illustrated since they are obvious.

A third, more catastrophic possibility is that the agents predate upon all the other individuals in the simulation, allowing a population explosion that eventually results in

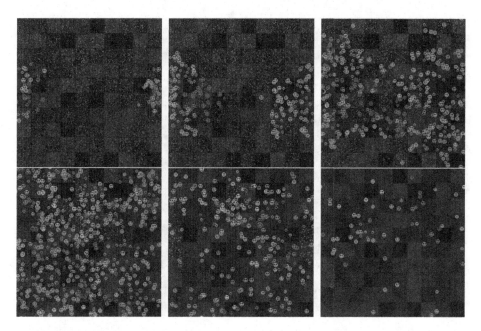

Fig. 7. A sequence of world snapshots of an invasion of agents (faces) into a 'plant' ecology (dots) with fast rate of migration, causing self extinction due to elimination of 'plants'

the consumption of all other entities in the world, after which the agents gradually starve. This is the sequence illustrated in Fig. 7.

A fourth possibility is that some kind of spatial predator-prey dynamics emerge for a while between agents and other entities. An illustration of this is in Fig. 8. Here "waves" of agents develop, consuming all in their path but in such a pattern that new clumps of entities develop in the patches they have disappeared from (due to the previous elimination of food). This is a spatial "cat and mouse" situation, which depends upon the agents not spreading evenly but accidently leaving patches and those patches being able to be seeded by other entities and thriving there.

A graph of their numbers may look like classic predator-prey dynamics such as in Fig. 9, although this apparently simple summary might not reflect what is happening within a more complex spatial dynamic. There are, of course, more complex mixes of dynamics where the pattern is not so distinguishable to the eye.

Some Illustrative General Results. As we see from Figs. 10 and 11 below, the agents have a consistent and negative impact upon the ecologies of other entities they invade, but, generally, a higher negative impact at higher levels of migration, which tends to make the ecologies more uniform. However, as Fig. 10 indicates, this is far from a uniform effect, reducing the diversity incrementally. Rather it indicates an increasing proportion of ecological catastrophes (the green proportion in Fig. 11) that occur in many cases.

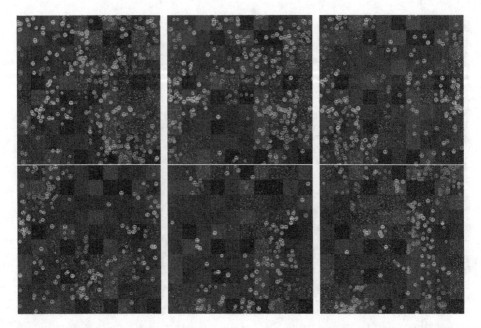

Fig. 8. A sequence of world snapshots with slower migration with the 'human' agents (faces) eating all resources as they go, but new 'plant' entities (dots) re-growing after they have left

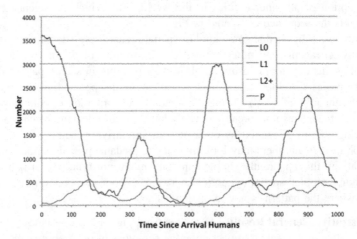

Fig. 9. Number of agents and 'plant' entitiess in a run of the simulation starting from a rich plant ecology, from the point at which humans were introduced, where: L0 = trophic level 0 entities (plants, top line), L1 = level 1 (herbivores, none), L2 + predators (none), and P (bottom line) is the number of 'human' agents.

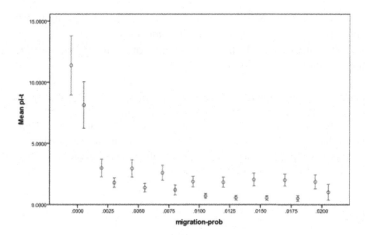

Fig. 10. Mean diversity for different migration rates with (bottom series) and without (top series) human agents (error bars indicate a 95 % confidence interval).

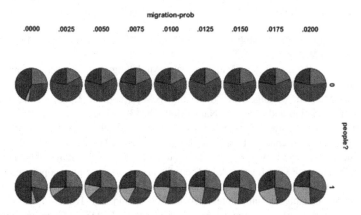

Fig. 11. Proportions of final ecological states at final tick over independent runs for different migration rates, with and without agents, where: lighter grey = plants only, darker grey = with higher trophic levels, darkest grey = monoculture, lightest grey = non viable (Color figure online).

5   Conclusion – A Challenge

Multi-agent simulation could apply its expertise in terms of specifying and exploring the cognitive/social abilities of agents with respect to such a test bed, and start to tease out the complex and often counter-intuitive effects of such abilities. Knowledge about this could play a real part in helping us understand our own, fragile and complex, relationship with the ecologies we inhabit and exploit. It is time to show that multi-agent based simulation can deliver tangible results that can significantly contribute to the challenge of surviving on our planet and living with a variety of other species.

The Challenge to all in the MABS community it to discover how human-like agents might be organised and so: (a) understand some of the possible consequences of various survival strategies and (b) help select which of the many possible strategies are worth trying out for real.

Acknowledgments. This research was partially supported by the Engineering and Physical Sciences Research Council, grant number EP/H02171X/1. Many thanks to Emma Norling, who first worked on these kinds of models at the CPM, Nanda Wijermans and JP Hofestede more recently, and all those I have discussed this and previous versions of this model with, including those at the Manchester Complexity Seminar, especially Alan McKane, and those at iEMSs conference in 2012 for discussions on this subject.

References

1. Bousquet, F., Cambier, C., Morand, P.: Distributed artificial intelligence and object-oriented modelling of a fishery. Math. Comput. Modell. **20**(8), 97–107 (1994)
2. Bousquet, F., Barreteau, O., Le Page, C., Mullon, C., Weber, J.: In: Blasco, F., Weill, A. (eds.) Advances in Environmental and Ecological Modelling, pp. 113–122. Elsevier, Paris (1999)
3. Bousquet, F., Le Page, C.: Multi-agent simulations and ecosystem management: a review. Ecol. Model. **176**(3–4), 313–332 (2004)
4. Caldarelli, G., Higgs, P.G., McKane, A.: Modelling coevolution in multispecies communities. J. Theor. Biol. **193**, 345–358 (1998)
5. de Aguiar, M.A.M., Baranger, M., Baptestini, E.M., Kaufman, L., Bar-Yam, Y.: Global patterns of speciation and diversity. Nature **460**, 384–387 (2009)
6. Deffuant, G., et al.: Data and models for exploring sustainability of human well-being in global environmental change. Eur. Phys. J. Special Topics **214**(1), 519–545 (2012)
7. Diamond, J.: Collapse: How Societies Choose to Fail or Succeed. Viking, New York (2004)
8. Drossel, B., Higgs, P.G., Mckane, A.J.: The influence of predator-prey population dynamics on the long-term evolution of food web structure. J. Theor. Biol. **208**, 91–107 (2001)
9. Edmonds, B.: Complexity and context-dependency. Found. Sci. **18**(4), 745–755 (2013)
10. Edmonds, B.: A test-bed ecological model (Version 1). CoMSES Computational Model Library. https://www.openabm.org/model/4204/version/1. Accessed 4 May 2014
11. Eldridge, N.: Life in the Balance: Humanity and the Biodiversity Crisis. Princeton University Press, Princeton (2000)
12. Kummer, H., Daston, L., Gigerenzer, G., Silk, J.: The social intelligence hypothesis. In: Weingart, P., Mitchell, S.D., Richerson, P.J., Maasen, S. (eds.) Human by Nature. Between Biology and the Social Sciences, pp. 157–179. Erlbaum, Mahwah (1997)
13. Loret, J., Tancredi, J. (eds.): Easter Island: Scientific Exploration into the World's Environmental Problems in Microcosm. Kluwer/Plenum, New York (2003)
14. Reader, J.: Man on Earth. Penguin Books, London (1990)
15. Turner, B.L., Sabloff, J.A.: Classic Period collapse of the Central Maya Lowlands: Insights about human–environment relationships for sustainability. PNAS **109**(35), 13908–13914 (2012)

Modelling Environments in ABMS: A System Dynamics Approach

Reza Hesan[(✉)], Amineh Ghorbani, and Virginia Dignum

Faculty of Technology, Policy and Management, Delft University of Technology,
Delft, The Netherlands
R.Hesan@tudelft.nl

Abstract. Environment is a basic concept of agent-based modeling and simulation (ABMS), in which agents exist and interact, can perceive and act. Common approaches to model environment in ABMS consider environment as a physical space (typically a 2D grid) or as a virtual space that supports agent to agent interaction. In this paper, we introduce a method for modeling the environment in agent-based simulations that integrates both its physical and social aspects. Borrowing from System Dynamics, we specify environment as a set of stocks and flows. Stocks represent physical resources, spatial locations and social structures in a uniform way. Stocks can be perceived and modified by agents through flows. Our method considers and describes the environment as a combination of spatial space (or network), physical structure, and social structure, which makes the inter-relation between the global state environment variables and the behavior of the agents explicit. We illustrate the use of the method through its application to a case study in consumer lighting.

Keywords: Agent-based modeling · System dynamics · Environment

1 Introduction

Agent-based models provide insights into the social systems they represent. A social system consists of social and physical structures, external to the actors, that facilitate or constraint actors behaviors and interactions. These components, and their link with the agent however, are often implicit in agent-based models.

The social and physical components of an agent-based model make up the environment which is generally defined as independent abstraction providing the conditions for the agents to exist, enabling access to resources and facilitating interaction between agents [19]. Even though, environment is commonly viewed as a purely spatial entity in ABMS literature (e.g., in Netlogo), some researchers have defined the social and physical aspects of agent-based models [9,11,13,15]. For example, [11] defines physical environment in terms of physical components (e.g., computer, street, house). These components are connected to each other and to the agents. The social environment in these models is defined on the

© Springer International Publishing Switzerland 2015
F. Grimaldo and E. Norling (Eds.): MABS 2014, LNAI 9002, pp. 41–52, 2015.
DOI: 10.1007/978-3-319-14627-0_4

basis of institutions (e.g., eating norms, driving rules). These concepts define the environment around an individual agent. The limitation of their conceptual definition however, is in defining environment variables, whether social and physical, that are global to the whole simulation, influencing all agents behaviors and being influenced by them. This limitation also holds for other research in the literature because in ABMS, the system is generally viewed as bottom-up and global variables that define the overall state of the system are not explicitly defined.

Besides the lack of definition for global state variables, another drawback of the current practices for modeling agent environments, is that the interrelation between the global level and individual level is also not captured. According to Coleman's bathtub model [7] however, global variables influence the perception of individuals in a social system, which in turn affect their decision making behavior that changes the initial state of the environment. Therefore, to provide a comprehensive definition of environment in agent-based models, we need to have an explicit definition of social and physical environment variables that show the global state of the system. In addition, we also need to capture the interrelation between these variables and the agents.

To define global state variables and their interrelation with the agents, we propose to look at the variables and relations in terms of stocks and flows. For example, if *food resource* is an environment stock, we define *flow of food* that goes to the agents which in turn influences the availability of food in the environment. Likewise, a social environment stock such as *fashion*, affects agents perception about a certain product, and the agents behavior in turn determines what stays in fashion. In fact, this can also be considered as an indirect interaction between agents through the environment [13,19].

In this paper, we propose an approach to model global environment variables and their interrelation with agents using a system dynamics perspective. The reason we propose this solution is that system dynamics views the system in terms of aggregate values [18]. Tracking these type of values would help us study the influence of individual behaviour on global parameters of interest (e.g., resource availability, general acceptance of a product). These parameters show the general behaviour of a social system which are commonly the points of interest for many simulations and policy problems in general.

The structure of this paper is as follows. In Sect. 2, we look into environment modeling more in depth, we explain system dynamics and present the concepts that we will be using to define our modeling approach. In Sect. 3, we present an example case which we will be using in Sect. 4, to explain our proposed approach. In Sect. 5, we will explain the consumer lighting model. In Sect. 6 we will finish with some discussion and concluding remarks.

2   Background

2.1   Environment in Agent Systems

In ABMS, agents interact with each other and with the environment to perform tasks that represent actual events in the system. Although the concept of agent as a social entity is relatively clear for modelers, the concept of the environment and its function and responsibility remain unclear [5].

The common approach in ABMS considers environment as a spatial entity that facilitates interaction between agents and enables different forms of networks between agents. In fact, [2] emphasize that environment in ABMS is a first order entity when the spatial dimension are important to be considered. Furthermore, [13] introduces environment in ABMS as a physical environment that imposes restriction on the location of agents. This kind of environment can be built by defining a 2D or 3D virtual space which is especially important in cases where spatial dimension is important (e.g., land use modeling). Besides the spatial definitions of the environment, [5] investigate the role of environment in agent-based models by assigning regulation functions to the environment.

In contrary to ABMS, in multi-agent systems (MAS) literature, many studies have been conducted that indicate the role of environment as a first-class abstraction for the modeling of MAS [19]. Some of these studies propose conceptual models of the environment similar to the work of [11] for ABMS (e.g., [2]). Reference [4] proposes a multi-layered framework called: Multi Agent Situated System (MMASS) which provides a representation of the environment. In MMASS, an environment is modeled as a set of interconnected layers so that every layer's structure is an indirect graph of sites. These layers can be abstraction of the physical environment or can also be related to the logical aspects. In addition, connections can be specified between layers. Reference [16] proposes a model of agents and artifacts. Artifacts are dynamically constructed and shared by the agents. Their research eventually lead to the CArtAgo (Common Artifacts for Agents Open framework) for prototyping artifact-based environment [17] which emphasizes the functionality of tools and objects (artifacts) and how agents work with these objects and tools in a system.

In both ABMS and MAS literature, besides the spatial representation, environment is viewed and used at the level of individuals through the definition of entities such as artifacts, physical components, norms and institutions. Such physical and social components are recognized by individual agents as entities that they can use or posses, or ones that for example restrict them. Therefore, although these concepts are external to the agents, they are viewed locally by them and they do not represent the global state of the environment in terms of aggregate variables (e.g., sum of all light bulbs in society, general perception about LED lamps). Nor do these concepts provide insights about how aggregate values in the environment would influence the agents or be influenced by them.

2.2   System Dynamics

System dynamics modeling is an equation-based approach for constructing simulations especially at the macro level. We use the general concepts of system dynamics modeling [8,18], namely stock and flow to extend the conventional environment in agent-based models.

Stocks represent specific elements of a system whose values depend on the past behavior of the system. Stocks accumulate inflow minus outflow and their value represents the state of system.

Flows represent the rate that changes the value of stocks in a system in every instance of time. Flows can be either inflow, increasing the stocks value or can be outflows, decreasing the stocks. The value of stocks are changed by their related flows.

The concepts of stock and flow are familiar concept that are being used in our daily lives. For instance, *bank balance* is a stock that is increased by the flow *deposit* and decreased by the flow money *expenditure*.

A global state variable of an agent-based environment can also be defined using stocks and flows at the macro level because the aggregation of agents' behaviors results in emergent states that are at a higher level than the agents themselves.

3   Working Example

As a running example,we take a consumer lighting case to explain our approach for modeling global state variables and their interrelations with the agents in ABMS.

Developments in electric lighting technology have increased the life time of the bulbs and their energy efficiency [10]. For example, over 98 % of the electricity used in the traditional incandescent bulbs is converted into heat and not into light. However, Compact Fluorescent Lamp (CFL) or Light-Emitting Diod (LED) are nowadays the more efficient alternative lighting products.

Nonetheless, consumers have only partially adopted CFL and LED technology because of a number of obstacles [14]. First, CFL and modern LED saving lamps are characterized by high up-front costs for consumers and poor light quality. Second, halogen lamps are more attractive than CFL and LED lamps because they fit in popular designs and have favorable color and size.

Different studies have been conducted about how different policies may change the people's preference to buy more efficient lamp [6]. The European Union's phase-out of incandescent lighting is a clear strategy that will change the sector. It involves regulations designed to remove the cheapest forms of inefficient household lighting from stores. Reference [1] developed an agent-based simulation to study adoption of LED and CFL lamp technology by consumers in a virtual society. This model encompasses consumers that buy lamp, based on the available luminaries in their houses, their personal preferences and the preferences of their acquaintances. Furthermore, retailers sell different lamps and producers produce lamps in the model. The behavior of all these agents is affected by the government agent who implements different policy in the system with the goal of moving the society towards more efficient lighting choices. Reference [1] investigate three policies in their work: banning light bulbs, taxing light bulbs, or subsidizing energy efficient alternative.

In this paper, we explain how our proposed method can be used to model global environment variables in an agent-based model of the consumer lighting example in order to study the effect of various policies on the global outcomes of the system.

4   A System Dynamics Agent Environment

In conventional ABMS, environment refers to the spatial space in which every agent has a location or is connected to other agents via a network [13]. This definition however, does not provide an explicit representation of social and physical variables that represent the global state of the system.

We use the definition of social and physical structures in [11], to extend environment for ABMS by defining global variables and specifying their interrelation with the agents in the system.

Physical Environment. The physical environment is composed of physical components [11]. Physical components have properties such as shape, color and price. These physical components may be used by agents to perform actions. We define *physical state variables* as variables that show the global state of the aggregation of such physical components. Therefore, while at the individual level, a physical component such as a lamp can be produced, bought, and sold by the agents, at the global level, the sum of all these lamps, which is affected by the same agent actions, influences their availability in the market or their popularity. For instance, when a producer agent produces a lamp, he decreases the amount of different raw material (stock) and increases the number of products in his inventory (stock).

Social Environment. We consider institution as the building block of the social environment [11]. An institution is a rule, norm or strategy that is followed by agents in a simulation. We use institutions as flows that change the *social state variables*. Therefore, to define a *social state variable*, we define a variable that is influenced by a number of institutions. For example, if an institutional rule says that "the government must give subsidy to producers who produce LED lamps", we define a social state variable that has an inflow of subsidy based on this institution and name it as *government support*. The rule "the government bans production of light bulbs" also relates to this social state variable. As another example, if a norm in the society is that "consumers talk to their neighbors about their experiences with lamps", a social state variable that would take this norm as a flow, is *awareness*.

Both social and physical state aspects of the environment are defined as stock and linked to agents as we will explain in the next section. While the physical elements of an environment are tangible, the social elements are the less tangible part of the system. For instance, in our working example *awareness* about a product in society is an intangible part and the amount of products which are available in shops or market are the tangible part of the environment.

The physical and social state variables are both essential for modeling and testing policies which are in fact the goal of many agent-based models. We will discuss this issue later on in the paper.

Another point to mention here is that besides the immediate outcome of local interaction between agents (e.g., immediate outcome of buying lamp = ownership of lamp by buyer), agent interaction may also have global outcomes that are important to capture as state variables. For instance, the *awareness* variable defined previously, is the global result of agents communicating their opinion about lamps among each other.

The Conceptual Model

Figure 1 shows the UML class diagram of our proposed model of the environment. For the purpose of this paper, we assume that the physical components owned by the agents or the institutions they follow are defined in the agent class[1], in order to have a clearer focus on how we define the state variables and how they are connected to agents.

The environment consists of agents, stocks and flows. There are two types of stocks: physical state variable and social state variable. Flows are the means to connect these variables to the agents. The agents are the active entities whose actions, and perceptions of environment lead to changes in the physical and social stocks of the environment.

The state of the environment in every instance of time is a series of stocks' value that can be characterized as $S_t = \{s1_t, s2_t, s3_t, ...\}$. For example $s1_t$ is the value of stock number 1 at time t. Agents perceive the environment state and

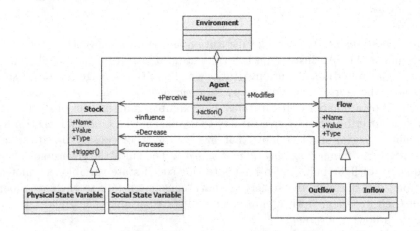

Fig. 1. The class diagram of the system dynamics environment

---

[1] Following the definition of [11], physical components and institutions are external to the agents. However, since in this paper we are making a distinction between local and global entities, for now, we assume that all the local entities are within the agents.

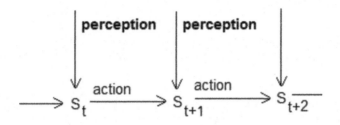

Fig. 2. Perception and Action Sequence

perform actions based on their decision mechanism. Agents' actions will change the value of stocks through the flows. We have two kind of flows: inflow, which increase the value of stocks, and outflow, which decrease the value of stocks. We can represent environment's state as the following:

$$\{s1_{t+1}, s2_{t+1}, s3_{t+1}, ...\} = \{s1_t + \sum_{i=1} inflow1_{a_i} - \sum_{j=1} outflow1_{a_j}, s2_t + \sum_{i=1} inflow2_{a_i} - \sum_{j=1} outflow2_{a_j}, s3_t + \sum_{i=1} inflow3_{a_i} - \sum_{j=1} outflow3_{a_j}, ...\} \quad (1)$$

Figure 2 illustrates how the state of the environment is changed by the agents activities. We use the consumer lighting example in the next section to show how this method works in more detail.

5   Consumer Lighting Model

Figure 3 illustrates the consumer lighting model. In this model, the rounded rectangles represent the stocks, the arrows show the flows and the dashed arrows show where the perceptions of the agents from the environment is coming from.

There are four types of agents in the model: `consumer`, `retailer`, `producer` and `government`. `Awareness`, `government support`, `retailer price` and `producer price` are the social state variables in the system. `Available lamps in shops`, `available lamps in market` and `lamps in society` are the physical state variables in the environment of the consumer lighting model. The goal of the `consumers` is to buy lighting products in order to have pleasant light in their house. The goal of the `producers` is to produce different kinds of lamps to offer in the market in order to have income. `Retailers` will sell lamps to `consumers` in order to increase their income. `Government` wants to reduce electricity consumption through different policy implementations. The agents actions which are defined according to their goals affect the environment's flows which in turn result in changes in the state of the system (environment stocks).

Consumers consider several criteria in their lamp purchase decision: preference for subjective lamp qualities (color, price, efficiency, and life time), opinions (perception) on the lamp's characteristics (lamp model, brand, and technology

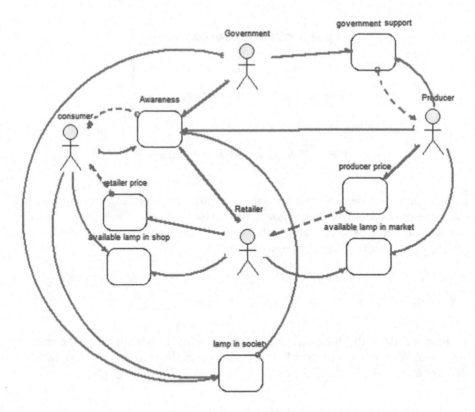

Fig. 3. Lighting Case Model

type), and popularity of LED lamps which is defined as **awareness** in the environment. **Consumers** buy lamps which declines **available lamps in shops** and they will change the **awareness** about the new efficient lamp by word of mouth. Consumers are influenced by the **price of products**, and **awareness** about the product in the whole environment.

Retailers will decrease **available lamps in market** by buying products and transferring them to shops. They will change the **retailer price** in shops and they will also affect the **awareness** about a product in the environment by advertising (shown as a flow between **retailer** and **awareness**). **producer price** influences the **retailers** decision making process about setting a price on the lamps in the shop.

Producers increase the **available lamps in market** by producing more lamps. They will change the **producer price** and influence the **awareness** about a product in the environment by advertising, similar to the **retailers**. The amount of **government support** is changed by the **government** by providing subsides to the **producers**. Besides, the amount of **government support** will encourage producers to produce more subsidized products. There is also a link between **lamps in society** and the **producer** which we will discuss later.

Government will intervene in society to support efficient lighting products. The link between the **government** and **awareness** shows that the **government** can increase **awareness** in society by some activity like advertising. In addition, the **government** increases **available lamp in society** by buying efficient lighting products for public area which triggers some important dynamics in the consumer lighting system.

Dynamics of the Model

Feedback is an important feature of a dynamic system: a system whose behavior changes over time [3]. The notion of feedback refers to a situation in which two or more variables of the system are influencing each other which may lead to growth or decaying behavior. As we are studying the dynamic behavior of the lighting case, it is worthwhile to study the feedbacks which determine the dynamic behavior of system.

The first clear feedback happens between **consumers** and **awareness** in society. More **awareness** in society about efficient products results in increased popularity of the products, which will in turn increase the **awareness** in the environment. The second feedback is between **consumers** and the **available lamp in society** either in consumer's home or in public places. Ubiquity of a technology in society can influence the preference of consumer about a product. Therefore, if the government buys efficient lighting products, this triggers the feedback between amount of lamp in society and the preference of consumers.

One of the obstacles that discourages people to buy new efficient lamps is their high up front costs. Since people do not buy these new costly products, producers cannot produce them in an economic scale. Economic scale has a significant effect on the price of products. The cost per unit of product decreases with increasing scale since the fixed costs are spread over more products. The final important feedback that we will mention happens between **consumers**, the **available lamps in society**, the **producers**, and the **retailers**. Due to economic scale, when people buy more products, the price will go down which will then encourage people to adopt new efficient lamps instead of non-efficient ones.

Modeling Policies

As previously mentioned, many agent-based models are built for testing policies. Policies are implemented with a set of policy instruments which can be social (e.g., speed limit rule) or/and physical (e.g., speed camera) [12]. Policies also have goals which are usually aimed at achieving desired global outcomes through individual behavior (e.g., decrease number of deaths by car accidents) [12]. Both the instruments and the goals are covered in an agent-based model that is extended with the state variables.

Reference [1] propose three policies: banning light bulbs, taxing light bulbs, or subsidizing energy efficient alternatives. All these three policies were aimed at intervening in the supply part of the system. Along with these three policies, we propose two new policies in order to influence the demand part of the system: (1) increasing the awareness about the new lighting products by advertising and (2) increasing the number of lamps in society by installing efficient lamps in public areas. These policies can activate the word of mouth dynamics and economics scale dynamics which we discussed in the previous section.

6   Discussion and Conclusion

In this paper, we proposed a method for modeling the global aspects of the environment in agent-based models and capturing the interrelation between the global states and local entities including the agents. We illustrate this method by applying it to a consumer lighting scenario.

In ABMS, the environment in which agents behave and interact in, is commonly considered as a spatial space to visualize agents and their interaction in the system. Nonetheless, some researchers define an agent-based model in terms of the social and physical aspects surrounding the agents, influencing their behavior and being influenced by them. However, even when the social and physical aspects are defined in the agent-based model, their level of abstraction is at the individual level.

The global aspects of the environment are essential for studying social systems because they provide insight into how individuals influence the system as a whole and how the global state of the system is perceived by the agents and influences their behavior. Therefore, in this paper, we proposed a method to add global social and physical variables to agent-based models in order to address this requirement. Since system dynamics modeling also has a global perspective on the system, we were inspired from this modeling approach in our proposed method.

The proposed method contributes to ABMS is several aspects. Firstly, since we extended the definition of physical components and institutions in [11], our definition of an agent environment now has two levels: one at the agent level with concepts like house, driving norm etc., and one at the global level where aggregate concepts such as general awareness are defined. We have also defined the relationship between these two levels to show how the local environment can lead to aggregate states in the system. Secondly, the global outcomes of agent interaction can also be captured with our proposed method, which provides further insights into how individuals influence the system as a whole. Thirdly, the method provides enhancement in implementing policies and testing them. As mentioned previously, with the global state variables introduced in this paper, the modeler can study how individuals influence the goal of a policy which can in fact be modeled as (a) stock(s). Of course, agent-based modeling platforms such as Netlogo and Repast already facilitate the definition of global variables. However, our contribution lies in the fact that we are using system dynamics as the method to implement such variables. Fourthly, by providing a visual representation of the environment as illustrated in Fig. 3, it becomes easier for modelers to study the interrelations and feedbacks in the system.

One final contribution of this method is that since we are taking two fundamental elements of system dynamics modeling (stocks and flows), ABMS can become more within the reach of the system dynamics community. Although system dynamics modeling, as a macro-level approach, is traditionally constructed by stocks that are changed by flows, we propose that the concept of stock and flow is compatible with agent based modeling and can be integrated with the concept of agent. In practice, system dynamics modeling assumes agents to be all homogeneous and therefore takes one representative for the whole population. However, with our proposed method, system dynamics modelers can use the advantage of considering heterogeneous agents and different decision making processes.

In this paper, we viewed agents as black boxes and did not go into the details of decision making processes or local interaction. However, it appears that the concept of stock and flow can also be considered in the decision making process of agents and their local interactions. Therefore, our next goal is to find out how the internal perception of the agents and their decision making behavior can be captured through this perspective.

References

1. Afman, M.R., Chappin, E.J.L., Jager, W., Dijkema, G.P.J.: Agent-based model of transitions in consumer lighting. In: Proceedings of 3rd World Congress on Social Simulation, Kassel, Germany (2010)
2. Amblard, F., Mailliard, M.: Review of e4mas 2004–2005 proceedings (2007)
3. Aström, K.J., Murray, R.M.: Feedback Systems: An Introduction for Scientists and Engineers. Princeton University Press, Princeton (2010)
4. Bandini, S., Manzoni, S., Vizzari, G.: A spatially dependent communication model for ubiquitous systems. In: Weyns, D., Van Dyke Parunak, H., Michel, F. (eds.) E4MAS 2004. LNCS (LNAI), vol. 3374, pp. 74–90. Springer, Heidelberg (2005)
5. Bandini, S., Vizzari, G.: Regulation function of the environment in agent-based simulation. In: Weyns, D., Van Dyke Parunak, H., Michel, F. (eds.) E4MAS 2006. LNCS (LNAI), vol. 4389, pp. 157–169. Springer, Heidelberg (2007)
6. Chappin, E.J.L.: Simulations of Energy Transitions. Ph.D. thesis, Delft University of Technology (2011). ISBN: 978-90-79787-30-2
7. Coleman, J.: Social theory, social research, and a theory of action. Am. J. Sociol. **91**(6), 1309–1335 (1986)
8. Forrester, J.W.: Industrial Dynamics, vol. 2. MIT Press, Cambridge (1961)
9. Garro, A., Russo, W.: EasyABMS: a domain-expert oriented methodology for agent-based modeling and simulation. Simul. Model. Pract. Theory **18**(10), 1453–1467 (2010)
10. Gendre, M.F.: Two centuries of electric light source innovations. 143 (2003). http://www.einlightred.tue.nl/lightsources/history/light_history.pdf
11. Ghorbani, A., Bots, P., Dignum, V., Dijkema, G.: MAIA: a framework for developing agent-based social simulations. J. Artif. Soc. Soc. Simul. **16**(2), 9 (2013)
12. Ghorbani, A., Dechesne, F., Dignum, V., Jonker, C.: Enhancing ABM into an inevitable tool for policy analysis. J. Policy Complex Syst. **1**, 61–77 (2014)
13. Gilbert, N., Terna, P.: How to build and use agent-based models in social science. Mind Soc. **1**(1), 57–72 (2000)
14. Menanteau, P., Lefebvre, H.: Competing technologies and the diffusion of innovations: the emergence of energy-efficient lamps in the residential sector. Res. Policy **29**(3), 375–389 (2000)

15. Pavon, J., Gomez-Sanz, J., Fuentes, R.: The INGENIAS methodology and tools. Agent-Oriented Methodol. **9**, 236–276 (2005)
16. Ricci, A., Viroli, M., Omicini, A.: Programming MAS with artifacts. In: Bordini, R.H., Dastani, M., Dix, J., El Fallah Seghrouchni, A. (eds.) PROMAS 2005. LNCS (LNAI), vol. 3862, pp. 206–221. Springer, Heidelberg (2006)
17. Ricci, A., Viroli, M., Omicini, A.: CArtAgO: a framework for prototyping artifact-based environments in MAS. In: Weyns, D., Van Dyke Parunak, H., Michel, F. (eds.) E4MAS 2006. LNCS (LNAI), vol. 4389, pp. 67–86. Springer, Heidelberg (2007)
18. Sterman, J.: Business Dynamics. Irwin-McGraw-Hill, Boston (2000)
19. Weyns, D., Omicini, A., Odell, J.: Environment as a first class abstraction in multiagent systems. Auton. Agent. Multi-Agent Syst. **14**(1), 5–30 (2007)

Simulation of Social Behaviour

Modeling Culturally-Influenced Decisions

Loïs Vanhée[1,2(✉)], Frank Dignum[2], and Jacques Ferber[1]

[1] Université Montpellier 2, Montpellier, France
[2] Utrecht Universiteit, Utrecht, The Netherlands
`lois.vanhee@gmail.com`

Abstract. This article proposes a model of culturally influenced decision processes. In particular, cultures influence individual motivation, jointly with human nature and personality. The use of this model is then illustrated by a simulation model of the impact of cultural differences on organizational performance (efficiency, flexibility and member satisfaction) in two organizational structures (bureaucracies and adhocracies). This model is validated against empirical evidence from social sciences.

Keywords: Social simulation · Simulation techniques · Tools and environments · Artificial societies

1 Introduction

"Leaders dictate, subordinates obey". Well, not the same everywhere. The acceptance of such a statement, which describes a collectively accepted social pattern, is shown to be highly correlated with culture. More generally, strong correlations between cultures and social patterns have been discovered. But, obviously, cultures do not directly influence societies. They influence individuals, whose collective action influences societies.

Sometimes, explaining how social phenomenon arise from the influence of culture on individuals is straightforward. For instance, the first sentence is easily explained by the individual sensitivity towards statuses, which is known to be culturally driven. Some other times, explaining correlations is far more complicated (e.g. determining the influence of culture on trading). Simple explanations may not be sufficient to cope with this complexity. So, more complex models such as agent based models (ABMs) are developed: by describing how cultures influence individuals, social patterns emerging from such a model can provide insights leading to new explanations.

Trivially, cultures influence individual practices (e.g. greeting in bowing or shaking hands). But, in cultures also influence inner motives, driving individual and collective action much more subtly while remaining quite strong. This article aims at producing the simplest possible agent decision model where individual motives are culturally-influenced, while not being only dependent on culture. Because culture is a very complex concept, we only use its core aspect, which can be seen as determining the preferences over a set of (fixed) values which influence motives.

© Springer International Publishing Switzerland 2015
F. Grimaldo and E. Norling (Eds.): MABS 2014, LNAI 9002, pp. 55–71, 2015.
DOI: 10.1007/978-3-319-14627-0_5

This model is then illustrated on a simple concrete case. This case reproduces social science observations, that individuals in cultures promoting openness to change are more satisfied in adhocracies, while those promoting conservatism are more satisfied in bureaucracies. This illustration, while not providing an explanation for a rather unknown social phenomena shows instead a concrete application of our model of culturally influenced motives in a well documented situation. Consequently, this illustration supports that our model allows to obtain results that are coherent with social science findings.

In Sect. 2, we present our culturally influenced motivation model jointly with their theoretical foundations. Then, our culturally influenced motivation model is applied to build a model of agents performing in organizations in Sect. 3 and finally the comparison between the output of this model and social science findings is described in Sect. 4.

2 Modeling Culturally-Influenced Motivated Decisions

2.1 Theoretical Foundations

Culture and Motives. Reference [7] suggests that motives are influenced by three sources: human nature (e.g. survival needs), shared by all humans; culture, shared within communities; personality which are unique. The distinction between these three sources is also related to Maslow's hierarchy of needs [7]: lowest levels are highly correlated with human nature while the order of highest levels is influenced by cultures and personalities.

As an important notice, motives, inspired by [2] are abstract drives or desires. All individuals have the motive to eat and the importance given to this motive can be culturally dependent. Then, these motives are turned in concrete goals or intentions: for instance, individuals can intend to have lunch. These intentions can be made concrete through plans (which can also be culturally dependent, like eating with sticks or forks and knives). In this article, we focus only on the abstract influence of culture on motives, leaving more concrete action for future work. To that extent, in our model, plans leading to concrete action are "predefined", but can of course be generated dynamically or make evolving.

Conceptualizing Cultures. Culture has been defined numerous times without reaching a consensus. Nonetheless, there is a general agreement that cultures are pieces of knowledge shared within communities. Reference [7] defines culture as the importance given to *values* (what is important for individuals, e.g. "being good" or "being rational") and *practices* (how to behave, e.g. shaking hands or bowing for greeting) shared within communities. Schwartz [9] proposes a set of values that is supposed to be fixed for all people: Self-Transcendence (Universalism, Benevolence), Conservation (Conformity, Tradition, Security), Self-Improvement (Achievement, Power) and Openness to Change (Stimulation, Self-direction). Values drives individuals towards reaching some type of situation. To that extent, values influence inner individual motives, while not influencing concrete plans pursued by agents.

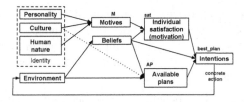

Fig. 1. Conceptual representation of the decision model

Cultural Dimensions. In spite of consensus on a formal definition, some research [6, 7] empirically discovered the existence of cultural preferences, referred to as cultural dimensions, that can be measured via a cultural dimension score. As an example of such a dimension, Uncertainty Avoidance (UAI) measures the cultural sensitivity with regard to uncertainty. Cultures promoting high UAI tend to prefer regulated and stable environments while those promoting low UAI are likely to prefer trying out new solutions in less constrained environments. Note that these dimensions are related to national cultures: they do not necessarily reflect individual preferences, but rather indicate individual tendencies. Cultural dimensions can be related to values by indicating that they lead to preferences for certain types of values from the Schwartz values classification. Thus, UAI can be conceptually correlated with a preference for conservation (conformity, tradition) or openness to change (stimulation, self-direction).

Former ABMs. Reference [12] uses cultural dimensions to model inter-cultural trade. This model expands a former trade model in using culture to instantiate numerical parameters (e.g. an UAI variable influencing the tendency to double-check received products when dealing with unknowns). On a similar track, [3] investigates modeling the influence of culture on norm emergence, trying to provide explanations about why the European smoking ban is accepted in some countries but not all. Finally, [4] describes how cultural values influence the plan selection process in considering them constraints imposed to agents. Although some of this work already considers culture in terms of preferences over values, none of this work combines the influence of culture with that of other motivational sources directly, which is the aim of the present paper.

2.2 Model

In this model, we aim at enriching the representation of the influence of culture on decisions by going beyond using cultural dimensions to influence surface behavior. We want cultures to influence decisions from a deeper motivational aspect, by representing them as preferences towards values. In addition, we want that other aspects of individuals (namely, human nature and personality), play a role in motivation. A global depiction of this model is represented in Fig. 1.

Identity and Motives. As said before, we assume three sources of influence over motives, referred as identity: human nature, (cultural) values and individual preferences (personality). In the case study presented in this article, motives represented by: m_s survival drive, only influenced by human nature; m_{otc} openness to change and m_c conservatism, both only influenced by culture. The set of motives is $M = \{m_s, m_{otc}, m_c\}$. For simplicity, each motive is influenced by only one part of the identity and the influence of personality over motives is discarded in this article.

Motive Satisfaction. Agent beliefs evaluate each motive satisfaction, modeled by the function $sat_a : M \rightarrow MS$ for each agent a from the set of agents A, where MS is a set of motive satisfaction. If MS is ordered, the lower $sat_a(m)$, the least m is satisfied. In the case study, MS is $[0, 1]$. sat allows modeling needs possibly independently satisfiable: agents can feel safe and bored at the same time.

Importance. Depending on their identity, agents can give more or less importance to different motives. This importance is represented by $imp_a : M \rightarrow I$, where I is the set of importance. Unlike sat which changes depending on agent beliefs, imp is expected to remain constant. In the illustration I is $[0, 1]$. In addition, imp is normalized: $\forall a \in A, \sum_{m \in M} imp_a(m) = 1$.

If I is partially ordered, the higher $imp_a(m)$, the more $m \in M$ is important for a. With such a representation, it becomes easy to model Maslow properties such as survival drives are more important than values. In addition, in this model, *cultures* are represented by changing the relative importance between values.

Desires. The inclination of an agent to act because of some motive is influenced both by the satisfaction and the importance of this motive. Desires are represented by $des_a : MS \times I \rightarrow D$, where D is the set of desires. If MS, I and D are ordered, des_a should be monotonically decreasing with regard to its first argument and increasing with regard to its second. In the illustration, I is $[0, 1]$. $des_a(ms, i) = (1 - ms) \times i$. An agent desire towards some motive is represented by $des_a : M \rightarrow D$ such that $des_a(m) = des_a(sat_a(m), imp_a(m))$.

This models capture the property that important or unsatisfied motives become more desirable for agents. Consequently, less important motives can become desirable if unsatisfied and more important motives are satisfied. In addition, lower level needs from the Maslow pyramid can be made are more easily desired than others. Idem for culturally important values.

Global Satisfaction. The global satisfaction of agents is determined by each motive satisfaction and importance. Formally, agent satisfaction is represented by: $Sat_a \in GS$, where GS represent the set of global satisfactions. If MS, I and GS are ordered, Sat_a should monotonically increase with regard to sat_a and des_a. In the illustration, $Sat_a = \sum_{m \in M} sat_a(m_s) \times imp_a(m_s)$. Since imp is normalized, this representation captures the property that more important motives have more impact on global satisfaction.

Plan Satisfaction. In order to select which action to perform, agents have to be capable of estimating how plans satisfy their motives. This estimation is represented by $sat_a : P \times M \rightarrow MS$, where P is the set of plans. sat_a can be expanded by $sat_a : P \rightarrow GS$ by determining global agent satisfaction from each motive estimated satisfaction. sat_a is just an estimation. Complex aspects, such as uncertainty are also part of the estimated satisfaction of a plan, represented by GS.

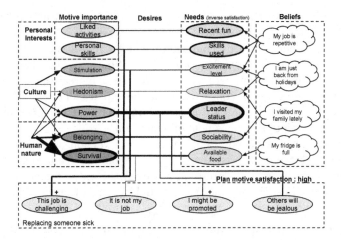

Fig. 2. Illustration of the evaluation of situations and plans (using line thickness). Human nature, culture and personality influence motive importance, beliefs influence motive satisfaction; importance and satisfaction influence desires; beliefs and desires influence estimation of plan satisfaction, influencing plan selection.

Plan selection. Finally, agents select the most satisfactory plan. Given the set of available plans AP, the selection is represented by $best\_plan_a \in AP$. If GS is partially ordered, then $best\_plan_a$ should belong to $(argmax_{p \in AP} sat_a(p))$. In the illustration, $best\_plan_a = argmax_{p \in AP} \sum_{m \in M} sat_p(m) \times des_a(m)$. This model represents the traditional utility function maximization. Note that $best\_plan_a$ is indirectly influenced by agent preferences and thus by culture.

Overview of Agent Decision Dynamics (Fig. 2). Agents desires result from the combination of beliefs (obtained through perception) and their motives. Then, desires are combined with available plans (resulting from beliefs) to determine how satisfactory a plan can be. The output of this combination depends on the organization as well as on agent beliefs. Then, the most satisfactory plan is selected for the next agent action.

2.3   Modeling the Influence of Culture on Decisions

Cultural Importance. Our model integrates the influence of human nature, cultures and personalities on motivation via the imp function. Changing culture is done by modifying imp. While the signature of imp permit a wide range of functions, imp implementation is kept simple in the use case.

Human nature influence is represented by $hn \in [0, 1]$, culture by $c \in [0, 1]$ and personality by $p \in [0, 1]$ such that $hn + c + p = 1$. For our simulations p is set to 0 to prevent personalities to blur results, hn is set to 0.6 and c to 0.4. Human nature influences on the importance given to survival drives: $imp(m_s) = hn$ and cultures on values: $imp(m_{otc}) + imp(m_c) = c$.

Conform to cultural theories [7], our representation of cultures influence the relative importance given to values. In the use case, since imp is normalized, the relative preference towards conformity can be represented via $\alpha \in [0,1]$. $imp(m_{otc}) = \alpha \times c$ and $imp(m_c) = \alpha \times (1-c)$. So, if $\alpha = 0$, extreme cultural importance is given to openness to change. When α increases, cultural importance is increasingly given to conservation at the expense of openness to change. Note that this representation captures the property that cultures and human nature are differentiated (α does not influences hn).

Additional values can be used: in previous version we integrated self-enhancement (achievement, power) and self-transcendence (universalism, benevolence) Schwartz values. They are removed from the current model in order to keep experimentations simple and concise. If $V \subseteq M$ is the set of values, their importance should respect this property: $\sum_{v \in V} imp(v) = c$

Designing Cultural Importance. A few important properties have to be considered when designing imp. First, in order to match Maslow hierarchy of needs, human nature, which emphasize the importance of human drives, should be given more importance than cultural values or personal aspirations. Nonetheless, the model still captures scenario where culture can be more influential than nature (e.g. agents capable of self-sacrifice).

Another important design aspect is the differentiation between the three sources of motivation: human nature should be the same for everyone, while culture is shared within communities and personalities are unique.

Changing culture just by altering the single α parameter can appear to be overly simple. Actually, this very particular implementation is on purpose designed to be simple. It serves as demonstration that easy and simple representations can be sufficient to obtain coherent results when using our model. Of course, more values can be integrated. Plus, a lot of freedom is given on designing evaluators, such as sat_p, des (which relies on imp). For interested readers, an illustration of the design of complex decision processes influenced by preferences over values can be found in [10].

3   Case Study: Culture and Organizational Performance

This section serves as an illustration the motivational model described in Sect. 2. This illustration investigates the influence of cultures of individual satisfaction and on collective performance in various types of organizations. In particular, two cultures are studied: conservatism and open to change as well as two organizational patterns: bureaucracies and adhocracies.

This model purposefully investigates a research question which has a clear answer from social sciences. Namely, conservative cultures and bureaucracies combine well, as well as open to change cultures and adhocracies. Nonetheless, there is, up to our knowledge, no simulation model which emerges this collective behavior from individual cultures. The main aim of this model is *not* to provide an answer to a controversial social science question. Instead, we want to show that our motivation model can be used on a concrete case, by being capable of observing expected collective properties from an expected cultural influence on individual behavior.

In addition, this illustration simplifies on purpose numerous aspects of the theory. While modeling in detail interactions occurring within organizations can be of great interest for providing explanations, going too far into detail would increase the model complexity while not better illustrating the motivation model. This simplification also avoids the risk for modelers to integrate culturally-driven bias into implementation details[1]. Second, culture seems to impact less on lowest-levels details, which are generally more environmentally constrained. In addition, abstracting away from lowest level details prevents results to be specific for a peculiar environmental or organizational detail. Finally, simplification avoids integrating very technical aspects which impact on organizational performance and sensitivity to culture are not yet extensively studied by former research. Instead, more importance can be given on clearly influencing aspects.

3.1 Previous Work

Organizations. Organizations have received a large amount of attention from social sciences. Reference [8] proposes a description of 5 typical organizational patterns (simple structure, machine bureaucracy, professional bureaucracy, divisionalized form and adhocracy). Each of these organizational pattern is fits for some type of environment (simple/complex, static/dynamic).

This article makes use of machine bureaucracies and adhocracies. While trying to define them is far out of the scope of this article, some key aspects are to be highlighted. Machine bureaucracies cooperation is promoted by standardization: behavior is restricted by procedures, which leads to repetition of action, allowing to improve individual efficiency and reducing necessary communication. In addition, a strong hierarchy is generally in place in order to centralize information and decision at various level of importance (e.g. team level, factory level, nation level). Adhocracies relies on informal structures. Individuals gather in working groups depending on tasks to be solved. Due to the volatile nature of these groups, rules of behavior tend to be rare and formal structure (such as leadership) have little benefits.

Reference [1] simulates of two organizational patterns (simple structure and adhocracy) in various environments. Each structure is in turn better than the other depending on the environmental conditions. Our illustration expands this idea in also integrating some cultural influence on individual behavior and thus on collective performance.

Culture and Organizations. Reference [7] links cultural dimensions and Mintzberg's archetypal organizations. The acceptance of some organizational patterns (and thus its coordination mechanism) depends on cultural preferences. For instance, bureaucracies, enforcing standardization are preferred in cultures which are sensitive to uncertainty. These preferences are summarized in Fig. 3. Our illustration model aims at providing explanations about how correlations

---

[1] Actually, the design of this model lead us to some culturally-motivated debates.

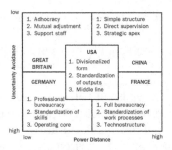

Fig. 3. Cultural dimension and preferred organizational form (conceptual)

between cultures and organizations emerge from the individual-based cultural influence, in the case of adhocracies and machine bureaucracies. Conceptually, conservatism is linked to high UAI and high PDI[2], while openness to change is linked to low UAI and low PDI. To that extent, adhocracies are expected to be preferred in open-to-change cultures while bureaucracies to be preferred in conservative cultures. On a similar track, [11] conceptualize the influence of culture on numerous organizational aspects such as coordination structure, communication processes, failure handling. This work was used to check whether aspects of the illustration model where coherent with theories.

3.2 Simulation Model

In order to ground investigated organizations and to give some meaning to numerical values, the model represents the functioning of an IT department. The department provides three kind of services: maintenance (e.g. keeping email servers running), user support (e.g. helpdesk) and software development (e.g. providing code for other organizations). This organization receives requests from users for each of those services. Each request is treated as an independent task, represented by the *task set* T. Tasks are solved by the intervention of a single agent for some amount of time. This amount of time is lowered if agents have the right expertise (represented by the *expertise set* E). Tasks have a deadline, hidden to agents, after which they are failed if not handled. Successfully resolving tasks influences organization success $OS \in [0, 1]$. Maintenance tasks are critical, making them more influential on organizational success than others.

Organizations can be either bureaucracies or adhocracies. In case of bureaucracies, a special entity, the leader, order subordinates to do some specific task (referred as t_l). Subordinates can still reject t_l for another task.

Agents either select tasks or work on them. This task selection is made using our motivation mechanism, depending on agent's environment (e.g. OS, t_l) and beliefs (domain of expertise).

Environment. The environment represents the set of requests made by users to the IT organization, treated as the set of tasks T and the organizational success, represented by OS.

---

[2] PDI refers to "power distance", the importance given by individuals to statuses.

Task Origin: Tasks originate from one of the three proposed services. Origins are represented by the set $O = \{o_m, o_s, o_d\}$, where o_m stands for maintenance tasks origin, o_s for support tasks and o_d for software development tasks. Task origins, represented by $origin : T \rightarrow O$, are randomly drawn from O.

The main distinction between task origins is that maintenance tasks have more impact on OS than others. The distinction between o_s and o_d is important for an extended version of the current model which includes Self-Transcendence and Self-Enhancement values (promoting cooperation and competition). For simplicity and space, these distinctions are removed from the current model.

Expertise: Tasks require some expertise in order to be resolved more efficiently. This expertise is represented by $exp : T \rightarrow E$, where E is the set of expertises. Task expertises are randomly drawn.

Task Deadline: Tasks can be failed if not being processed quickly enough. Deadlines, which are not visible by agents, is failed is represented by $dl : T \rightarrow \mathbb{N}$. In our simulations, deadlines occur 20 rounds after tasks are issued. This parameter is high enough for expert workers to easily resolve tasks but low enough for making not experts agents or maladapted resolutions to risk failures.

Task resolution: Tasks can be resolved in various ways: quickly r_q, procedurally r_p or creatively r_c. The set of task resolutions is $R = \{r_q, r_p, r_c\}$. This model simplifies reality: in practice not any resolution is allowed every time, but we assume that agents have always the choice.

Time to completion: Tasks require some time for being completed, which depends on several parameters: the task, resolver's expertise and the selected resolution. This time is represented by $ttc : T \times R \times E \rightarrow \mathbb{R}$ such that: $ttc(t, r, e) = btd(t) \times emf(t, e) \times rf(p, e)$ where $bdt : T \rightarrow \mathbb{R}$ represents the base task duration, $emf : T \times E \rightarrow \mathbb{R}$ represents the expertise match factor and $rf : T \times R \times E \rightarrow \mathbb{R}$ represents the influence of the type of resolution on the task resolution.

$\forall t \in T, bdt(t) = 3$, so tasks have the same base duration, which is set in relation with the task deadline. $emf(w, t) = 1$ if $exp(t) = e$, otherwise $emf(w, t) = 2$. This function represents the gain from performing a task the agent is expert at. rf represents the impact of the task resolution on the time required for solving tasks with the following formula: $rf(t, r, e) = 1$ iff $(r = r_q) \vee (r = r_p \wedge exp(t) = e$, otherwise $rf(t, r, e) = 3$ if $r = R_p \wedge exp(t) \neq e$ and $rf(t, r_c, e) = 1.5$. Quick resolution are more efficient. Procedural resolution can be as fast as a quick resolution if the agent is an expert, otherwise much less efficient. Finally, creative resolutions are slightly less efficient than quick resolutions but more efficient than an inexpert procedural resolutions.

Organizational success: represented by $OS \in [0, 1]$. Maintenance task are the main mission of the IT service and are thus more important for organizational success than others. When maintenance tasks are failed, OS is set to $OS \times 0.95$ and to $OS \times 0.99$ for other task origins. When a maintenance task is successfully performed OS is set to $OS + (1 - OS) \times 0.02$ and to $OS + (1 - OS) \times 0.01$ otherwise. The main property of this representation is that OS increases when workers perform well decrease otherwise, with a discounted memory over time.

Available Tasks: AT is the set of available tasks, which are issued but not yet done, failed or being processed.

Agents. Agents perform tasks received by the organization. The set of agents is A. In our experiments, $|A|$ is set to 15, creating a multi-worker setting while keeping reasonable computational complexity[3].

Expertise: Agents have expertise domains, represented by $exp : A \to E$. Agents are more efficient when solving tasks within their field of expertise. In our simulations, exp is uniformly drawn from E. This representation is a simplification of reality (e.g. expertises can be related), it captures capture the benefits of expertise on worker performance. Moreover, $|E|$ also models the fitness between agents and their environment: since task expertise are also uniformly drawn, the probability for a task-worker matching expertise between is $|E|^{-1}$.

Current task: The task on which an agent a is currently working is represented by $t_a \in T \cup \bot$. $\bot$ represents "no task" if no task is available.

Leader orders: Bureaucracies comprise leaders that propose tasks to subordinates. Proposed tasks are represented by $t_l : A \to \{T \cup \bot\}$. $t_l(a)$ is uniformly drawn from $\{t \in AT | exp(t) = exp(a)\}$ if this set is not empty. Otherwise, t_l is randomly drawn from AT. This model represents bureaucracy-like task allocation: experts are allocated tasks within their field of expertise if possible.

Implementation of Culturally-Influenced Decision Process. A few elements from the motivation decision process remain to be defined for this particular setting. Namely, how agents evaluate their satisfaction for each motive and how they estimate the satisfaction resulting from their actions.

Motive Satisfaction: The satisfaction of the survival drive m_s is represented by $sat_a(m_s) = \frac{1}{1+e^{-4(2OS-1)}}$. This formula links m_s to OS with a sigmoid function. Thus, $sat(w, m_s)$ is high for high OS values and decreases quickly when OS decreases below a threshold (around 0.7). This formula represents that satisfaction of survival needs is high when the organization performs well and depletes quickly when organizational success decreases too much.

Conservatism drives are satisfied in following standards, being obedient and acting like others, while open to change drives are satisfied when acting creatively. Openness to change and conservatism values satisfaction depends on two beliefs variables e_c and e_p recording past activity evaluation. e_c records the amount of creatively action in the past and e_p records the time spent acting conform to procedures. At the end of every round, e_c increases by $0.05 \times (1-e_c)$ when acting creatively and $e_c \leftarrow 0.99 \times e_c$ otherwise. Similarly for e_p. These update functions discount with time the importance of oldest actions. Motive satisfactions of m_{otc} and m_c are represented by $sat_a(m_{otc}) = e_c$ and $sat(w, m_c) = e_p$. These formula have the property to increase when doing appropriate behavior and decrease over time. The importance of events is discounted over time.

---

[3] The simulation complexity is proportional to $|A|$, times the amount of rounds per simulation and the number of simulations to run. To that extent, $|A|$ is set to a reasonable value.

Plans: Agent plans is a task and its desired resolution, represented by the set $P = T \times R$. The set of available plans is $AP = \{(t,r)|t \in AT, r \in R\}$.

Estimated Plan Satisfaction: The organizational structure influences the way individuals satisfy their motives. Organizational archetypes, in addition to their impact on formal coordination structures, also influence on how individuals satisfy their drives. In both organizations, openness to change is satisfied by creative task resolution. But, the satisfaction of conservatism motives is more sensitive to the organization. Since adhocracies have no leader, thus conservatism motives cannot be satisfied via obedience. Instead, these motives can be satisfied by satisfying conformity and tradition, that is, performing similar tasks as others and following professional standards. In machine bureaucracies, instead of preferring performing similar tasks as others, conformity is satisfied by obeying leaders. Concerning survival needs, in adhocracies one's job is directly correlated to organizational survival. Thus, survival drives are satisfied in performing critical (maintenance) tasks. Conversely, machine bureaucracies tend to empower leaders. Thus, obedience is a better solution to satisfy survival drives.

Formally, for survival drive m_s, $sat_p((t,r), m_s) = 1$ if $t = t_l$ (the agent obeys the leader) in machine bureaucracies or if t is a maintenance task in adhocracies. Otherwise $sat_p((t,r), m_s) = 0$. For openness to change drive m_{otc}, $sat_p((t,r_c), m_{otc}) = 1$. $sat_p((t,r), m_{otc}) = 0$ if $r \neq r_c$. For conservatism drive m_c, $sat_p((t,r), m_c) = 1$ if r is a standardized resolution and if $t = t_l$ in a hierarchical organization or if the origin of t is the most frequently performed by other workers. Otherwise, $sat_p((t,r), m_c) = 0$.

Then, rewards are discounted by the estimated time to completion for this task, that is divided by $ttc(t, r, exp(a))$ for plan (t,r) and agent a.

Simulation Loop. The model iterates over a loop, where each round corresponds to one hour. Each round, incoming requests are added as tasks; agents work on their allocated task t_a; finished and failed tasks are removed; task-less agents decide on picking an available and how to resolve it.

Each time step, some new tasks are processed by the organization by the organization. In our simulations 5 tasks are issued each turn. This parameter is correlated to organizational processing capacity (depending on the number of agents). This value is high enough for workers to be busy but low enough for workers to be confronted to tasks they are not expert at.

3.3   Key Dynamics of the Model

Dilemmas: The environment forces agents into dilemmas: shall they botch a task with a quick resolution, with high efficiency, avoiding discounting expected survival reward over too long? Or shall they prefer to be creative, costing more time but allowing to satisfy their self-direction motives? Or to follow procedures, at any cost? What makes a decision change from one to another?

Since culture influences on individual preferences towards openness to change and conformism, agents are more likely to favor one decision over another. This lead to various patterns at the individual and collective level.

Maslow Hierarchy of Needs: These dilemmas happen only when survival needs are satisfied. Since human nature motives are more important than higher level cultural aspects, survival, when not satisfied, is always given more importance than higher levels, more influenced by culture.

Agent Satisfaction and Organizational Structure: A core mechanism of this model is that individual motives are satisfied differently depending on organizational structure. Thus, this structure influences individual decisions. For instance, agents tend to obey leaders in bureaucracies because that is the way their survival motive are satisfied. In adhocracies, this motive is satisfied in instead in performing maintenance tasks.

Organizational structure influences in turn satisfaction influences collective patterns. In bureaucracies, subordinates are allocated tasks they are expert at if available. In this case, workers can generally satisfy their conservation motives "for free". Conversely, openness to change, requiring creative solutions[4] are slightly less efficient than procedural resolutions unless workers are not experts. In case of high survival desire and not expert tasks, workers can prefer a quick resolutions, reducing the time to completion. In adhocracies, in spite of being given more freedom, agents are driven to perform maintenance tasks when OS is low. Thus, opportunities to perform tasks they are expert at can be lost, potentially leading to performance loss.

Environmental Complexity: Finally, in altering $|E|$ (which represents environmental complexity), tasks and agent expertise can be more or less in accordance. Since procedural resolution efficiency suffers the most from lack of expertise, conservation is likely to be less efficient (and thus less satisfied) than openness to change in complex environments.

4   Experiments

4.1   Setup

Experimental Variables and Measures. Experiments investigate the impact of culture on collective organizational performance (efficiency, flexibility, member's satisfaction), depending on organizational structure (adhocracy or bureaucracy) and environmental complexity. Cultural preferences are determined by $\alpha \in [0, 1]$, the relative preference towards conservation and openness to change from Schwartz values. The higher α the more workers prefer conservatism on openness to change. Environmental complexity represents the fitness of the organization with regard to its environment, here represented by $|E|$, lowering the probability of having a matching expertise between agent expertise and task requirements. The higher $|E|$ the more complex is the environment.

Efficiency is measured by the organizational success OS at the endrun. Flexibility correspond to the degree to which the organizational efficiency decreases

---

[4] In a former version, some "original" tasks could satisfy creativity. Open to change workers were occasionally insubordinated in well-doing organizations.

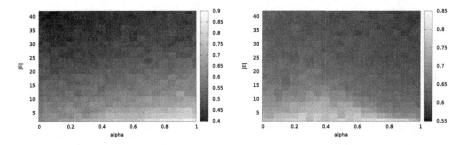

Fig. 4. Efficiency in bureaucracies (left) and adhocracies (right) depending on culture and environmental complexity

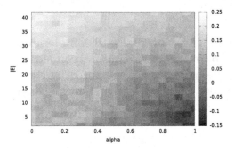

Fig. 5. Differences in OS between performance of bureaucracies and adhocracies in similar environmental setups

when the environment gets more complex. It is measured by $OS_{n+2} - OS_n$ where OS_i is the organizational success (and thus efficiency) when $|E| = i$. Individual satisfaction is measured by the average over Sat of agents. Each result is the average of 20 runs of 150 rounds each. Organizations contain 15 workers.

Studied Hypotheses. These experiments are conducted in order to test the conformity of our model of culturally influenced motivations with regard to well-studied social science observations. These observations provide a stable and well-studied "benchmark" to show the dynamics of our model of culturally-influenced motives. Consequently, if the output is not conform to expectations (and a stable theory provides a lot of expectations), then the only reason is that our model is faulty: we cannot hide behind subjective interpretation of theories. While not providing new answers about social sciences, we reinforce the As suggested by theories in Fig. 3, positive correlations are expected between efficiency and satisfaction in bureaucracies and conservative cultures. Idem, positive correlations are expected with adhocracies and open to change cultures. In addition, for both organizations, positive correlations between flexibility and openness to change are expected. Finally, Mintzberg's culturally-independent property that adhocracies are fitter for complex environment while bureaucracies are fitter for simpler ones is also expected to be retrieved.

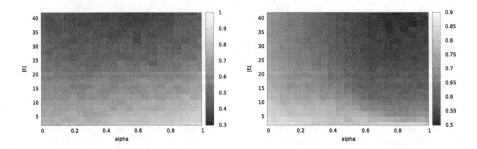

Fig. 6. Individual satisfaction in bureaucracies (left) and adhocracies (right)

4.2 Results

Culture, Organizational Structure and Efficiency. Figure 4 presents the relationship between culture (α), environmental complexity ($|E|$), organizational structure and organizational efficiency measured by the organizational success variable OS. In this figure, lighter cells represent higher efficiency. A horizontal polarization for bureaucracies can be seen: given any environmental complexity, higher conservatism leads to higher performance. For adhocracies, moderate level of conservation leads to higher efficiency for lowest complexity. The positive influence of conservation decreases when the complexity increases. This result is explained by the low cost of following standards in low complexity. In both cases, efficiency is correlated to conservation in bureaucracies and openness to change in adhocracies. This observation underlies a correlation between culture and preferred organizational structure.

Reference [5] shows evidence that "power distance moderated the relationship between empowerment practices and performance, such that there was lower performance for countries assumed to be high in power distance". In order to investigate if our model replicates this observation, bureaucracy and adhocracy efficiency are compared in Fig. 5. Lighter cells mean that adhocracies are more efficient than bureaucracies. For any given environmental complexity level, higher preference towards conservation leads to darker zones. So, adhocracies are less and less efficient than bureaucracies when preference towards conservation (higher power distance) increases, which correlate with the aforementioned evidence.

Culture, Organizational Structure and Satisfaction. Figure 6 depicts individual satisfaction in adhocracies and bureaucracies depending on culture and environmental complexity. Lighter cells represent higher satisfaction. Both figures display a horizontal polarization. In bureaucracies, satisfaction is correlated with conservatism while in adhocracies, satisfaction is correlated with openness to change. Once again, a correlation between satisfaction, organizational pattern and culture is observed. This observation also matches with [5]: "the relationship between empowerment and satisfaction differed across levels of power distance, such that empowerment was negatively associated with satisfaction in high power distance samples". In our model, satisfaction is negatively

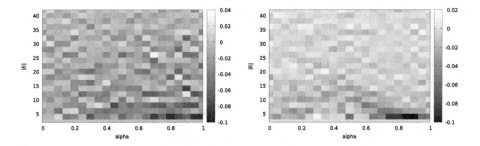

Fig. 7. Gradient of OS along $|E|$ in bureaucracies (left) and adhocracies (right)

associated with power distance (conformism) when individuals are empowered (in adhocracies).

Note the particular case of low environmental complexity and openness to change preference: individuals are more satisfied with in spite of lower efficiency (so, lower survival satisfaction). This case correspond to organizations confronted to a friendly environment: since survival is mostly satisfied, agents gain more satisfaction in value satisfaction.

Flexibility. Figure 7 represents the derivation of efficiency of organizations along increasing level of environmental complexity. Dark zones represent important performance drop due to environmental complexity increase. Both organizational structures display a similar pattern. Darkest zones are darker or more frequent in higher conformity. So, in conservative cultures, performance drops due complexity increases are more frequent and important. Consequently, organizations in conservative cultures are less flexible than organizations in more open to change cultures. This correlation suggested in [7, 11], which describe that PDI and UAI have a negative impact on flexibility.

Mintzberg's Properties. Our model also replicates culturally independent phenomena described by Mintzberg [8]. Figure 5 replicates that, yet slightly influenced by culture, machine bureaucracies have higher organizational success (OS) than adhocracies in simple environments but less success in complex environments.

5   Conclusion

This article presents an agent decision model which explicitly links the influence of culture on motivation. Motivation is also non-cultural influenced by human nature and personality. Human nature, culture and personality influence the relative importance between motives. This importance, combined with need satisfaction, determines agent desires. These desires are influence in turn plan to be selected. Then, this model is illustrated by replicating the influence of culture on organizations as observed by social sciences.

Our decision model differs from the conceptual approach of recent social simulation cultural models such as [12]. Instead of representing culture using cultural dimension scores, which correspond to a cultural tendency to display some type of behavioral response, we represent cultures by the relative importance given to values. This model, which is directly inspired by theories of culture [7], allows to go beyond altering surface level behaviors, but rather uses cultures as a factor of agent motivation thus influencing fundamental motives. This makes our approach more generally applicable and independent of specific applications.

By treating culture as preferences over values, our model can capture interesting properties of cultures. For instance, power distance and collectivism are empirically shown to be related. Since, in our model, cultural dimensions are to be inferred from individual behavior[5], correlations between these dimensions can easily be reproduced by our model: these two dimensions are related by some shared (or at least closely related) underlying cultural values.

The current paper shows a first step towards building computational models of culture that are conceptually closer to the theory of culture: a culture made of values and practices influencing individuals from their desires to their actions, while not discarding the influence of their own personalities and survival drives. Our model opens the way towards more elaborated and complex models of individual decision processes which integrate cultural aspects.

More complex models can enrich our simple model of culturally-driven motivations. As tracks for future work, we propose to integrate culturally-driven practices into agent decision (e.g. how to greet, how to eat), which provides immediately observable aspects of culture. In addition, ABMs appear to be a suitable tool for modeling dynamic aspects of culture, for instance how culture is acquired when entering into a new social environment, but also how individuals "switch" cultures when they change social context. Finally, we also propose to investigate the case where agents are heterogeneous, capable or representing different personalities, but also to acquire different aspects of culture.

Acknowledgments. The first author wishes to thank (anonymous) reviewers for their rich and constructive feedback.

References

1. Aldewereld, H., Tranier, J., Dignum, F., Dignum, V.: Agent-based crisis management. In: Guttmann, C., Dignum, F., Georgeff, M. (eds.) CARE 2009/2010. LNCS, vol. 6066, pp. 31–43. Springer, Heidelberg (2011)
2. Bratman, M.E.: Intention, Plans, and Practical Reason. Center for the Study of Language and Information (1999)
3. Dechesne, F., Di Tosto, G., Dignum, V., Dignum, F.: No smoking here: values, norms and culture in multi-agent systems. Artif. Intell. Law **21**, 79–107 (2012)
4. Dignum, F., Dignum, V.: Emergence and enforcement of social behavior. In: Anderssen, R.S., Braddock, R.D., Newham, L.T.H. (eds.) 18th World IMACS Congress and MODSIM09 International Congress on Modelling and Simulation, pp. 2942–2948 (2009)

---

[5] As in social sciences: dimensions are inferred from behaviors, not the reverse.

5. Gibson, C.B., McDaniel, D.M.: Moving beyond conventional wisdom: advancements in cross-cultural theories of leadership, conflict, and teams. Perspect. Psychol. Sci. **5**(4), 450–462 (2010)
6. Hampden-Turner, A., Trompenaars, C.: The Seven Cultures of Capitalism: Value Systems for Creating Wealth in the United States, Japan, Germany, France, Britain, Sweden, and the Netherlands. Currency Doubleday, New York (1993)
7. Hofstede, G., Hofstede, G.J., Minkov, M.: Cultures and Organizations: Software of the Mind, 3rd edn. McGraw-Hill Professional, New York (2010)
8. Mintzberg, H.: The Structuring of Organizations: A Synthesis of the Research. Prentice-Hall, Englewood Cliffs (1979)
9. Schwartz, S.H.: A theory of cultural value orientations: explication and applications. Comp. Sociol. **5**(2), 137–182 (2006)
10. van der Weide, T.: Arguing to motivate decisions. PhD thesis, Utrecht Universiteit (2011)
11. Vanhée, L., Dignum, F., Ferber, J.: Towards simulating the impact of national culture on organizations. In: Alam, S.J., Van Dyke Parunak, H. (eds.) MABS 2013. LNCS, vol. 8235, pp. 151–162. Springer, Heidelberg (2014)
12. Verwaart, D.: Agent-based Modeling of Culture's Consequences for Trade (2011)

Gender Differences: The Role of Nature, Nurture, Social Identity and Self-organization

Gert Jan Hofstede[1(✉)], Frank Dignum[2], Rui Prada[3], Jillian Student[1],
and Loïs Vanhée[2]

[1] Wageningen University, Wageningen, The Netherlands
gertjan.hofstede@wur.nl
[2] Utrecht University, Utrecht, The Netherlands
f.p.m.dignum@uu.nl
[3] INESC-ID, Lisbon, Portugal
rui.prada@tecnico.ulisboa.pt

Abstract. This paper describes an agent-based model to investigate the origins of gender differences in social status. The agents' basic behaviour is modelled according to Kemper's sociological status-power theory. Differences in the socializing forces of the surrounding society are modelled using Hofstede's dimensions of culture. Particulars of play behaviour are modelled using experimental child development studies from various cultures. The resulting model is presented and discussed. Social identity as a group of either non-gendered children, boys, or girls, seems a powerful force, multiplying the effect of biological differences. The model is actually general enough to be applicable to a wide range of social behaviours with minimal changes.

Keywords: Agent-based model · Gender · Aggression · Rough-and-tumble · Social identity · Status-power theory · Culture · Self-organisation · Emergence

1 Introduction

"Poor Toby! He was so eager to join the big kids in their evening games of Capture the Flag and Kill the Pill. It's a great tradition among the kids at the marine biology lab where we've spent many summers. But little did Toby know that he would soon become "the pill". He came home in a fury, bruised, crying and as angry as I've ever seen him. Luckily, his injuries weren't serious, but when I interrogated him to find out who'd done this, the real source of his rage became clear. It wasn't all the tackling and roughhousing he was upset about. It was that he'd been beaten by... a girl!" [7] (p. 264 – Toby is a ten-year old US boy, the author is his mother).

In all the populous societies in the world, there is a degree to which men receive more status or wield more power than women, according to various criteria such as visibility in public life, representation in well-paying jobs, sexual prerogatives, violence and crime rates. The difference could be small, as e.g. in Sweden, or large, as in Saudi Arabia. It could be generally accepted, contested, or denied.

Our concern in this paper is to explore whether an agent-based model about the micro-dynamics of play between pre-puberty girls and boys can throw light on the

© Springer International Publishing Switzerland 2015
F. Grimaldo and E. Norling (Eds.): MABS 2014, LNAI 9002, pp. 72–87, 2015.
DOI: 10.1007/978-3-319-14627-0_6

origins of gender differences in power. We concentrate on children under the assumption that they may come closer to a 'tabula rasa' than do grown-ups, that their behaviours may be more guileless and observable, and less affected by external circumstances, than those of grown-ups.

What are the main possible influences on these differences? The traditional opposition is between 'nature' and 'nurture'. The 'nature' point of view is that biological differences between the sexes cause the power balance – or imbalance, if you will. The 'nurture' point of view is that gender differences are a product of socialization. At birth, socialization has yet to begin. Boys are slightly bigger and fussier at birth, but parents react in vastly gendered ways to their babies' sex, even before birth. The opening quote about Toby shows that by ten years of age, children can be keenly aware about gender and its status aspects.

Agent-based models allow exploring the interaction between nature and nurture in a process of self-organization or emergence. This means the gender differences could start small but be enlarged to various degrees in various societies by interaction with those already socialized into the mainstream culture, and by the institutions of that culture.

In this article we describe an agent-based modelling framework to investigate the roles of nature, nurture and self-organization for the emergence of gender differences. We model a mixed-sex playground with ten-year old children and some minimal prototypical interaction activities, and look at the emerging patterns of interaction.

The model requires several types of theories as its foundation. This is important because we aim for a generic model of social reality, of which the playground example is just one instantiation. First, we need a theory that tells us what motivates the children. We selected the sociological status-power theory by Kemper [19], for its simplicity and universality. We supplement it with notions from Tajfel's Social Identity theory [28]. Next, we need a theory to span the cultural spectrum of socializing influences. For this we took Hofstede's [13] dimensions of culture because they are the society level indicators with the largest nomological network, i.e. validity. Third, we need to use specific theory on child development and play. Here we use a variety of books and articles, with a central role for Eliot's recent study [7].

The core elements of Kemper's theory are highlighted in our choice of concepts. First, Hofstede's work on culture shows a strong influence of the dimension of masculinity-femininity on comparative gender status. This dimension actually distinguishes status-based versus power-based social organization, and fits Kemper's framework well. Hofstede [15] argued that the same distinction was found to be important for social organization in non-human primates by Hemelrijk [10, 11] in agent-based models of dominance interactions. Second, there is ample evidence from child development literature that points at important roles of both rough and tumble and fighting for hierarchical relations between children within and among genders.

The bodies of theory used are briefly introduced in the next sections. After this we explain how they are used in our agent based model. Because that model operationalizes agent behaviours such as playing and quarrelling, it also requires variables and mechanisms that the theory does not specify. After a summary of the research questions in the second section, the third section describes our design, including links to the theories. After that the results of preliminary simulation runs are presented and conclusions are drawn for further work.

2 Research Questions

We are investigating the emergence of differences in status across genders, and the emergence of specializations in social role among boys and girls. To do this we consider a number of possible causal factors:

- biological, innate differences between boys' and girls' characteristics, assuming individual variation;
- behavioural differences between the sexes, again assuming individual variation, and in belief update,
- differences in social identity between boys, girls and 'generalized children', as apparent in penalizing or rewarding certain behaviour;
- cultural influences on the previous factors;
- self-organized ('emergent') outcomes of interaction.

The means to study these questions is a simulation that allows varying the first four of the above factors. This modelling exercise creates two levels of aggregation: the individual children (agents), and the simulated world (playground). Based on variations in the agents and the rules of interaction, different gender patterns can occur. We build the agents in this simulated world as faithfully as possible based on the theories that we selected, create rules for the agents' interaction as far as possible also based on these theories, then run the simulation to study the results at system level.

We created one version "boy-girl" in which reference groups are simply modelled by a systematic bias in favour of the gender with the highest average status, and another one 'ref-group" with full-fledged reference group logic. At the time of writing, we managed to test the first much more thoroughly than the second version. The paper therefore deals with the boy-girl version unless otherwise specified.

Our main hypothesis is that the effect of nurture (operationalized through culture and reference group norms) will dominate the effect of nature (operationalized through kindness, beauty and power). In particular:

1. Social status will correlate with kindness in feminine cultures.
2. Social status will correlate with power in masculine cultures.
3. Rough-and-tumble will boost social status.
4. Categorical differences in status accord based on gender will enlarge any tendency to gender-based status differentiation.

3 Theory Base

3.1 Status-Power Theory

US sociologist Theodore D. Kemper [19] proposes that our social behaviour revolves around the concepts of status and power. It could be summarized as "Make status, avoid power".

Status as Kemper uses it is not just a pecking order variable, though it includes that element. It is something that we continually both claim from one another and confer upon one another through our actions. An example may illustrate this. If, at the office,

I greet Linda upon entering her room unannounced, I confer status on Linda; how much will be determined by the modalities of the greeting. My choice of greeting will depend on things such as our hierarchical and personal relationship, what preceded between us, my personality, the nature and urgency of the issue at hand, and whether others are present. At the same time, by entering unannounced I make the status claim of being somebody entitled to enter Linda's room. Formally, status is the voluntary compliance with the wishes of another.

Power comes into play when we want someone to do things and they do not voluntarily comply: we can then coerce them in some way, by pleading, lying or violence. Many actions have both a power and a status component. For instance in our example, if Linda does not want to confer status upon me by hearing me, she could look up, say "Excuse me, but I'm, very busy, could you come back later?" and then resume working; this might be a status move, indicating that I have not enough status to enter. I'd probably also interpret Linda's action of resuming work as a power move – I would have wanted Linda to continue looking at me to hear my reason for entering, and I expect Linda to know this..

Reference group is another important notion in Kemper's theory. Sociologically speaking, our actions are influenced by a committee of reference groups.. Sometimes this can be quite complex; e.g. when the greeting rules from the tennis club, where I play in a team with Linda, differ from those of the office, which ones to use?

Kemper's theory posits that people attempt to maximize their status while protecting themselves from the power of others. People are also driven to confer status on the deserving. Status is earned by a proper dose of status conferral upon others, refraining from over-claiming status with them, and using power in ways backed by authority granted by the reference groups.

3.2 Social Identity Theory

In accordance to reference groups in Kemper terms, Social Identity Theory [28] has some elements that can be used in our simulation. It states that part of the self-concept is built in terms of membership of social categories. Social categories define a set of features that drive and regulate conduct of behaviour of its members. These features represent the ideology, such as values and norms, that members should follow, therefore sustaining a frame for status worthiness. A member that behaves according to the ideal is worthy of status, but one that deviates is blamed and disregarded.

The influence that a social identity has on the behaviour of a person depends on how salient it is in a situation. The theory postulates that certain situations, such as the presence of an out-group, make social identities more salient, thus raising the influence of its ideology in the person. In such cases, the person behaves more like a member of the group and less like an individual. In addition, the strength of this effect is related to the emotional commitment of the person to the social identity. A person is more likely to activate a social identity if (s)he is positively committed to it. The commitment, as well as the construction and identification of the ideal into one's social reality, comes from experience and socialization processes.

The social identity defines a frame of social structure as well, including status order and social relationships. By activating different social identities the social structure changes as well. This partially explains why certain approaches to Linda, of the example in the previous section, may work in the tennis club and not in the office. It could be the case that according to the social identity that is salient in the office the status difference is higher than it is in the frame of the social identity that is salient in the tennis club.

3.3 Cultural Dimensions of Values

For the cultural component of our model we follow the theory of Geert Hofstede. In the most recent version of that theory [13] there are six dimensions of culture, each of which represents one of the big issues of social life that the members of a society have to contend with. The associated dimensions are bipolar continua, on each of which each society takes a position. These societal traits are not to be confused (but, alas, often are) with personality traits such as those found by McCrae et al., although there are national-level correlations [14].

If social life revolves around status and power, then this should be reflected in dimensions of culture. We would expect different societies to have different propensities to use power, for instance; power sanctioned by a society being known as authority. The dimensions point to systematic differences in how the people in a culture tend to act – thus both enacting and perpetuating their culture, and sometimes modifying it.

In what follows we present each dimension of culture in Kemperian terms.

Individualism. Individualism-collectivism is a society's specification for the unit that has the right to claim and receive status. In an individualistic society, individuals are the units. In a collectivistic one, groups are.

In an individualistic society, there will be more reference groups, differing in their reach of control over the agent's mind. Ideals in these groups might include heroes, friends, or one's nuclear family members, deities and fiction characters. In a collectivistic setting, one inclusive reference group, the extended family, clan, or people, is likely to take priority over the others.

Power distance. Large versus small power distance is the willingness to accept status and/or power domination. It is about voluntary status-accord and granting of authority, based on ascribed characteristics, not on actions. The net effect is that default status-accord in an interaction will be asymmetric: participants will seek to find out their respective status, and if they deem themselves inferior in ascribed status, they will give way. Some status markers are age and gender. Note that the term 'power' in Hofstede differs from Kemper's 'power' In this paper we follow Kemper's meaning except in the name of the 'power distance' dimension of culture.

Masculinity. Masculinity versus femininity is a preference for either power-oriented or status-oriented social relations. It is about voluntary status-accord to others based on their performance in competitive settings – in other words, based on their power *sensu* Kemper. The net effect is that people in interaction tend to seek status either by winning competitive sequences, or by aligning themselves with powerful 'winners' (presidential candidates, deities, sports heroes). The converse, femininity, stands for voluntary status-accord to those who refrain from using or showing power. A feminine culture may also penalize overt power moves and status displays.

Uncertainty Avoidance. This is the degree of anxiety in a culture in relation to strange things or unfamiliar situations. It leads to status conferral on the familiar and status withdrawal from the unfamiliar.

Masculinity-Femininity and gender roles. The Anglo-saxon and Scandinavian world are culturally much alike but for the dimension of masculinity – femininity. This makes them comparable to Hemelrijk's despotic and egalitarian macaque societies, as proposed by Hofstede [15]. On average, men hold more masculine values than women, confirming the 'Mars – Venus' hypothesis. Curiously, there seems to be a tendency for women in more masculine societies to more often achieve prominence in the pecking order in companies. In masculine societies, career women hold more masculine values than other women in these societies [13]. This probably reflects a selection process: women without such values quit the rat race. In political life, the trend is different: in government, women are more numerous in feminine societies than in masculine ones. The difference between business and politics is that in business, women are promoted by co-optation: existing alpha persons, usually males, have to accept newcomers among or above them. In politics, the anonymous voting system can promote women to the top. In the Netherlands, a country with a very feminine culture, the trend for women to be less prominent in business than in politics is clear.

3.4   Empirical Studies of Child Behaviour

Infants. Brain scientist Lise Eliot made a grand sweep through the literature on gender [7]. Her conclusion is that at birth, biologically speaking the variation within each sex is a lot greater than the differences between the sexes. The only reliable difference at birth is that boys are a bit bigger and more active. A meta-study of 46 studies [3] found boy babies to be 0.2 standard deviations more physically active than girls.

In contrast to the small biological differences found at birth, socialization by parents shows obvious and large effects. Haviland and Malatesta [9] show that when baby girls were cross-dressed as boys, observers were more likely to ascribe anger or distress to them, and vice versa. In another study with 3- to 6- months' old New York babies and their mothers, Haviland and Malatesta found that mothers showed a conspicuous lack of responsiveness to their baby sons' expressions of pain, as well as to their baby girls' expressions of anger [22].

Aggression. Starting at about age 4, boys are found to be more physically aggressive than girls [24]. For some time, this finding led to reduced attention to aggression in girls, until it was found that girls used 'relation aggression' more, such as exclusion from peer groups.

Crick assessed aggression and prosocial behaviours in a school in the US Mid-West. Physical and relational aggression and prosocial behaviours were found to be separate behavioural categories stable across time. Children that were aggressive and lacked prosocial behaviours developed social maladjustment [5].

Lansu [20] investigated popularity and aggression among 10–12 year olds. Popular peers evoked subliminal avoidance response in a joystick task. For unpopular peers, the response was gender-biased: girls evoked approach, whereas boys evoked avoidance. In a second study she found that popular peers attract unconscious attention, especially from other popular peers. Popular boys especially attracted attention from girls. A third study investigating explicit likeability and implicit avoidance/approach found the following (ibid. p. 164, or see [21]):

"Prosocial adolescents were evaluated more positively, and evaluated others more positively, on the explicit likeability ratings. There were implicit effects for aggressive girls. Girls who were known for their bullying and relational aggression such as gossiping, ignoring others and excluding others evaluated their peers negatively at the implicit level. They tended to avoid their peers in the joystick task. Aggressive boys did not show this tendency".

Lansu carried out a fourth study that showed adolescents to be on their best behaviour when interacting with more popular peers in a discussion task.

Rough and tumble. Rough and tumble (R&T) is defined as "a physically vigorous set of behaviours, including chasing, jumping and play fighting, accompanied by positive feelings from the players towards one another" [6, 17]. R&T is found among all human cultures and more generally among non-human primates, as well as other social mammals and birds. It happens a lot in peer groups of children, such as one finds on playgrounds. R&T involves reciprocal behaviour often observed in role change, such as chasing and being chased [26]. Jarvis [17] cites a number of studies that find R&T to involve much social learning, particularly among male primates. A very robust finding is that R&T is more common among boys than girls [6, 27, 29, 30]. In her review DiPietro [6] found R&T to occupy for 3%–5% of play time at preschool time, 7%–8% between 6–10 years of age, and to peak at 10% between 7 and 11 years. It then rapidly fell to 5% at 11–13 years and 3% at 14 years, to almost disappear in adulthood.

R&T can lead to enjoyable play, or it can lead to fighting. Anthony Pellegrini, in a South-eastern US school with children aged 5, 7 and 10, found that popular children's use of R&T was positively correlated with social problem solving [25].

Children who engage in R&T tend to be friends, and tend to be of equal status, until adolescence when slightly stronger children approach slightly weaker ones [16, 27]. Together with the finding that among all human cultures, as well as among non-human animals, males do more R&T than females, this suggests a role in preparing for sexual selection.

The line between rough-and-tumble and aggression is sometimes a contested one, as shown by RuthWoods [31] in an ethnography of a London primary school. Girls will claim aggression where boys claim friendly intent.

Culture. It can be assumed that biological sex (boy or girls) and norms for behaviour (boyish or girlish) are correlated to a degree that varies with cultural masculinity. The research on children so far has almost entirely been from culturally masculine societies. This is recognized by some authors. Hilary Aydt and William Corsaro, for instance, comparing preschool children from Italy (Bologna and Modena) and the USA (African American and white American), say (p. 1309) "we can infer that the level of segregation of children would vary according to the degree the adult culture considers men and boys to be aggressive and women and girls to be passive" [1].

Do child studies from Sweden, the world's most feminine society according to the Hofstede database, yield a different picture? Evaldsson [8] studied 11–12 year-olds in a multi-ethnic school in Sweden. The immigrant children at the school were fluent in Swedish and had been there for 3–7 years. The environment was decidedly culturally feminine: "In contrast with American school settings (...) girls' participation in team sports such as handball, basketball and soccer were promoted through physical education classes in cross-sex groups during school hours and same-sex sport clubs outside school" (ibid, p. 479–480). Evaldsson found that when playing foursquare, girls used 'slams' freely with boys but would 'throw like girls' to physically less skilled girls. Cross-sex games were quite common. She compares her findings to those of Thorne (1993) in the USA: "In contrast to what Thorne (p. 67) found, cross-sex games such as 'boys against girls' remained relatively stable and often lasted for several weeks. (...) The boys did not enter the girls' groups with the intention of disrupting the game, as Thorne found (...)".

Even in this gender-egalitarian atmosphere there was still a degree of gender separation; one group of 10–13 year old boys played football with only occasionally girls joining, some less physically skilled girls avoided mixed-sex games, and some less physically skilled boys avoided boys-against-girls games. Also, symbolic gender identity management took place. In particular, physically unskilled boys were discounted by the other boys, so that only the skilled ones became representative of the social category of boys (p. 493). Generally however, it was clear to these children that "differences in physicality within the girls' (and the boys') group were even greater than the differences across the gender groups".

This latter statement reflects what Eliot found in her review: as far as nature goes, boys and girls seem much more heterogeneous within their class than between; but socialization dramatically draws the genders apart in the USA. Girls tend to underperform if their social identity as girls is stressed [2, 4, 18]. It would seem that this is much less so in Sweden. Because girls and boys mixed there, they learned that girls and boys are in most respects not categorically different, but similar with overlapping variation. They learned to see one another as 'children' instead of 'boys' or 'girls'.

Finally, in a cross-cultural study among six-year olds, Martínez-Lozano et al. [23] found that Dutch children in a dyad were more likely to leave after a conflict if they did not get their way, whereas Spanish children were more likely to submit to the demands of their playmate. This could reflect a difference in power distance, larger in Spain, and/or in individualism, stronger in the Netherlands.

4 Agent-Based Model Design: The Boy-Girl Version

4.1 Representing Status-Power Theory in Child Behaviour

Status. Children are driven to confer and receive appropriate status: more is better, receiving too little status evokes the urge to use power in retaliation. The agents all start at status = 0.5 and converge on a dynamic status distribution that may or may not show a gender status gap (GSG; see Fig. 1).

Individual characteristics. Agents have a tendency to confer status, which we called their kindness in our model. They have a tendency to be found worthy of status conferrals, which we called their beauty, which might also be thought of as attractiveness or charisma. They have a capacity to use power *sensu* Kemper called their power. Power maximizes potential rough-and-tumble. All of the agent attributes are  normally distributed on a 0..1 scale, and we can vary their means separately for boys and girls. They are depicted in the interface: smile for beauty, big eyes for kindness, power as the leftmost number, status as size.

Dyadic relationship. Each agent maintains a directed friendship indicator towards each of the others. This takes the form of a vector called *has-been-nice* of all agents with which it has played, in which it stores the memory of whether the other agent conferred adequate status. At each interaction, the existing value of has-been-nice is discounted against the new value depending on the parameter status-volatility. Thus, both agents in a dyad have a has-been-nice for one another that need not be symmetric. We can vary the update rate of girls and boys separately.

Reference groups: social identity. The model has two agent groups: boys and girls. A switch sex-factor-on-conferral (SFoC) decides whether boys and girls act in a gender-aware manner. If it is on, boys and girls will subtract the SFoC from their conferrals to children of the other sex. The SFoC thus acts as a social identity-related modification of status conferrals that is updated on each tick.

Power exchange. The three kinds of aggression found in the literature are distinguished. Physical aggression is modelled in two ways. First, rough-and-tumble bonus parts of status conferrals may be disregarded by the recipient but never by the sender, so that the two may disagree about how much status was conferred. Second, and more seriously, there can be open power exchange in fights. A fight benefits the stronger child's status, unless it is blamed by the group, in which the attacker loses status.

Relational aggression in our simulation can also be modelled as fights. Besides it can occur if a child stays away from another one based on their mutual history (negative 'has-been-nice'). Lack of prosociality is modelled simply as a low kindness level.

Rough-and-tumble. The fact that R&T usually happens between friends and is enjoyable has led us to model it as an aspect of status conferral rather than as power move. Humphreys and Smith [16] (p. 208) have a nice way of putting it:

"This suggests that a rough-and-tumble initiation was more in the nature of an invitation to which the recipient was free to respond in any manner or not at all than a challenge which had either to be met or refused".

4.2 Representing Nurture Through Culture

Four of Hofstede's dimensions of culture are operational in the simulation. They are used for system-wide parameters ranging from 0 to 100 that symbolize the social environment internalized by the agents. The dimension scores were taken from [13]. This approach was shown to be feasible by Hofstede et al. [12].

Individualism. IDV moderates the likelihood that a child will leave a group when unhappy with the conferral it received, or the fight it was subjected to.

Power distance. PDI determines the likelihood that a child will pick a fight or leave a group, depending on its status. Low-status agents in large-power-distance cultures will be subdued and less likely to leave the group or pick a fight.

Masculinity. MAS moderates the likelihood of fighting (depending on the agent's power) and of conferring status rewards or penalties to fighters based on reference group ideals.

Uncertainty avoidance. Large UAI increases the likelihood that a group will blame a child for picking a fight against a child of the opposite sex.

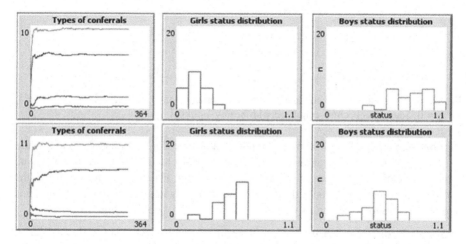

Fig. 1. Conferrals and resulting status distribution after 301 ticks for the same school class of 20 boys and 20 girls under different parameters. Left: conferrals per tick; green = happy, blue = mildly unhappy, black = fight condoned by group; red = fight blamed by group. Top row: MAS = 100, SFoCn;resulting GSG = 0.6. All boys dominate all girls. Bottom row: MAS = 0, SFoC off; resulting GSG = 0. No trace of a glass celling (Color figure online).

Cultural masculinity and social identity. Rough-and-tumble and fighting are subject to norms of praise or blame from the reference group, depending on the ideal. In a culture with MAS = 0, fighting is usually blamed, and this probability goes down when MAS goes up according to the formula:

```
to-report attacker-blamed-by-group?
report (random-float 1 > 1 – affront – 0.5 * sex-gap? * segregation-tendency –
                0.5 * (1 – MAS / 100) +
                ([status] of receiver – [status] of giver) * PDI / 100)
```

In which

- Affront = status deficit perceived by receiver.
- Segregation-tendency = (((100-IDV) + UAI)/200).

4.3 Dynamics

The playground is an undifferentiated square. Children are randomly introduced at the outset, with equal status of 0.5, and then play during a run of a variable number of ticks. A tick represents something akin to a few seconds, enough to have a status exchange. 300 ticks would constitute a school break (Fig. 1).

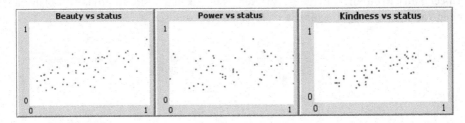

Fig. 2. Agent parameters (horizontal) vs status (vertical), after 301 ticks in a culture with MAS = 0. Status has become correlated with beauty and kindness.

Finding playmates. In each tick, each child that is alone looks for a child to play with. If it finds one it becomes 'attracted', which is a status claim. If the potential playmate accepts the claim and is 'attracted' back, they will join. If the playmate was alone, the two of them form a new group. If the playmate is already in a group, the first child joins that child's group, adopting its reference group's status bookkeeping.

Status exchange: conferral. Once in a group the child selects a group member at random to exchange status with, assuming that in a group, all children are playing together even if some might be more attractive than others. A status exchange involves a status conferral by the giver and an interpretation by the receiver. The conferral may include a rough-and-tumble action.

Status exchange: interpretation. If the receiver interprets the conferral as insufficient, that is, as lower than its current status in the reference group in action, then the receiver may, depending on the perceived status deficit ('perceived-affront') decide to pick a fight. Willingness-to-fight is dependent on culture.

Power exchange. In case of a fight, power of the two fighters becomes important in determining the outcome, along with perceived-affront. The winner gains status whereas the loser loses an equal amount.

Leaving a group. After a fight, one or both fighters may decide to leave the group. An agent could also leave if it was unsatisfied with a conferral it received but did not actually fight.

5   Model Results

The boy-girl version was tested with 20 runs per condition on classes of 30 girls and 30 boys. Figure 1 shows plots of univariate analysis of variance with gender-status-gap as the dependent variable.

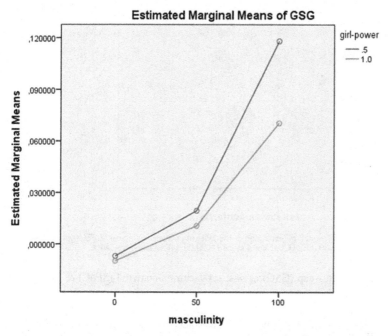

Estimated Marginal Means of GSG

Covariates appearing in the model are evaluated at the following values: girl-kindness = 1.250, individualism = 50.00, power-distance = 50.00, uncertainty-avoidance = 50.00

Fig. 3. ANOVA of gender-status-gap (GSG) against MAS and girl-power. No rough-and-tumble.

Hypothesis 1. "Social status does correlate with kindness in feminine cultures" is confirmed by Fig. 2. The figure averages runs with girl-kindness = 1 and girl-kindness = 1.5 (girls kinder than boys). Under MAS = 0 the GSG is negative, meaning boys have lower average status than girls. This is the case even if boys are stronger (girl-power = 0.5) (Fig. 3).

Hypothesis 2. "Social status will correlate with power in masculine cultures", is also confirmed. As MAS goes up, the GSG favours boys more, and the effect of differences in power is amplified.

Hypothesis 3. "Rough-and-tumble will boost social status" is not shown in a figure for lack of space. The same runs as in Fig. 1 but with R&T turned on yield higher GSG in all conditions, the difference increasing from 0.01 at MAS = 0 and girl-power = 1–0.55 at MAS = 100 and girl-power = 0.5.

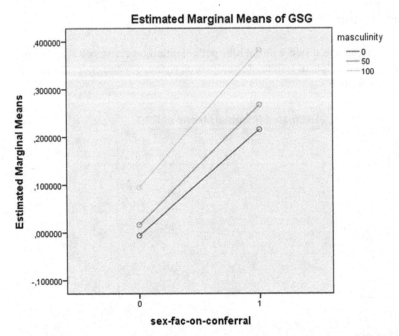

Fig. 4. Gender-status-gap (GSG) against sex-factor-on-conferral (SFoC) & MAS.

Hypothesis 4. "Categorical differences in status accord based on gender will enlarge any tendency to gender-based status differentiation" receives overwhelming support, to the extent that it can precipitate full glass ceiling phenomena in which no girls achieve high status. Switching SFoC on can lead to gender status gaps of .2 under MAS = 0, until .4 under MAS = 100 (Fig. 4).

6   Discussion

The playground simulation operationalizes 'nature' as possible differences in power between boys and girls, in tendency to perform power-related behaviours (rough-and-tumble and fighting), as well as in relationship updating. The effects of even large variations of these are modest.

The simulation operationalizes 'nurture' as culture parameters in combination with variable social identity. The combined effect is pervasive, since it strongly modifies the social reward to engage in the power-related practices. This combined effect materializes through self-organization of boys and girls. As such the model seems a promising way to study self-organization in all kinds of social settings, such as organizations, schools, and social life in general.

The results suggest that reference group dynamics are by far the most powerful causal factor for the establishment of glass-ceiling like phenomena. If girls receive less status just because they are girls, this has huge emergent effects. And they do, as illustrated by the case of little Toby with which this article began. Our social identity model version is a promising tool for future development.

The second most powerful factor in the simulation is culture, in this case a masculine value system that supports the use of power in the pursuit of status.

Nature, in the form of differences in 'in-born' kindness and power between the sexes, plays a modest role in itself. This role can be very strongly amplified by culture and by reference group logic, through emergent results of interaction.

One more remark can be made pertaining to gender roles. In feminine societies in our model, fighting is blameable. This leads to flatter status hierarchies, but not necessarily to gender equality, since any occurring gender gap will go uncontested. Masculine societies lead to larger gender gaps but with some strong girls fighting themselves to the top. This confirms [11] on macaques and [13] on humans.

Methodological remarks can also be made. This study operationalizes three major social scientific theories and a body of experimental work on development psychology. The integration of these three is new and tentative. The resulting model is a hypothesis-generating engine; it begs more questions than it answers. Here are some important questions for further investigation.

- How to model this system with actual reference groups, in which every child may have a different social status in every reference group? We have a version of a simulation that does this, but at the time of writing the results are too tentative to say much about them.
- How to integrate praiseworthiness or blameworthiness of fighting better with social identity theory? For instance, at present there is no concept of 'fair fighting', that is, refraining from fighting weak opponents, or children of the other sex.
- How to articulate the dynamics of membership of a group or category versus commitment to it?
- How do agents maintain their 'status landscape' across reference groups? This involves which groups to commit to and spend time in, and how to transfer status information between reference groups. The dynamics of commitment to reference groups are likely to be nontrivial.
- What are the system-level consequences of the previous point, i.e. how are statuses ranked between reference groups? Status and power relationships between reference groups might be called prejudices, prototypes, or ideal types.
- In connection with the previous one, what if a conferral to one member of a reference group is interpreted as a conferral to the identity of that group?
- To what extent can we re-use this model for other purposes, e.g. the social reality of the financial world?
- How far can these particular theories take our models? On what grounds should we change or supplement them?

7 Conclusion

The model introduced here confirms the importance of emergent patterns of behaviour in modifying differences due to both nature and nurture. Social identity issues seem more pervasive in bringing the effects of influences from both nature and nurture about. In the lives of children, nurture amplifies nature through self-organisation.

On a meta-level, the model convincingly shows that it is worthwhile to put social scientific theory in the centre of agent-based models that investigate theoretical points. This enables to both create convincing models and scrutinize the theories used.

This work is only the first step in what could be a rich area for further study of various areas of social reality, not just children's lives.

Acknowledgements. The authors are grateful to NIAS, Netherlands Institute for Advanced Study in the Humanities and Social Sciences, for offering a fellowship enabling the present study. The support of the Lorentz Center in Leiden is also acknowledged. Discussions with Theodore D. Kemper have been most valuable.

References

1. Aydt, H., Corsaro, W.A.: Differences in children's construction of gender across culture an interpretive approach. Am. Behav. Sci. **46**(10), 1306–1325 (2003)
2. Cadinu, M., et al.: Why do women underperform under stereotype threat? evidence for the role of negative thinking. Psychol. Sci. **16**(7), 572–578 (2005)
3. Campbell, D.W., Eaton, W.O.: Sex differences in the activity level of infants. Infant Child Dev. **8**(1), 1–17 (1999)
4. Cimpian, A., Mu, Y., Erickson, L.C.: Who is good at this game? linking an activity to a social category undermines children's achievement. Psychol. Sci. **23**(5), 533–541 (2012)
5. Crick, N.R.: The role of overt aggression, relational aggression, and prosocial behavior in the prediction of children's future social adjustment. Child Dev. **67**(5), 2317–2327 (1996)
6. DiPietro, J.A.: Rough and tumble play: a function of gender. Dev. Psychol. **17**(1), 50 (1981)
7. Eliot, L.: Pink Brain, Blue Brain How Small Differences Grow into Troublesome Gaps-And What We Can Do About It, p. 420. Mariner Books, Boston (2009)
8. Evaldsson, A.C.: Throwing like a girl?: situating gender differences in physicality across game contexts. Childhood **10**(4), 475–497 (2003)
9. Haviland, J.J., Malatesta, C.Z.: The development of sex differences in nonverbal signals: fallacies, facts, and fantasies. In: Henley, N.M., Mayo, C. (eds.) Gender and Nonverbal Behavior, pp. 183–208. Springer, New York (1981)
10. Hemelrijk, C.K.: Simple reactions to nearby neighbors and complex social behavior in primates. In: Menzel, R.F.J. (ed.) Animal Thinking: Comparative Issues in Comparative Cognition, pp. 223–238. MIT Press, Cambridge (2011)
11. Hemelrijk, C.K.: The use of artificial-life models for the study of social organization. In: Thierry, B., Singh, M., Kaumanns, W. (eds.) Macaque Societies, pp. 295–313. A Model for the Study of Social Organization. Cambridge University Press, Cambridge (2004)
12. Hofstede, G.J., Jonker, C.M., Verwaart, T.: Cultural differentiation of negotiating agents. Group Decis. Negot. **21**(1), 79–98 (2012)
13. Hofstede, G., Hofstede, G.J., Minkov, M.: Cultures and Organizations. Software of the Mind. McGraw-Hill, New York (2010)

14. Hofstede, G., McCrae, R.R.: Personality and culture revisited: linking traits and dimensions of culture. Cross-Cult. Res. **38**(1), 52–80 (2004)
15. Hofstede, G.J.: Theory in social simulation: status-power theory, national culture and emergence of the glass ceiling. In: Social Coordination: Principles, Artefacts, and Theories, pp. 21–28. AISB, Exeter (2013)
16. Humphreys, A.P., Smith, P.K.: Rough and tumble, friendship, and dominance in schoolchildren: evidence for continuity and change with age. Child Dev. **58**, 201–212 (1987)
17. Jarvis, P.: Monsters, magic and Mr Psycho: a biocultural approach to rough and tumble play in the early years of primary school. Early Years **27**(2), 171–188 (2007)
18. Kang, S.K., Inzlicht, M.: Stigma building blocks how instruction and experience teach children about Rejection by outgroups. Pers. Soc. Psychol. Bull. **38**(3), 357–369 (2012)
19. Kemper, T.D.: Status, Power and Ritual Interaction: A Relational Reading of Durkheim. Goffman and Collins. Ashgate, Burlington (2011)
20. Lansu, T.: Implicit processes in peer relations: effects of popularity and aggression. Nijmegen University (2012)
21. Lansu, T.A., Cillessen, A.H., Bukowski, W.M.: Implicit and explicit peer evaluation: associations with early adolescents' prosociality, aggression, and bullying. J. Res. Adolesc. **23**, 762–771 (2013)
22. Malatesta, C.Z., Haviland, J.M.: Learning display rules: the socialization of emotion expression in infancy. Child Dev. **53**, 991–1003 (1982)
23. Martínez-Lozano, V.S.M., Sánchez-Medina, J.A., Goudena, P.P.: A cross-cultural study of observed conflict between young children. J. Cross Cult. Psychol. **42**(6), 895–907 (2011)
24. Parke, R.D., Slaby, R.G.: The development of aggression. In: Mussen, P.H. (ed.) Handbook of Child Psychology, vol. 4, pp. 547–641. Wiley, New York (1983)
25. Pellegrini, A.D.: Elementary-school children's rough-and-tumble play and social competence. Dev. Psychol. **24**(6), 802 (1988)
26. Pellegrini, A.D.: School Recess and Playground Behavior: Educational and Developmental Roles. SUNY Press, Albany (1995)
27. Pellegrini, A.D., Smith, P.K.: Physical activity play: The nature and function of a neglected aspect of play. Child Dev. **69**(3), 577–598 (1998)
28. Tajfel, H.: Social Identity and Intergroup Relations. Cambridge University Press, Cambridge (1982)
29. Thorne, B.: Gender Play. Girls and Boys in School. Rutgers University Press, New Brunswick (1993)
30. Warden, D., Mackinnon, S.: Prosocial children, bullies and victims: an investigation of their sociometric status, empathy and social problem-solving strategies. Br. J. Dev. Psychol. **21**(3), 367–385 (2003)
31. Woods, R.: Children's Moral Lives: An Ethnographic and Psychological Approach, p. 238. Wiley-Blackwell, Chichester (2013)

Partner Selection Delays Extinction in Cooperative and Coordination Dilemmas

Pedro Mariano[(✉)] and Luís Correia

LabMAg – Departamento de Informática, Faculdade de Ciências,
Universidade de Lisboa, Lisbon, Portugal
plmariano@fc.ul.pt, luis.correia@di.fc.ul.pt

Abstract. Multiagent systems have been used to model and study social systems. Such studies have focused on cooperation and coordination dilemmas. The goal was to investigate how a population of agents could escape those dilemmas. Typically those studies assume large populations either fixed size or infinite. However, when we introduce variable sized population, a new risk arises consisting on population extinction, which is a stable point of the corresponding dynamics. We present the Energy Based Evolutionary Algorithm, a model where agents are born, interact, reproduce and die. Interaction is mediated by some game which is the sole means of acquiring energy needed for reproduction. In this paper we show that when an agent is capable of selecting its partners based on knowledge of successful interactions, the population is able to survive longer when compared with random partner selection. We present results using a set of well known games.

1 Introduction

Cooperative and coordination dilemmas have been used to model economic or biological scenarios [5,10]. Given the mismatch between experimental outcomes and behavioural prediction of Game Theory, there is a wealth of work to explain these results [1,14,16,25,27,28,33]. A common denominator in the majority of these works is either infinite population or finite but constant size population. However these features are unrealistic because real populations fluctuate due to internal or external influences.

There are population models that allow variable population. Most of them use Agent Based Models (ABM) [11], or are artificial ecosystems [15,30]. Often they deal with specific problems and generalisation to other games may be difficult.

While standard Evolutionary Game Theory (EGT) models use either infinite populations or constant finite populations, ABMs have been used to model scenarios where populations could go extinct. This can happen because agent's actions do not provide him enough resources to reproduce. Since such models are often used in specific problems it is important to create a general evolutionary algorithm that can be applied to any game and where extinctions can occur independently of game characteristics.

© Springer International Publishing Switzerland 2015
F. Grimaldo and E. Norling (Eds.): MABS 2014, LNAI 9002, pp. 88–103, 2015.
DOI: 10.1007/978-3-319-14627-0_7

In this paper we present a population model called Energy Based Evolutionary Algorithm (EnBEA) with variable population size, that can be applied to any scenario modelled by a game. In our model agents are born, interact with each other, reproduce and die. When we apply our model to a set of cooperative and coordination dilemmas, they produce extinction dilemmas. As such, our model is suitable to study how a population can avoid extinction.

The ability to select partners based on knowledge of previous interactions can explain the prevalence of cooperation in many cooperative dilemmas [1]. As such we analyse its influence on the occurrence of extinctions in EnBEA.

2   Related Work

The prevalence of cooperation has been studied using models based on differential equations such as the replicator equation or the Moran process [22]. There are a set of assumptions behind the replicator equation [31]. One assumes a considerably large or infinite population. Another assumes a well mixed-population such that everybody plays with everybody else. A similar approach is randomly pairing players. These are unrealistic assumptions and have led to alternative proposals. Among them are structured populations where players are placed in the nodes of some graph and interactions are restricted to links between nodes [23,37]. In structured populations, agents have the possibility of selecting their partners [33]. Other approaches include finite but constant size population whose dynamics are modelled by a Moran process. Despite not allowing varying population size, they have been used to model scenarios that may cause extinctions such as climate change [34].

ABM address the difficulties of creating a formal model of a complex system [8]. After investigation of artificial ecosystems populated [15,29] specific protocols to construct such systems have emerged [11].

There are ABMs that analyse the possibility of extinctions but they do that in specific contexts such as modelling population growth of endangered species [3], tree mortality [17], impact of logging activities in bird species [39]. Some of these models are characterised by using specific differential equations or operate at higher level than the individual. Often they are specific to their case study and their methods are not directly transferable to another scenario.

McLane et al. provide in [21] a review of ABM used in the literature of ecology to address the issues of managing ecosystems. They presented a set of behaviours that individuals can choose in their life cycle: habitat selection, foraging, reproduction, and dispersal. In the papers that they reviewed, some used all the behaviours in the set while others used just one. Such a set of behaviours could constitute the set of actions of some generic game played by animals. Moreover we can roughly divide them in two sets, one where an animal obtains energy (foraging) and a second where an animal spends energy (habitat selection, reproduction, and dispersal).

Partner selection is one of the possible explanations for the prevalence of cooperation [24,36]. This characteristic is also combined with the possibility of refusing an interaction. The selection mechanism is usually dependent on the game: in Prisoner's Dilemma (PD) it depends on the partner defecting or not [1], in trading networks it depends on the trading offer [38]. However, there was no concern to generalise the mechanism to be applied to any game, which is a problem that our work tackles.

3   Description of the Evolutionary Algorithm

3.1   Population Model

In this section we will give a formal description of EnBEA. It is a population model where agents are born, interact, reproduce and die. Agent interaction is mediated by some game. Interaction is essential because agents acquire or lose energy when playing games and energy is necessary to reproduce. Agents can die because of old age, starvation (lack of energy) and overcrowding.

We use games as an energy transfer process. This means a redefinition of the payoff function. A game G is a tuple (N, A, E) where N is a set of n players, $A = \{A_1, \ldots, A_n\}$ and each A_i a set of actions for player i, and $E = \{e_1, \ldots, e_n\}$ is a set of energy functions, with $e_i : A_1 \times \ldots \times A_n \to \mathbb{R}$ being the energy obtained by player i given the actions of the n players.

An agent α is characterised by a strategy s which he uses to play game G, an energy level e and an age. We thus have $\alpha = (s, e, a)$. In each iteration t of EnBEA a population of agents, $\mathcal{P} = \{\alpha_1, \ldots\}$ is updated through three phases.

play in this phase all agents play the game and update their energy. Partners can be randomly selected or agents can choose them.

reproduction in this phase the agents whose energy is above some threshold produce one offspring by cloning and mutation, and their energy is decremented by some value.

death in this phase the entire population goes through death events that depend on population size, on agent's age and agent's energy. Age of surviving agents is incremented by one.

In the play phase, the game is used as energy transfer. Regarding the relation between the payoff function and the energy function, we have extended the approach followed in [19] and considered the case where the obtained energy is scaled and translated to the interval $[-1, 1]$:

$$e \leftarrow e + \frac{\pi}{\max(\overline{\pi}, |\underline{\pi}|)}, \qquad (1)$$

where π represents the payoff obtained by an agent, and $\overline{\pi}$ and $\underline{\pi}$ are the highest and lowest payoffs obtainable in game G.

Scaling allows us to compare the evolutionary dynamics of games with different payoff functions, e.g. comparing the number of offspring per iteration or the number of iterations until an extinction occurred. We could remove scaling, if we made energy range equal to payoff range.

With Eq. (1) we introduce the possibility of an agent dying through starvation when the energy drops below zero, thus augmenting the risk of extinction. Instead of zero, we could have used another energy threshold in the decision to remove agents, which would only amount to one more parameter in our model. This case is more realistic as the payoff value reflects gains and costs of an agent. Consider for instance, the costs of providing in the Public Good Provision game or of being exploited in the PD game.

When an agent's energy reaches the reproduction threshold e_R, it is decremented by this value, and a new offspring is inserted in the population. Moreover, we have to deal with the possibility of an agent's energy dropping below zero. Similarly to [1] we remove an agent when its energy drops below zero. The energy of newborns could be zero, but this puts pressure on the first played games to obtain positive energy, otherwise infancy mortality may be high. Instead we opt for providing each newborn with e_B units of energy. Therefore, the dynamics of an agent's energy depends on two parameters, namely e_R and e_B.

In order to avoid exponential growth, in each iteration of the algorithm all agents go through death events. We consider two events: one depends on population size and a second that depends on agent's age. The probability of an agent dying due to overcrowding is:

$$P(\text{death population size}) = \frac{1}{1 + e^{6\frac{K - |\mathcal{P}|}{K}}}, \tag{2}$$

where $|\mathcal{P}|$ is the current population size and K is a parameter that we call carrying capacity. This probability is a sigmoid function. The exponent was chosen because the logistic curve outside the interval $[-6, 6]$ is approximately either zero or one. In the event of the entire population doubling size, it will not go from a zero probability of dying to certain extinction. This assumes that each agent has at most one offspring per simulation iteration.

The probability of an agent dying because of old age is:

$$P(\text{death agent's age}) = \frac{1}{1 + e^{\frac{L - a}{V}}}, \tag{3}$$

where L is agents' life expectancy and V controls the variance in the age at which agents die through old age.

3.2   Partner Selection

The play phase of EnBEA does not specify how agents select their game partners. In this paper we test and compare two scenarios. One with random partner selection and a second where agents can select partners. Since EnBEA can be applied to any n-player game, we also need a partner selection model that is independent of the game. We choose the model presented in [18]. An agent in this partner selection model has a vector of size l. Each position of this vector contains a probability and a set of $n-1$ candidate partners. When an agent needs to play a game, he selects a set from a position in this vector. Sets with higher probability have more chance of being picked. After playing the game the agent compares the payoff obtained with threshold π_T. If the payoff is higher the vector is not changed. Otherwise, the selected set of candidate partners is replaced by a random set and its associated probability is multiplied by factor $\delta < 1$. Since the probability decreases, in order to maintain unit sum, the decreased amount is distributed evenly among the other positions in the vector.

As long as the population remains stable, the net effect of this partner selection is that good sets of candidate partners absorb the probabilities of discarded sets of candidate partners. Whenever an agent that is in a set of candidate partners dies, a random set with live candidate partners is inserted in the corresponding vector position.

In this model we can have random partner selection whenever the vector size is zero. This allows us to study the evolution of partner selection. This partner selection is generic as it can be applied to any game, which contrasts with other approaches (e.g. [35]).

4   Experimental Analysis

In this section we will present the experimental analysis that we have performed with EnBEA. We will start by describing the set of standard games that we used. We finish with the description of EnBEA related parameters.

4.1   2 × 2 Symmetric Games

The class of 2-player 2-action symmetric games comprises several cooperative and coordination dilemmas. These games are Prisoner's Dilemma (PD), Stag Hunt, Snowdrift or Hawk-Dove, and Harmony. In [1] the authors have studied the evolution of cooperation in PD with a tailored partner selection model. In [34] the authors investigated networks of contacts to promote coordination in Snowdrift. The payoff matrix of this class can be characterised by two parameters if players' payoff when both cooperate is one and when both defect is zero. Parameter T is named *temptation* and represents the defecting player's payoff when the opponent cooperates. The payoff of the opponent is represented by parameter S and is named *sucker*. The analysis of the population dynamics can be restricted to the set $(T, S) \in [0, 2] \times [-1, 1]$. This divides the parameter space in four quadrants: the upper-left corresponds to Harmony, the upper-right to Snowdrift, the bottom-left to Stag Hunt and the bottom-right to PD. To handle these games we need to add to the agent's chromosome a single gene representing the probability to cooperate, p_c. When this gene is mutated, p_c is perturbed by a Gaussian distribution with mean zero and standard deviation 0.1. The resulting value is truncated to remain in interval $[0, 1]$.

In order to analyse the population dynamics of this class of games under EnBEA we varied payoffs T and S from their lower values to their higher values in 0.2 increments. The initial population was homogeneous and the probability to cooperate varied between zero and one in 0.2 increments. Table 1a summarises the parameters used in this experiment.

Table 1. Game specific parameters used in the experiments.

T	temptation	$\{0, 0.2, 0.4, \ldots, 2\}$
S	sucker	$\{-1, -0.8, \ldots, 1\}$
p_c	cooperate probability	$\{0, 0.2, 0.4, \ldots, 1\}$
$|\mathcal{P}_0|$	size of initial population	10

(a) Parameters used in 2×2 symmetric games.

n	number players	$\{3, 4, 5, \ldots, 8\}$
c	provision cost	$\{0.1, 0.2, \ldots, 0.9\}$
p_c	provision probability	$\{0, 0.2, 0.4, \ldots, 1\}$
$|\mathcal{P}_0|$	size of initial population	10

(b) Parameters used in PGP.

n	number stages	$\{4, 6, 8, \ldots, 14\}$
d	pot increase	$\{0.2, 0.3, \ldots, 0.7\}$
p_s	pot share	$\{0.6, 0.65, \ldots, 0.9\}$
	number of odd players in $\mathcal{P}_0$	10
	number of even players in $\mathcal{P}_0$	10

(c) Parameters used in Centipede.

p_0	money pot size	$\{4, 6, 8, \ldots, 14\}$
d	dictator strategy in $\mathcal{P}_0$	$\{0, 2, 4, \ldots, p_0\}$
a	serf strategy in $\mathcal{P}_0$	$\{0, 2, 4, \ldots, p_0\}$
	number of dictators in $\mathcal{P}_0$	10
	number of serfs in $\mathcal{P}_0$	10

(d) Parameters used in Ultimatum.

4.2   Public Good Provision

We have also performed simulations using the PGP game [4,13]. This game is commonly studied to analyse cooperative dilemmas. It is considered a generalisation of PD to n players. In previous work [18] we have shown that partner selection avoided extinctions. However, in that work there was no death by starvation. In the PGP game, a player that contributes to the good, incurs a cost c. The good is worth g for each player. We fixed the good value to $g = 1$ and varied the other game parameters n and c. Similarly to 2×2 games, to handle PGP we need to add a single gene, with the probability to provide p_p to the agent's chromosome. The mutation operator adds to p_p a random value from a Gaussian distribution with mean zero and standard deviation 0.1. The resulting value is truncated to remain in interval $[0, 1]$.

In this game, we have varied the number of players in the game, the provision cost, and the composition of the initial population. All agents were homogeneous and their probability to provide the good varied between zero and one in 0.2 increments. Table 1b summarises the parameters tested in the simulations.

4.3   Centipede

The Centipede game is a sequential game of perfect recall where in each stage a player decides if he keeps a higher share of a pot of money or decides to pass the pot to the other player [20,27,32]. If the player keeps the higher share the game stops. If he passes the pot is increased by some external entity. The game has some fixed number of stages. In the last stage if the deciding player stops he receives the higher share of the pot. Otherwise the pot is increased but he receives the lower share. The payoff structure is constructed such that the payoff the deciding player obtains at stage t is higher than he obtains at stage $t + 1$. This raises a cooperation problem since backward induction results in a player stopping the game in the first stage thus obtaining a lower payoff. Recently [19] we have witnessed in the Centipede game that players are able to survive extinctions when they are generalists, that is they can play both roles of this asymmetric game, but we have not analysed the impact of partner selection on preventing or delaying extinctions.

The game can be characterised by the initial size of the pot, p_0, how the pot is increased, d, and the pot share given to the player that decides whether to stop or not, p_s. In this paper we use an arithmetic progression for pot size. Since Centipede is an asymmetric game, we considered two types of players: *odd* represents the players that decide in odd stages; *even* represents the players that decide in even stages.

The chromosome contains two genes. The first gene (binary) represents the player type while the second gene (natural number) represents the stage where he decides to stop the game. The first gene is never mutated, while the second gene is perturbed by a discrete Gaussian distribution with mean zero and standard deviation one. Recall that in our current implementation of the algorithm, if players of the same type are paired, they obtain zero energy. Otherwise, they play the game.

To decrease the number of parameters, we set the initial size of the pot to one, $p_0 = 1$. The number of stages varied between four and 14 in increments of two. The pot increment varied between 0.2 and 0.7. The pot share varied between 0.6 and 0.9 in 0.05 increments. The initial population had ten odd players and ten even players. Both players stopped the game at the last stage. Table 1c shows the parameters used in the experiments.

4.4   Ultimatum

The Ultimatum game is an one shot game where a dictator proposes a division of a pot of money to a serf. If the serf accepts the division, both players get the share, otherwise they get nothing. This game has many Nash Equilibria (NEs) all of them having the serf accepting some division. The serf strategy of accepting any division is the only one that is subgame perfect. This contrasts with experiments involving people with different quantities of money [5]. These showed acceptance with fair divisions of the pot and refusals of unfair divisions. Regarding formalisation, the pot size p_0 is a natural number. The dictator strategy, d, belongs to the set $A_1 = \{0, 1, \ldots, p_0\}$ where each number represents a pot share he keeps to himself. The serf action space can also be represented by the same set, $A_2 = A_1$, but in this case it represents the threshold, a, for accepting a division. This game is different from the previous in that an agent has a type meaning he is either a dictator or a serf. Moreover, in our simulations an offspring's type is always equal to the parent's type. This means that if a type goes extinct, the other type follows suit. An agent's chromosome has two genes. One represents his type (either dictator or serf) and another represents the corresponding strategy (either d or a).

Only the strategy gene is perturbed by a discrete Gaussian distribution with zero mean and standard deviation 1. The resulting value was truncated to remain in the integer set from zero to p_0.

In order to analyse the population dynamics, we have varied the pot size, p_0 from 4 to 14 with increments of 2. The initial population has ten dictators and ten serfs with all dictators identical and all serfs identical. We tested combinations $(d, a) \in \{0, 2, \ldots, p_0\} \times \{0, 2, \ldots, p_0\}$ such that the initial serfs accepted the proposals of the initial dictators. Table 1d shows the parameters tested in the experiments.

4.5   Partner Selection Parameters

We have performed simulations with – agents can select partners (ASP) – and without the partner selection model presented earlier – random partner selection (RPS). Simulations with the partner selection model add to the agent's chromosome three more genes. One for the vector size, l, one for payoff threshold π_T and a third for the probability update factor, δ. Whenever the mutation operator is applied to any of these genes, the first gene is perturbed by a discrete Gaussian distribution with mean zero and standard deviation one, while the second and third genes are perturbed by a Gaussian distribution with mean zero and deviation 0.1. In any case, the resulting value is truncated to a valid value. In these simulations, the values of these genes in the initial population were the following: $l = 0$, $\delta = 0.5$ and $\pi_T = 0.5$. The rationale was to see if partner selection could evolve and then avoid or delay extinctions.

4.6   EnBEA Parameters

In the experiments that we performed we used panmictic population. Although unrealistic, given that we used a carrying capacity, K, of 100, it is reasonable to assume that all agents can potentially interact with each other. When agents are capable of choosing with whom they will play, networks of agents can be formed. The initial population size depends on the game. In symmetric games it is 10 and in asymmetric games (Centipede and Ultimatum) it is 20, because agents have a role.

In this work we are interested in analysing different versions of the games we have used and to measure the occurrence of extinctions. With reproduction energy, e_R, set to 50, an agent that obtains per game the highest payoff, reproduces in less than 50 iterations. Since life expectancy, L, is set to 150, such agent can produce on average three offspring during its lifetime. Offspring were subject to a single-gene mutation with 10 % probability. This is an evolutionary model with clonal reproduction subject to mutation.

The number of iterations was set to 10000, two orders of magnitude higher than an agent's average lifetime, in order to have a duration enough to observe an extinction or not. In order to obtain statistical results, we performed ten runs for each parameter combination. Table 2 shows the values of these parameters.

Table 2. Common parameters used in all games.

K	carrying capacity	100
e_R	reproduction energy	50
	energy birth	10
L	old age	150
	mutation probability	10%
	number of iterations	10000
	number or runs	10

5 Results

For each simulation run we recorded the number of iterations it lasted[1]. We assume that if a simulation reaches the maximum number of iterations (10000) there is no extinction. Figure 1 shows the average number of iterations ratio between ASP and RPS simulations for some parameter combinations of the tested games. Some simulations with ASP lasted four times longer than RPS simulations. In the 2×2 Harmony game there is no visible effect of partner selection. In this game there is no cooperation nor coordination dilemma and as a consequence extinctions occur only when the initial population is entirely composed of exploiters.

Figure 2 shows the cooperation level versus the number of iterations. The cooperation level is computed either from the initial population parameters or from the game parameters. In 2×2 games the cooperation level equals agents' cooperation probability, and in PGP it equals agents' provision probability. In Centipede we define it as a weighted average of pot share and pot increase, $2(1 - p_s) + 1 - p_i$. This expression means that a game is more cooperative when payoffs are equally distributed both among players and stages. In Ultimatum we define it as $(1 - 2|d' - 0.5|)(1 - 2|a' - 0.5|)$ where d' and a' are the normalised dictator and serf's strategies, with respect to p_0. This means that cooperation level is higher in the case of high and similar division and acceptance thresholds of dictator and serf. Overall, the higher is the cooperation level in the initial population, the higher is the number of iterations. Except for the 2×2 games there is a general tendency for partner choice to increase the duration of simulations, in some cases avoiding extinction altogether. There are some parameter combinations that always result in extinctions independently of whether random partner selection is used or agents can select their partners. These combinations correspond to PD, to PGP with high provision cost or an initial population with low probability of providing the good, to Centipede with high pot share, and to Ultimatum with division proposal higher than the acceptance threshold.

– Extinctions occur in PD because defectors exploit cooperators who cannot acquire enough energy to reproduce and will die of starvation or old age.

---

[1] The simulation was implemented in Mercury, a declarative language, and is available at http://github.com/plsm/EBEA.

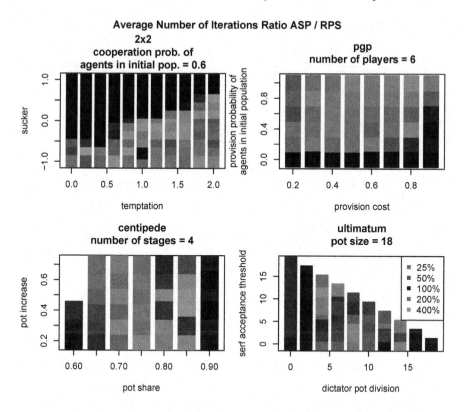

Fig. 1. Average number of iterations ratio between ASP and RPS simulations for some parameter combinations. The greener the point, the longer is the corresponding set of ASP simulations.

In this particular 2×2 game the payoff of defection is negative. As cooperators die, exploiters take over the population, but when they play among themselves, they obtain zero energy. This means they die of old age without any offspring.

– PGP is an extension of PD to multiple players. The reason for extinctions is the same as in PD: exploiters take over the population but they cannot acquire any energy when playing among themselves.

– The reason for extinctions in Centipede with high pot share are due to one type of player rapidly achieving the reproduction threshold. This type reproduces faster and replaces the other type, which cannot achieve the reproduction threshold. Agents with the latter type die of old age without producing sufficient offspring. Afterwards agents with the former type do not have anyone to play with thus earn no energy to reproduce.

– In Ultimatum when the initial population has serfs or dictators that receive a large share of the pot, they reproduce faster. This is similar to exploiters taking over the population in PD or PGP, and likewise, they will go extinct. When the pot is equally divided among players (cooperation level equal to one), neither role is benefited, and they reproduce at the same pace. Partner

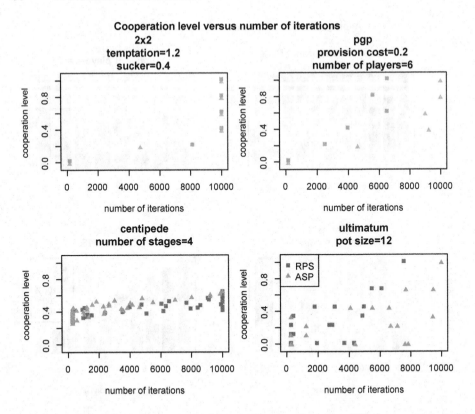

Fig. 2. Cooperation level versus number of iterations between ASP (green triangles) and RPS simulations (red squares) for some parameter combinations. Each point represents an average over a set of parameter combinations. For visibility purposes squares are slightly displaced upwards while triangles are slightly displaced downwards (Color figure online).

selection allows each role to promote a cooperative strategy in his partner. Notice that this game is very sensitive to the cooperation level. Only very slight variations from the optimal cooperation level are able to sustain the population. A particular case should be noticed. A fair dictator offering 50 % break and serfs accepting 50 % or less constitute a perfect balance and last for a long time, before mutations change this balance (see bottom rightmost triangles in Ultimatum results in Fig. 2).

We have performed a Kolmogorov–Smirnov test between two sets of simulation lengths. One set was taken from simulations with only RPS, while the other set was taken from simulations whith ASP. Other parameters had the same value. Figure 3 shows the p-value of this statistical test for some parameter combinations of the tested games. A triangle means the null hypothesis was rejected meaning the distribution of the number of iterations was different. If the triangle points upward, then the average number of iterations of ASP simulations is

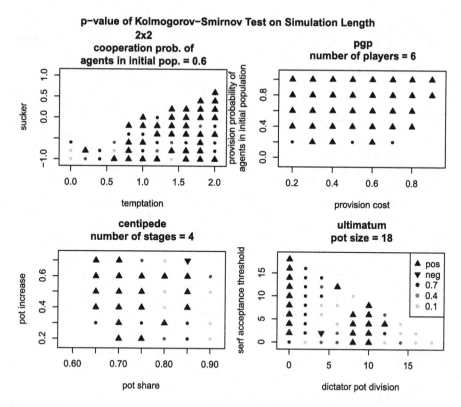

Fig. 3. Results of the Kolmogorov-Smirnov test on RPS and ASP simulation lengths. A circle means simulation lengths belong to the same distribution (null hypothesis). The lower is the p-value, the darker is the circle. Lowest p-values are represented by triangles which correspond to accepted hypothesis. A triangle pointing upwards (downwards) means partner selection increased (decreased) simulation length.

higher than RPS. This means that partner selection can delay extinction. The percentage of statistical tests where the null hypothesis was rejected was 23.4 % for 2 × 2 games, 65.5 % for PGP, 32.9 % for Centipede and 30.7 % for ultimatum. One can see that partner selection has different effects depending on the game. It is more prominent in PGP where ASP simulations lasted longer.

6   Discussion

We have applied the core evolutionary algorithm that we have described in the previous section in a set of well known games. In the simulations that we have performed we have observed the occurrence of extinctions only due to old age or starvation. In Harmony, Snowdrift, Centipede and Ultimatum there is no death by starvation because the payoffs are always positive. By comparison to [19] where there was only death by overcrowding, we noticed an expected increase in the cases of population extinction, since there are more death causes.

Simulations with partner selection last longer than simulations with random partners. The improvement depends on the game with PGP showing the best results. Population dynamics are sensitive to initial conditions. If agents in the initial population cannot gain any energy because they are pure exploiters, no pot division is accepted, or only one type (serfs or even) is present, then the population is condemned from the start. For instance, in Ultimatum there is no point in having an initial population with dictators and serfs that do not reach an agreement. On the other hand, in Harmony there is no dilemma, so it does not matter if agents are capable of choosing their partner or not. Therefore Harmony acts as a neutral control game whose population dynamics are the same for any parameter combination.

The increase in the number of iterations in ASP simulations was not greater because the parameters of the partner selection model of agents in the initial population was set to random selection. Therefore, agents had to evolve the capability of selecting partners. This requires a combination of mutations in the genes that encode partner selection. However, mutation may introduce a defector that exploits existing cooperators thus leading the population to extinction. If instead the initial population had the right combination of partner selection parameter values, then a simulation can last longer. For instance, in Ultimatum the average number of iterations increases around 15 %. If we increase the maximum number of iterations to 50000, then simulation length increases last 200 % in Ultimatum and 12 % in PGP.

7   Conclusions

In our evolutionary algorithm, reproduction depends on the amount of energy obtained in games. Offspring do not replace parents but compete for time to obtain the necessary energy to spread their genes. This process allows for varying population size, either at the edge of the carrying capacity or down to extinction. This algorithm is similar to an agent-based approach [2,6] in that we have a simple model of the lifetime of an agent: birth, growth, reproduction and death. However, our approach using a game as an energy transfer process is general enough to be a model of biological [9] or economical [12] systems.

Extinctions are a dilemma at the population level that agents must deal with. Players do not have explicit knowledge of the extinction dilemma as they have of direct payoffs. Therefore extinction is an implicit phenomenon. In this paper we have extended previous work [18,19] to study extinctions under different conditions: starvation, no offspring, and no partner with adequate role.

Our algorithm can also be used to analyse the population dynamics of specialised versus generalised players. Consider the case of asymmetric games such as Centipede or Ultimatum where players can be specialised in one of the two roles of these games. On the other hand, generalists can play any role of the game and thus are able to cope better with population perturbations [26]. This reasoning can be extended to cooperation and coordination dilemmas. Exploiters have to prevent the death of their targets otherwise both will go extinct. Lack of coordination results in players not receiving any energy thus they risk dying of old age without any offspring.

This process (energy dynamics and population control) is different from other approaches [1,15]. Even when they use energy, the focus is not the evolutionary algorithm and extinctions are not possible. Interactions between players are mediated by some game, which determines how much energy a player obtains. Therefore it is applicable to any game, either some simple game such as Iterated Prisoner's Dilemma [1] or a complex game where strategies are computer programs [15]. Population control is also independent of the game as it only depends on population size and agents' age.

In this paper we have shown that a set of cooperation dilemma games turn out to be population level dilemmas because agents can go extinct. We have compared random partner selection and the capability of selecting partners. In both cases, agents start with the capability of selecting partners randomly. This is a hard condition for the second case, in that evolution has to find the correct partner selection parameter values. Once they appear in a population agents can live longer. If we soften the starting conditions for the second case (agents start with the correct values), preliminary results show even higher number of iterations.

Regarding future work, we plan to investigate what type of network connections arise with partner selection, how stable a population is, and additional features that delay or avoid extinctions. There are many societal problems such as resource management [7] that can be better analysed with EnBEA. This can be implemented if we introduce a fourth step in EnBEA that given agents' actions, current game parameters and common parameters such as carrying capacity, returns the set of parameters to be used in the following iteration of EnBEA. One can investigate how agents could be organised, what norms they should follow, which institutions should exist in order to avoid a collapse in the resource base. High game payoffs or carrying capacity values can be interpreted as a stable resource. Lower values can be interpreted as a polluted or depleted resource.

Acknowledgments. This work was partially supported by FCT, Portugal (PEst-OE/EEI/UI0434/2011) and by EU-ICT project ASSISIbf, nr 601074, of FP7-ICT-2011-9.

References

1. Aktipis, C.A.: Know when to walk away: contingent movement and the evolution of cooperation. J. Theor. Biol. **231**, 249–260 (2004)
2. An, L.: Modeling human decisions in coupled human and natural systems: review of agent-based models. Ecol. Model. **229**, 25–36 (2012)
3. Beissinger, S.R., Westphal, M.I.: On the use of demographic models of population viability in endangered species management. J. Wildl. Manage. **62**(3), 821–841 (1998)
4. Boyd, R., Gintis, H., Bowles, S., Richerson, P.J.: The evolution of altruistic punishment. Proc. Nat. Acad. Sci. **100**(6), 3531–3535 (2003)
5. Camerer, C.: Behavioral Game Theory. Princeton University Press, Princeton (2003)

6. Dawid, H.: Evolutionary game dynamics and the analysis of agent-based imitation models: the long run, the medium run and the importance of global analysis. J. Econ. Dyn. Control **31**(6), 2108–2133 (2007)

7. Ehrlich, P.R., Ehrlich, A.H.: Can a collapse of global civilization be avoided? Proc. R. Soc. B Biol. Sci. **280**(1754), 2012–2845 (2013)

8. Forrest, S., Jones, T.: Modeling complex adaptive systems with echo. In: Stonier, R.J., Yu, X.H. (eds.) Complex Systems: Mechanism of Adaptation, pp. 3–21. IOS Press, Amsterdam (1994)

9. Frey, E.: Evolutionary game theory: theoretical concepts and applications to microbial communities. Phys. A Stat. Mech. Appl. **389**(20), 4265–4298 (2010)

10. Gintis, H.: Game Theory Evolving - A Problem-Centered Introduction to Modeling Strategic Interaction, 1st edn. Princeton University Press, Princeton (2000)

11. Grimm, V., Berger, U., Bastiansen, F., Eliassen, S., Ginot, V., Giske, J., Goss-Custard, J., Grand, T., Heinz, S.K., Huse, G., Huth, A., Jepsen, J.U., Jørgensen, C., Mooij, W.M., Müller, B., Pe'er, G., Piou, C., Railsback, S.F., Robbins, A.M., Robbins, M.M., Rossmanith, E., Rüger, N., Strand, E., Souissi, S., Stillman, R.A., Vabø, R., Visser, U., DeAngelis, D.L.: A standard protocol for describing individual-based and agent-based models. Ecol. Model. **198**(1–2), 115–126 (2006)

12. Hall, C.A.S., Klitgaard, K.A.: Energy and the Wealth of Nations - Understanding the Biophysical Economy. Springer, New York (2012)

13. Hauert, C., Monte, S.D., Hofbauer, J., Sigmund, K.: Volunteering as red queen mechanism for cooperation in public goods games. Science **296**, 1129–1132 (2002)

14. Izquierdo, S.S., Izquierdo, L.R., Vega-Redondo, F.: The option to leave: conditional dissociation in the evolution of cooperation. J. Theor. Biol. **267**(1), 76–84 (2010)

15. Lenski, R.E., Ofria, C., Pennock, R.T., Adami, C.: The evolutionary origin of complex features. Nature **423**(6936), 139–144 (2003)

16. Levine, D.K., Pesendorfer, W.: The evolution of cooperation through imitation. Games Econ. Behav. **58**(2), 293–315 (2007)

17. Manusch, C., Bugmann, H., Heiri, C., Wolf, A.: Tree mortality in dynamic vegetation models - a key feature for accurately simulating forest properties. Ecol. Model. **243**, 101–111 (2012)

18. Mariano, P., Correia, L.: Evolution of partner selection. In: Lenaerts, T., Giacobini, M., Bersini, H., Bourgine, P., Dorigo, M., Doursat, R. (eds.) Advances in Artificial Life, ECAL 2011, pp. 487–494. MIT Press, Cambridge (2011)

19. Mariano, P., Correia, L.: Population dynamics of centipede game using an energy based evolutionary algorithm. In: Liò, P., Miglino, O., Nicosia, G., Nolfi, S., Pavone, M. (eds.) Advances in Artificial Life, ECAL 2013. MIT Press, Cambridge (2013)

20. McKelvey, R.D., Palfrey, T.R.: An experimental study of the centipede game. Econometrica **60**(4), 803–836 (1992)

21. McLane, A.J., Semeniuk, C., McDermid, G.J., Marceau, D.J.: The role of agent-based models in wildlife ecology and management. Ecol. Model. **222**(8), 1544–1556 (2011)

22. Nowak, M.: Evolutionary Dynamics : Exploring the Equations of Life. Belknap Press of Harvard University Press, Cambridge (2006)

23. Nowak, M., Bonhoeffer, S., May, R.: Spatial games and the maintenance of cooperation. Proc. Nat. Acad. Sci. **91**, 4877–4881 (1994)

24. Orbell, J., Dawes, R.: Social welfare, cooperators' advantage, and the option of not playing the game. Am. Sociol. Rev. **58**(6), 787–800 (1993)

25. Pacheco, J.M., Traulsen, A., Nowak, M.A.: Active linking in evolutionary games. J. Theor. Biol. **243**, 437–443 (2006)

26. Ponge, J.-F.: Disturbances, organisms and ecosystems: a global change perspective. Ecol. Evol. **3**(4), 1113–1124 (2013)

27. Rand, D.G., Nowak, M.A.: Evolutionary dynamics in finite populations can explain the full range of cooperative behaviors observed in the centipede game. J. Theor. Biol. **300**, 212–221 (2012)

28. Rand, D.G., Tarnita, C.E., Ohtsuki, H., Nowak, M.A.: Evolution of fairness in the one-shot anonymous ultimatum game. Proc. Nat. Acad. Sci. **110**(7), 2581–2586 (2013)

29. Ray, T.S.: An approach to the synthesis of life. In: Langton, C.G., Taylor, C., Farmer, D., Doyne, J., Rasmussen, S. (eds.) Artificial Life II: Proceedings of the Second Conference on Artificial Life, pp. 371–408. Addison-Wesley (1992)

30. Ray, T.S.: Evolving complexity. Artif. Life Robot. **1**(1), 21–26 (1997)

31. Roca, C.P., Cuesta, J.A., Sánchez, A.: Effect of spatial structure on the evolution of cooperation. Phys. Rev. E **80**, 046106 (2009)

32. Rosenthal, R.W.: Games of perfect information, predatory pricing and the chain-store paradox. J. Econ. Theory **25**(1), 92–100 (1981)

33. Santos, F.C., Pacheco, J.M., Lenaerts, T.: Cooperation prevails when individuals adjust their social ties. PLoS Comput. Biol. **2**(10), e140 (2006)

34. Santos, F.C., Vasconcelos, V.V., Santos, M.D., Neves, P., Pacheco, J.M.: Evolutionary dynamics of climate change under collective-risk dilemmas. Math. Models Methods Appl. Sci. **22**(1), 1140004 (2012)

35. Savarimuthu, S., Purvis, M., Purvis, M., Savarimuthu, B.T.R.: Mechanisms for the self-organization of peer groups in agent societies. In: Bosse, T., Geller, A., Jonker, C.M. (eds.) MABS 2010. LNCS, vol. 6532, pp. 93–107. Springer, Heidelberg (2011)

36. Stanley, E.A., Ashlock, D., Smucker, M.D.: Iterated prisioner's dilemma with choice and refusal of partners: evolutionary results. In: Morán, F., Merelo, J.J., Moreno, A., Chacon, P. (eds.) ECAL 1995. LNCS, vol. 929, pp. 490–502. Springer, Heidelberg (1995)

37. Szabó, G., Hauert, C.: Phase transitions and volunteering in spatial public goods games. Phys. Rev. Lett. **89**, 118101 (2002)

38. Tesfatsion, L.: How economists can get alife. In: Arthur, W.B., Durlauf, S.N., Lane, D.A. (eds.) The Economy as an Evolving Complex System II. SFI Studies in the Sciences of Complexity, vol. XXVII, pp. 533–564. Addison-Wesley, Reading (1997)

39. Thinh Jr., V.T., Doherty, P.F., Huyvaert, K.P.: Effects of different logging schemes on bird communities in tropical forests: a simulation study. Ecol. Model. **243**, 95–100 (2012)

Group Size and Gossip Strategies: An ABM Tool for Investigating Reputation-Based Cooperation

Francesca Giardini[1], Mario Paolucci[1]([✉]), Diana Adamatti[2],
and Rosaria Conte[1]

[1] ISTC-CNR, Roma, Italy
{francesca.giardini,mario.paolucci,rosaria.conte}@istc.cnr.it
[2] Universidade Federal Do Rio Grande - FURG, Rio Grande, Brazil
dianaada@gmail.com

Abstract. In an environment in which free-riders are better off than cooperators, social control is required to foster and maintain cooperation. There are two main paths through which social control can be applied: punishment and reputation. Using a Public Goods Game, we show that gossip, used for assortment under three different strategies, can be effective in large groups, whereas its efficacy is reduced in small groups, with no main effect of the gossiping strategy. We also test four different combinations of gossip and costly punishment, showing that a combination of punishment and reputation-based partner selection leads to higher cooperation rates.

Keywords: Evolution of cooperation · Reputation · Gossip · Punishment

1 Introduction

When cooperators can be easily exploited by those who reap the benefits of cooperation without paying its costs, free-riders will definitely outcompete altruists [18]. How is it possible to reduce the profitability of free-riding in a social dilemma, like a *public goods* game? Models of large-scale human cooperation show that cooperative behavior can be evolutionarily stable if free riders are punished, thus making defection less profitable by means of decreasing the cheaters' payoffs at a cost for the punisher.

There is a large body of evidence showing that humans are willing to punish non-cooperators, even when this implies a reduction in their payoffs [7]. According to "strong reciprocity" theory, punishment is a decentralized, spontaneous and effective solution against cheaters, a solution made possible by the presence of strong reciprocators, i.e., individuals who altruistically reward cooperative acts and punish norm violating behaviors [8]. This view has been recently questioned, and there is mounting evidence that the results on strong reciprocity obtained in the lab can be hardly generalized to what happens in the field [13]. Furthermore, punishment inevitably leads to a second-order collective problem

© Springer International Publishing Switzerland 2015
F. Grimaldo and E. Norling (Eds.): MABS 2014, LNAI 9002, pp. 104–118, 2015.
DOI: 10.1007/978-3-319-14627-0_8

because punishing is costly, therefore refusing to punish non-cooperators maximizes individual welfare. A solution to this has been proposed in [20], where the authors use reputation to link reciprocity and collective action, showing that large-scale cooperation can be stabilized. Using a combination of one-shot Public Goods game and a series of mutual aid games they show that the threat of exclusion from indirect reciprocity can sustain collective action. In this setting, social exclusion reduces free-riding and it has no costs for the punishers (what Panchanathan and Boyd call *shunners*), who can withhold help from free-riders without damaging their reputations.

In models of indirect reciprocity supported by reputation, individuals can base their decision to help others on the basis of observation of their past behaviors. Even without direct experience, cooperation can thrive thanks to the exchange of information based on direct observation of others' interaction [19], or on reported experience [1,19,23], even when group size increases. If punishing implies paying a cost in order to make the other pay higher costs for his defection, reputation works because information about agents' past actions becomes known to potential partners, and this allows cooperators to avoid ill-reputed individuals. In Axelrod's words [2]: 'Knowing people's reputation allows you to know something about what strategy they use even before you have to make your first choice' (p. 151). The importance of reputation for promoting and sustaining social control is uncontroversial, as demonstrated both in lab experiments [22], and in simulation settings, in which reputation has proven to be a cheap and effective means to avoid cheaters and increase cooperators' payoffs [9,10,21].

Moreover, prosocial gossip may effectively bypass the second-order free-rider problem, wherein the costs associated with solving one social dilemma might produce a new one [14,15]). Reputation-based theories of cooperation [1] consider reputation as a by-product of direct observation, thus equivalent to a label or a score, as the well-known *image score* theory developed in [19]. Agents, in that model, can choose whether to help another individual at a certain cost to himself, or to avoid this cost. This decision is based on agents' image scores which are publicly visible. An agent's image score increases when he donates to another agent and decreases in the opposite case, thus working as a reliable indicator of the agents' past behaviors and cooperative attitudes. In such a setting, cooperation can emerge because free-riders have low image scores, therefore they can be easily avoided by cooperators. However, the result depends on the public availability of accurate information:

> 'cooperation based on indirect reciprocity depends crucially on the ability of a player to estimate the image score of the opponent. In the above model, we assume that the image score of each individual is known to every other member of the population'. ([19] p. 575).

Although effective, image score is completely unrealistic, especially if used to account for the evolution of cooperation in human societies. In large groups of unrelated individuals, direct observation is not possible, and records of an individual's past behaviors are usually not freely and publicly available. What is abundant and costless among humans is gossip, i.e., reported information about others' past actions that can be used to avoid free-riders, either by refusing to interact with them, or joining another group in which free-riders are supposedly absent.

2 Gossip as a More Realistic Information Transmission

Unlike previous works [19,20], in which information about others is publicly available and is used to discriminate between cooperators and non-cooperators in a indirect reciprocity game [19], we design a model in which information is privately transmitted among gossipers. Also, we account for the fact that information is noisy and reputation is sticky, two features that characterize human societies, in which gossip does not necessarily have a positive effect. A third element of novelty of our work is the use of a multi-players game, such as the *public goods game* (*PGG* from now on), in which interactions happen in groups, with a conflict of interest among agents. In such a setting, our work is aimed at investigating whether different reputation-based strategies may have an effect on cooperation rates in mixed populations, and also to compare performances of gossipers, who exchange information about their peers, and punishers, who pay a cost in order to reduce cheaters' payoffs.

We are interested in contrasting benefits and costs of gossip with those of costly punishment, but we also aim at specifying how action strategies may complement reputation spreading. While punishing a free-rider is an action with immediate consequences on the free-rider's payoff, reputation spreading implies an information transmission, but the way in which this information is used is usually not specified. For a complete definition of the gossip and reputation behaviour, we have to define how agents are going to transform this information into action. Here, we propose three reputation-based strategies: gossipers can refuse to contribute to the group (strategy *refuse*, actively look for a better group (strategy *compare*), or apply a more refined form of partner choice. In this latter case, group formation is delegated to a single agent, randomly selected to act as a leader, and then allowed to choose its group mates (strategy *leader*). If the leader is a gossiper, it can use information received about others in order to select the most cooperative partners and avoid the uncooperative ones.

If we define the *object level* as containing all the actions that influence score directly, the *PGG* constitutes the main interaction at the object level for our model. Punishment also happens at the object level, as it is a response strategy influencing scores directly. Distinct from the object level, the *information level* contains observation results, for example compliance information as employed by punisher agents, but also inter-agent information diffusion by gossip. Note that a gossip strategy by itself is incomplete, because it is only specified at the information level; a complete mechanisms need to influence the object level just as punishments does (see Fig. 1). Thus, information is applied to the object level by means of costly punishment; by withholding participation to the next game (gossipers under *refuse* strategy); or by weak (gossipers with *compare*) or

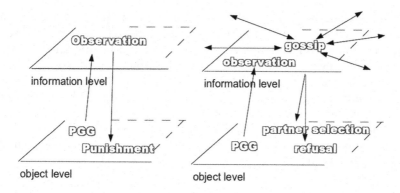

Fig. 1. Actions at different levels. Left: a punishment mechanism is complete as it contains both information specification (observation only) and action specification that effects the object level. Right: gossip and reputation mechanisms dictate how information is diffused and grows, but they don't have an unique response. In this work, we study responses as partner selection and refusal.

strong (*leader*) partner selection. These last three mechanisms constitute the application, or *response* as we will call it in the rest of the paper, at the object level of gossip and reputation information.

Building upon results obtained in previous work [3,11], our agents are cooperative at the object level (with the exception of the free-riders), but can change their behavior on the basis of their peers' actions. Agents start gossiping and punishing, respectively, when the number of free-riders in their group is considered too high, i.e., it exceeds a given threshold (which is set at 0.2 of the group size). The threshold represents an attempt to take into account the fact that free-riders may be difficult to discover and that some missed contributions can go undetected.

It is well known that group size can be a critical factor in models of social interaction. We are interested in understanding the interplay between our strategies and group size, so we report results obtained in small groups (5 agents), medium size group (10 agents), and large groups (25 agents).

To this purpose, we have implemented our model using NetLogo [24]. The implementation is general-purpose and highly customizable, even beyond the purposes of the present paper[1].

The paper is organized as follows: Sect. 2 explains the simulation model using an ODD protocol, Sect. 3 presents experiments and results, whereas in Sect. 4 the results are discussed and some conclusions are sketched.

3   The Model

Building up on the simulation framework developed in [11] using NetLogo, we added two new strategies in order to deepen our understanding of the role of

---

[1] The model can be downloaded at http://labss.istc.cnr.it/code/punishment-and-reputation.

reputation mechanisms in supporting cooperation in mixed populations in which different types of agents play a *public goods game* (*PGG*), the classical experimental model used to investigate social dilemmas [17]. In this game, agents in a group decide whether or not to contribute to a public pot at a net personal cost c, in order to create a benefit b (normally with $b > c$). The pot is then divided equally amongst all the participants in the group, without considering their contributions.

In compliance with the ODD protocol [12] for describing ABM models and simulations, the model will be described now in terms of purpose, entities, processes and objectives.

3.1   Purpose

Using a *PGG*, we investigate how cooperation can be maintained in mixed populations in which there are cooperators, free-riders, punishers and gossipers. While the former two populations play always the same strategy, irrespective of what other agents do, the latter types of agents are reactive. The group's total payoff is maximized when everyone contributes all of their private endowment to the public pool. However, game-theory predicts zero contributions because any rational agent does best contributing zero, regardless of whatever anyone else does.

It is well known that punishment reduces profitability of free-riding and increases cooperation [3,6], but less is known about the effect of gossiping, which is a kind a informal social control widely used in human societies. This is especially true if we refer to information transmission in a one-to-one way, instead of public information available through direct observation.

In a previous work [11], we have shown the effects of two gossip strategies on the emergence of cooperation: *defect* (a retaliatory strategy that agents played against those with a bad reputation), and *refuse*. Here we consider two alternative strategies, *compare* and *leader*, with the aim of introducing partner choice in the model and testing its performance on cooperation rates. Our hypothesis is that when partner choice is available, a reputation-based strategy for social control should be effective in promoting cooperation and selecting out free-riders. We also predict that there is an interaction effect between group size and gossip strategy, therefore in bigger groups a gossip-based strategy should perform better. For this reason, we test our model in a first experiment for three different group sizes: 5, 10, and 25 agents. To the best of our knowledge, this work is the first attempt to model different gossip strategies and to compare their performance on cooperation rates in a mixed population.

In a second experiment, we also measure different combinations of harsh and mild reactions, with the aim of understanding what happens when punishers and gossipers start defecting in a retaliatory way, and to what extent cooperation is robust to this behavior.

Our simulation allows to:

- explore three different ways of implementing gossip in a *PGG*, and to test the effectiveness of different gossip-based behaviors on cooperation rates, populations' scores and survival rates;

– identify the most effective combination of costly punishment and gossip in a situation in which Gossipers and Punishers may react to free-riding more or less harshly.

3.2 Entities, State Variables and Scales

The main entities in our model are agents, either non-reactive or reactive. In the former category we find *cooperators* (C), who always contribute to the common pool, and *free-riders* (FR), who never contribute. In the latter category, *punishers* (P) and *gossipers* (G) start as cooperators, but they change their behavior in response to the percentage of detected free-riders in their group: when the number of known defectors in a group exceeds a threshold set at 20 % of group size (following [3]), punishers and gossipers become *active* and apply a counter strategy defined below.

At the onset of the simulation, each agent is endowed with an initial amount of 50 points that can be put in the common pool, or used to punish others; regardless of the strategy, agents are culled from the game when their cumulated payoff goes to zero (*death* of the agent) and they are not replaced. The cost of contributing to the *PGG* is set to 1, the unit of our utility scale, and the sum of all the contributions is multiplied by a factor set to 3. The public good, i.e., the resulting quantity, is divided evenly among all group members, regardless of individual contributions.

As for counter strategies, punishment works by reducing the payoff of free-riders through the imposition of a cost sustained by the punisher. Punishers pay 1 unit in order to reduce free-riders's payoff by 5. Punishers keeps on punishing until they run out of resources.

Each step, a simple evolutionary algorithm is applied. Agents are ordered by score, and those sitting at the bottom of the ranking are removed and replaced with an identical number of clones generated by a random subset of the surviving ones. The replacement rate is set at 8 % of the population, and this kind of algorithm has been already used in the social sciences [3].

For each strategy we calculate the average *score* in time, as the accumulation of points obtained in the *PGG*, and the population for each strategy, as modified by evolution and death. We also calculate the *cooperation rate* as the ratio of agents who contributed to the last game, a value bounded between 0 and 1. Note that complete cooperation can be reached only if the *FR* population gets extinct.

Algorithm 1. Description of punishers behaviors

While {Number of Timesteps}
  * Random group formation of the population;
  * Agents take First Stage decision;
  * Gather and Distribution of the Public good in each group;
  * First Stage Decisions are made public within the group;
  * Agents make Second Stage decision;
  * Punishment Execution;

An important variable is group size, which is known to have an effect on cooperation rates in PGG [3]. We tested our strategies for three different dimensions of groups: small group (5 agents), intermediate group (10 agents) and large group (25 agents).

In the second study, we fine-tuned the reactions, dividing Punishers and Gossipers into two sub-sets [11]:

- Nice Punishers (Np) cooperate in the passive state; once active, they punish free-riders at a cost to themselves, but they continue to cooperate in the PGG. This behavior will continue until the agent eventually exits the active state when cheaters' rate goes below 0.2 of group size.
- Mean Punishers (Mp) contribute in the passive state; once active, they punish free-riders and free ride themselves in the PGG until they exit the active state.
- Nice Gossipers (Ng) are cooperative in the passive state; once active, they start spreading information about free-riders, and keep on cooperating in the PGG.
- Mean Gossipers (Mg) contribute in the passive state; once active, they spread information about free-riders, and always defect in the PGG until the agent eventually exits the active state.

Algorithm 2. Description of gossipers' behaviors - REFUSE

While {Number of Time-steps}
- * Random group formation of the population;
- * Gossipers check others' reputation;
- **If** number of bad images (known FRs plus anyone who defected and had been marked with a bad image) equals or is higher than beta * numagents
  - * Reputation diffusion
  - * Gossipers refuse the interaction
- * Gossipers take the First stage decision according to their active/passive status;
- * Gather and Distribution of the Public good in each group;
- * Images are updated (bad images added; there is no restoration of bad images if one cooperated)

3.3 Process Overview and Scheduling

The behavior of reactive populations is described in the Algorithms 1 to 4. Punishers punish after contributions are made public, whereas gossip reaction works as a proactive strategy that is triggered by agents' reputations.

4 Experiments and Results

We conducted two simulation experiments in which simulations lasted for 200 time steps. In the first set of simulations, we explore a 3×3 set of conditions, with three different group size of 5, 10, and 25 agents. We measured cooperation rates, populations' scores and population size in mixed populations with gossipers playing three different strategies: *compare*, *leader* and *refuse*. Each condition was repeated ten times, for a total of 90 simulation runs. The results are reported in Sect. 4.1.

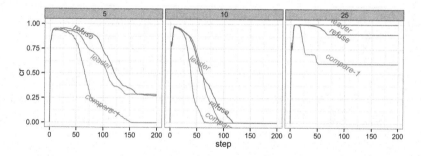

Fig. 2. Cooperation rate (cr) in time by response and group size. In large groups (25 agents), the final cooperation rate is higher, and this is especially true if compared to the intermediary group size (10 agents). Agents in 10-sized groups show the lowest level of cooperation.

The second experiment was performed in a $4 \times 2 \times 2$ set of conditions, again repeated 10 times each, for a total of 160 simulations. For all plots, points in time are averages over repetitions. Results are reported in Sect. 4.2.

4.1 First Experiment: Testing Responses

First, we wanted to test whether cooperation can evolve and be maintained in a mixed population in which gossip is the only means of social control. Given the strategies employed, cooperation can be generated by any mix of population in a non-active state, except for the *FR*. In Fig. 2, the average cooperation rate for all agents is presented. Large groups (25 agents) outperform the others for all responses. In intermediate size groups (10 agents) we observe the lowest cooperation rates. A possible explanation is that with 10 agents in group there are too many agents for direct reciprocity to be effective, but too few for reputation to work. With regard to response strategies, *compare* always leads to lower cooperation levels, while *leader* and *refuse* do not show a consistent ordering. The *leader* response prevails in larger groups and is the only strategy that supports full cooperation, while *refuse* prevails in smaller groups.

Algorithm 3. Description of gossipers' behaviors - COMPARE

While {Number of Time-steps}
  * Random group formation of the population;
  * Gossipers check other agents' reputation;
  If number of bad images (known FRs plus anyone who defected and had been marked with a bad image) equals
      or is higher than beta * numagents
        * Reputation diffusion
        * Gossipers evaluate another group at random, and join it if the percentage of known free-riders there
            is lower than in the current group. Another agent is randomly picked to join the original group of
            the shifting agent.
  * Gossipers take the First stage decision according to their active/passive status;
  * Gather and Distribution of the Public good in each group;
  * First Stage Decisions are made public within the group;
  * Images are updated (bad images added; there is no restoration of bad images if one cooperated).

Algorithm 4. Description of gossipers' behaviors - LEADER

While {Number of Time-steps}
  * A given number of agents (depending on the the total population and the group size g) are randomly selected
   to act as leaders
  If Leader is a gossiper
   * check agents without bad images and tries to build a group with them (if there aren't enough not-
    bad-image agents he will admits some bad-image to fill up the group)
  ElseIf Leader is not a gossiper
   * gather agents and form a group (G) = (groupsize-1)
  * Gossipers check other agents' reputation;
  If number of bad images (known FRs plus anyone who defected and had been marked with a bad image) equals
   or is higher than beta * numagents
   * Reputation diffusion (active gossipers inform other gossipers about known cheaters in the group (if
    gossip=10 they spread info ten times depending on the number of recipients available)
  * Gossipers take the First stage decision according to their active/passive status;
  * Gather and Distribution of the Public good in each group;
  * First Stage Decisions are made public within the group;
  * Images are updated (bad images added; there is no restoration of bad images if one cooperated).

To have a better understanding of the emergence of cooperation, we look into cumulated scores (the results of the PGG) for each strategy. These are shown in Fig. 3. Free-riders' payoffs are higher in groups of 5 and 10 agents, where, after an initial increase, all other populations reach a maximum score around step 60, followed by a collapse.

To the contrary, in larger (25 agents) groups reputation strategies are effective in keeping free-riders under control. This result supports our view of gossip as a powerful mean to sustain cooperation in large groups. In particular, when gossipers played the *compare* response they achieved the highest payoffs in the population, dominating all other strategies; when they used *leader* or *refuse*, they got the highest payoffs together with cooperators. Punishers, while being an essential ingredient for cheating control, obtain low payoffs in all situations.

Another measure of success is reported in Fig. 4 where the final population sizes are shown. For groups of size 5 or 10, the FR strategy outperformed other populations, being in several cases the only survivor after 200 steps. Larger groups (25 agents) showed a different pattern: the cooperative strategies, summed together, managed to contain them within the initial simulation steps, and ended out controlling the whole population.

Finally we run a conditional inference tree analysis [16], to isolate, among all the possible variables, the ones that have a major impact on our results. Conditional inference trees are used to estimate a regression between a set of variables, in this case group size and response strategy, ordering them on the basis of the strength of their association to the effect (in this case, cooperation rate).

As shown in Fig. 5, in large groups cooperation is higher (leaves 9, 10 and 11). Independent of group size, the group strategy is always divided between *leader* and *refuse* in one branch, and *compare* in the other. *Refuse* is a conservative strategy and *leader* allows for full partner selection, therefore they can promote cooperation and favour gossipers. On the other hand, agents playing the *compare* strategy have only one possibility to change their group, therefore they can end up in a group of strangers with a higher number of free-riders than in their original group.

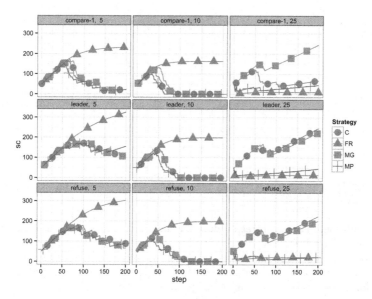

Fig. 3. Average strategy scores in time for each strategy. Rows: gossip response; columns: group size. Free-riders (*FR*) prevail in group size 5 and 10, while the cooperative strategies fare better in groups of 25 agents. Notice the special case of the *compare-1* gossip strategy separates gossipers (*Mg*) from punishers (*Mp*), the latter generally paying the cost of cooperation.

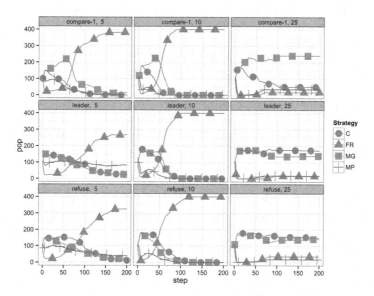

Fig. 4. Number of agents (*pop*) in time by group size and response. Rows: gossip strategy; columns: group size. The intermediate group level (10 agents per group) shows the higher extinction rate.

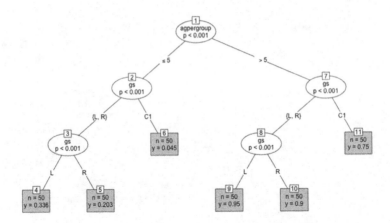

Fig. 5. Conditional inference tree on data for the last 20 steps of the first experiment. The group size (*agpergroup* variable) divides the tree between small groups (≤5) and large groups. Subsequently, the gossip response (*gs* variable) divides the tree between *leader* (*L*) and *refuse* (*R*) in one branch, and *compare* (*C1*) in the other. The better cooperation rates (*Y* variables) are in large groups.

4.2   Second Experiment: Severity of Mechanisms

In the second experiment, we wanted to compare two levels of severity for the mechanisms that support cooperation, that is, for punishment and reputation. As with the previous experiment, we record cooperation rates, scores and populations, with the aim to find out the best combination between harsh/mild punishment and harsh/mild gossip.

Results are reported for global cooperation rates in Fig. 6. Here, cooperation rates in time for the 4 combinations of Nice and Mean are displayed, in a 3×3 experiments setting with group size of 5, 10 and 25. Gossipers can adopt one of the three responses *compare*, *leader* and *refuse*. Each line shows the global cooperation rate for a single experiment with 100 agents per strategy in combinations of mean and nice variants. We remind that *mean* punishers (*Mp*) and gossipers (*Mg*) do not only react to known cheaters in their group by punishing or gossiping, but they also defect, while *nice* ones only apply the relative response.

In this experiment, cooperation was difficult to achieve when gossipers defected and punishers reacted without defecting. On the other hand, we observed very high cooperation rates, up to 1, with the combination of mean punishment and nice gossip in large groups. This suggests that once mean punishers had reduced the number of free-riders, a cooperating gossip (for the *compare* response) or any kind of gossip (for *leader* and *refuse*) was effective in promoting cooperation in large groups.

The conditional inference tree analysis [16], as shown in Fig. 7, confirms that in large groups cooperation could reach values close to or equal to 1 when the reactions were in combination, like Mean Punishment-Nice Gossip and gossipers

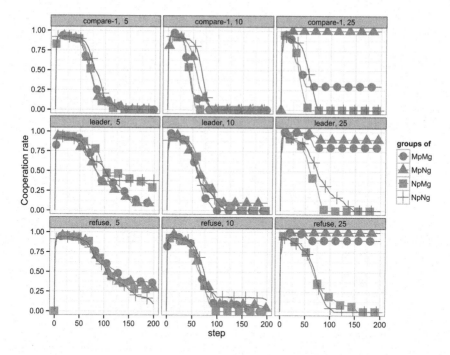

Fig. 6. Cooperation rates for mixed populations in which Punishers and Gossipers strategies are combined. Each line shows the global cooperation rate for a single experiment. The highest cooperation rates are reached in the population in which punishers also defect against known free-riders, whereas Gossipers adopt a milder strategy. This combination outperforms all the other strategies in small and large groups.

played either *compare* or *refuse* (leaves 10 and 11). This supported our hypothesis about the effectiveness of partner choice in promoting cooperation, especially when cheaters were selected out by punishers.

5   Discussion and Future Work

Among humans, gossip is a powerful tool for social control, and information transmission might have played a crucial role in the evolution of cooperation, as suggested by Robin Dunbar:

> 'Lacking language, monkeys and apes are constrained in what they can know
> ... But language allows us to seek out what has been going on behind our backs.
> Indeed, we can even be proactive about it and tell our friends and relations
> what we have seen when we think it might be in their interests to know' ([4],
> p. 103).

In the last decade, research on reputation-supported cooperation has unveiled the importance of getting information about others' past behaviors through direct

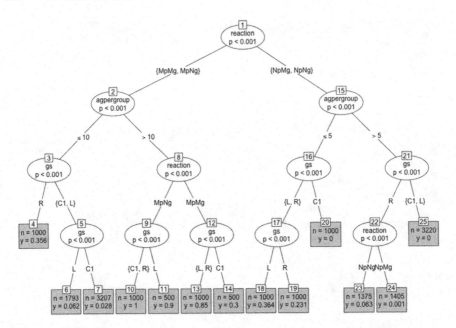

Fig. 7. The conditional inference tree on data for the last 20 steps of the second experiment shows that the main effect on cooperation rates is connected with Mean Punishment (Mp) in combination with both Mg and Ng. The second level of discrimination is due to group size, and the third mostly to reaction strategies. In general, the Mp branch leads to higher levels of cooperation with the exception of small groups for $C1$ and L reactions.

observation, but less is known about the role played by transmission. In an environment in which free-riders can be easily spotted because of some visible marker, like a score publicly visible, cooperation can easily emerge, but this model cannot be extended to human societies, where free-riders do not show any mark and they also have an incentive in concealing their tendencies and behaviors. In this work, we modeled gossip as information transmission among agents and we linked it with three different ways of using the information received. When we discover that someone is a free-rider we can react in several ways, like refraining from interaction (strategy *refuse* in our model), or avoiding that person and joining another group (strategy *compare*). There are also cases in which humans can actively select their partners, creating a new group in which only reliable cooperators are present (strategy *leader*).

Our data provide some additional insights into the role of gossip spreading on cooperation levels in mixed populations in which gossipers can transmit information and tune their behaviors on the basis of information received from their peers. We show that cooperation rates are higher when agents can compare their present situation and switch to a better one, i.e. they can avoid free-riders, and this solution allows gossipers to get the highest scores in large groups of 25 agents. We also show that the combination of punishment and gossip can lead cooperation to its maximum in large groups, irrespective of the specific gossip strategy. This result is especially interesting because it is in line with ethnographic studies of human societies in which material punishment and gossiping about free-riders usually go hand in hand [5].

Building upon previous work in which we modelled gossip in a more ideal-typical way [11], here we made an effort towards a more realistic modeling of gossip spreading, allowing agents to spread gossip at the beginning of each encounter, informing their peers (other gossipers) about the identity of known free-riders in the group. Preventive gossip is a way of warning one's peers against the risks of exploitation, but additional work is needed in order to identify the best conditions for the emergence of gossip. The model that we have developed is just one of several steps required in that direction. It should be supported by experimental and observation data, and, possibly with the help of these data, get refined and replicated.

Acknowledgements. We gratefully acknowledge support from PRISMA project, within the Italian National Program for Research and Innovation (Programma Operativo Nazionale Ricerca e Competitivitá 2007–2013. Settore: Smart Cities and Communities and Social Innovation Asse e Obiettivo: Asse II - Azioni integrate per lo sviluppo sostenibile).

References

1. Alexander, R.: The Biology of Moral Systems (Foundations of Human Behavior). Aldine Transaction, New York (1987)
2. Axelrod, R.: The Evolution of Cooperation. Basic Books, New York (1984)
3. Carpenter, J.P.: Punishing free-riders: how group size affects mutual monitoring and the provision of public goods. Games Econ. Behav. **60**(1), 31–51 (2007)
4. Dunbar, R.I.M.: Gossip in evolutionary perspective. Rev. Gen. Psychol. **8**(2), 100–110 (2004)
5. Ellickson, R.: Order without Law : How Neighbors Settle Disputes. Harvard University Press, Cambridge (2005)
6. Fehr, E., Gächter, S.: Cooperation and punishment in public goods experiments. Am. Econ. Rev. **90**(4), 980–994 (2000)
7. Fehr, E., Gachter, S.: Altruistic punishment in humans. Nature **415**(6868), 137–140 (2002)
8. Fehr, E., Schneider, F.: Eyes are on us, but nobody cares: are eye cues relevant for strong reciprocity? Proc. Biol. Sci. R. Soc. **277**(1686), 1315–1323 (2010)
9. Giardini, F., Conte, R.: Gossip for social control in natural and artificial societies. SIMULATION **88**(1), 18–32 (2012)
10. Giardini, F., Paolucci, M., Conte, R.: Reputation. In: Edmonds, B., Meyer, R. (eds.) Handbook on Simulating Social Complexity. Understanding Complex Systems, pp. 573–577. Springer, Heidelberg (2013)
11. Giardini, F., Paolucci, M., Villatoro, D., Conte, R.: Punishment and gossip: sustaining cooperation in a public goods game. In: Kamiński, B., Koloch, G. (eds.) Advances in Social Simulation. AISC, vol. 229, pp. 107–118. Springer, Heidelberg (2014)

12. Grimm, V., Berger, U., Bastiansen, F., et al.: A standard protocol for describing individual-based and agent-based models. Ecol. Model. **198**(1-2), 115–126 (2006)
13. Guala, F.: Reciprocity: weak or strong? What punishment experiments do (and do not) demonstrate. Departmental Working Papers 2010–23, Department of Economics, Business and Statistics at Università degli Studi di Milano, July 2010
14. Hardin, G.: The Tragedy of the Commons. Science **162**(3859), 1243–1248 (1968)
15. Heckathorn, D.D.: Collective action and the second-order free-rider problem. Ration. Soc. **1**(1), 78–100 (1989)
16. Hothorn, T., Hornik, K., Zeileis, A.: Unbiased recursive partitioning. J. Comput. Graph. Stat. **15**(3), 651–674 (2006)
17. Ledyard, J.O.: Public goods: a survey of experimental research. In: Kagel, J.H., Roth, A.E. (eds.) Handbook of Experimental Economics, pp. 111–194. Princeton University Press, Princeton (1995)
18. Maynard-Smith, J.: Evolution and the Theory of Games. Cambridge University Press, Cambridge (1982)
19. Nowak, M.A., Sigmund, K.: Evolution of indirect reciprocity by image scoring. Nature **393**(6685), 573–577 (1998)
20. Panchanathan, K., Boyd, R.: Indirect reciprocity can stabilize cooperation without the second-order free rider problem. Nature **432**(7016), 499–502 (2004)
21. Pinyol, I., Paolucci, M., Sabater-Mir, J., Conte, R.: Beyond accuracy. reputation for partner selection with lies and retaliation. In: Antunes, L., Paolucci, M., Norling, E. (eds.) MABS 2007. LNCS (LNAI), vol. 5003, pp. 128–140. Springer, Heidelberg (2008)
22. Rockenbach, B., Milinski, M.: The efficient interaction of indirect reciprocity and costly punishment. Nature **444**(7120), 718–723 (2006)
23. Wedekind, C., Milinski, M.: Cooperation through image scoring in humans. Science **288**(5467), 850–852 (2000)
24. Wilensky, U.: Netlogo. Center for Connected Learning and Computer-Based Modeling, Northwestern University. Evanston (1999). http://ccl.northwestern.edu/netlogo/

Data and Multi-agent-Based
Simulation

Automatic Generation of Agent Behavior Models from Raw Observational Data

Bridgette Parsons[1]([✉]), José M. Vidal[1], Nathan Huynh[2], and Rita Snyder[3]

[1] Department of Computer Science and Engineering,
University of South Carolina, Columbia, SC, USA
parsons@email.sc.edu
[2] Department of Civil and Environmental Engineering,
University of South Carolina, Columbia, SC, USA
[3] College of Nursing's Healthcare Process Redesign Center,
University of South Carolina, Columbia, SC, USA

Abstract. Agent-based modeling is used to simulate human behaviors in different fields. The process of building believable models of human behavior requires that domain experts and Artificial Intelligence experts work closely together to build custom models for each domain, which requires significant effort. The aim of this study is to automate at least some parts of this process. We present an algorithm called MAGIC, which produces an agent behavioral model from raw observational data. It calculates transition probabilities between actions and identifies decision points at which the agent requires additional information in order to choose the appropriate action. Our experiments using synthetically-generated data and real-world data from a hospital setting show that the MAGIC algorithm can automatically produce an agent decision process. The agent's underlying behavior can then be modified by domain experts, thus reducing the complexity of producing believable agent behavior from field data.

1 Introduction

Agent-based modeling has been used to simulate traffic patterns, markets, supply chains, wildlife ecology, and networking. It is a popular method for simulating complex systems because of its ability to show emergent behaviors, or behaviors that arise from the interaction between the different agents. Unfortunately, the creation of an agent-based behavioral model can be a difficult task, especially when modeling humans that are involved in complex processes. Frequently, simulation models involving human decision processes are created using observed behavior sequences. This model development paradigm requires that both the programmer and the domain expert work together to create a computational model which correctly reflects the observed behavior.

In this paper, we present MAGIC (Models Automatically Generated from Information Collected), an algorithm for extracting behavior models from raw observational data consisting of time-stamped sequential observations of the subject's behavior. Our behavior model, described in Sect. 3, resembles a Markov

© Springer International Publishing Switzerland 2015
F. Grimaldo and E. Norling (Eds.): MABS 2014, LNAI 9002, pp. 121–132, 2015.
DOI: 10.1007/978-3-319-14627-0_9

Decision Process (MDP), but with added support for cyclic behavior and additional nodes known as **decision points** that indicate when the agent requires outside input in order to proceed. In order to demonstrate the ease of modification of the behavior model for use in simulation, we have also developed an editing tool that allows the model to be altered, and illustrated its use in a 3D simulation of a nurse administering medications to patients on a hospital floor.

We test our algorithm both in a synthetic test setting and a hospital setting where we build a simulation of a nurse as she carries out a medication administration process in a hospital. Data for the nursing simulation was gathered by following several nurses for 6 weeks as they administered medications to their patients [7,8,13]. Our experimental results demonstrate that the MAGIC algorithm can automatically build appropriate behavioral models.

2 Related Work

One possible method of building a model of human behavior is by deep analysis of the human decision process and human cognition. This is, in essence, the goal of cognitive psychology, which tells us that the heuristics humans use to make decisions are highly varied and individualized [4]. This lack of a clear model of the human decision-making process made an alternate method of deriving a decision process an attractive alternative.

Agent decision processes that have instead been derived from sequences of behavior observed over time have proved successful in many areas, including human behavior modeling. For example, in smart home studies, sensor pattern readings have been used to determine human behavior patterns in order to automate heating and lighting systems in accordance with the owners' lifestyle [2,6,10]. In the RoboCup competition, a framework was developed not only to learn from logged human behavior, but to then train other agents by using the behavior it had learned [3]. The 2012 BotPrize competition, an Unreal Tournament DeathMatch-style game where human judges attempt to distinguish between AI-players and humans, had a tie for first place between two bots that used mirrored human behavior sequences, fooling more than 50 percent of the judges in the competition [12]. Thus, there is ample evidence in different settings that agents that effectively and believably simulate human behavior can be built by deriving decision processes from observed sequences of human behavior.

In robotic planning, there has also been some success in deriving decision processes from observed behavior. The learning of primitives [1] or low-level actions [5] using variations of HMM's enables robots to learn by imitating behavior, although these methods necessitate online rather than offline learning. More recently, a method has been proposed to enable robots to learn offline using human-readable text files [9]. This method, however, requires natural language processing and the careful construction of an appropriate ontology, unlike our research, in which the task names are provided by domain experts, and behavior is recorded by trained observers.

In simulation, agents have required the specialized skills of AI experts working together with domain experts to create the needed agent behaviors. In contrast, our research aims to develop algorithms and tools to automatically build these agents' behaviors using the raw observational data. That is, we want to take observed workflow data as input and output a generalized behavior model. Also, since these models will almost certainly require some modification, we propose to develop tools for domain experts, who are not AI experts or developers, to be able to modify these behaviors as needed.

3   Behavioral Model: Sequential Compressed Markov Decision Process

The type of behaviors we wish to model can almost be captured using a Markov Decision Process [11]. However, since MDP's do not allow for an internal state, they cannot be used to represent a finite loop of a length prescribed by an outside input. For example, in our healthcare domain, we need to represent the fact that a nurse will administer a fixed number of medications to a patient, so she will repeat a finite set of tasks some fixed number of times, such as 5 steps for each one of the 3 medications. We need a behavior model that can also represent these repeated sequences.

In this study, we created a variation of the Markov Decision Process that we will refer to as a Sequential Compressed Markov Decision Process, or **SCMDP**. This SCMDP extends the basic MDP by including decision points which have direct links to other states based on external inputs instead of a transition probability.

Definition 1. *(Sequential Compressed Markov Decision Process) An SCMDP consists of an initial state s_0 and an end state s_n both taken from a set S of states where $|S| = n$, a transition function $T(s, p, s')$, a set of decision points $D \subset S$, and a set of decision point transitions $P(d, s, e)$ where $d \in D$ and e is some external input.*

In the SCMDP, states correspond to tasks performed by the agent, such as "wash hands" or "enter room." The transition function T gives the probability p that the agent will transition from one state to another, therefore doing the corresponding task. All transition probabilities from any given state will always add to 1, as they do in an MDP. Start and end states s_0 and s_n are designated to account for the fact that only certain tasks are likely to occur at the beginning or end of a sequence.

The decision points D are a set of special states within the decision process. They represent the entrance to a cycle. Each decision point has at least two edges extending out from it. One edge goes to the first state in the cycle, and the other to the action that is to be taken after the cycle ends. The cycle begins and ends due to some external information e. The transitions out of decision points are represented by P. For example, a nurse agent might repeat the same set of tasks for each medication that must be administered to a patient. The external information in this case is the number of medications that the patient requires. The decision point keeps track of how many medications have been

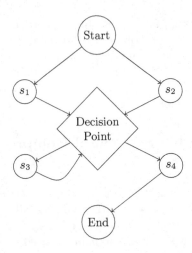

Fig. 1. Example SCMDP.

administered thus far and ends the cycle when there are no more medications to administer. It is possible to have more than one transition out of a decision point, therefore requiring more than one piece of external information, such as whether the medication the patient needs is available, and whether it is located in the medication room or the pharmacy.

Figure 1 shows a simple example of an SCMDP. Note that at the decision point, the agent can either repeat the cycle by going back to s_3 or end the sequence by choosing to go to s_4. In this example, the cycle consists of only one state, s_3, but there could be any number of states before the agent gets back to the decision point. The decision between s_3 and s_4 is made using external information not shown in the diagram. In practice, this external information will depend upon the domain that the SCMDP is modeling.

3.1   The MAGIC Algorithm

The MAGIC algorithm, shown in Fig. 2, takes as input a text file of sequential task observations and outputs an SCMDP. This input text file consists of a sequence of observations O, where each observation $o \in O$ is a sequence of tasks, $o_i = (t_1, t_2, \ldots t_{ki})$, that we have observed a person perform. For example, one observation corresponds to the sequence of tasks that we watched a nurse perform from the time she entered a patient's room on Monday 9:32 am until the time that she left the room. We assume that all of the observations have recognizable start and end points. In the nursing example, these start and end states correspond to a change in the patient's room number.

The MAGIC algorithm tries to identify and extract cycles in the raw input data, which is especially difficult given the fact that the data might contain errors in the form of transposed tasks. For example, in the observation $t_1, t_2, t_3, t_4, t_5, t_6,$ t_7, t_3, t_5, t_4, t_8 the set of tasks t_3, t_4, t_5 should be recognized as a cycle because

MAGIC (O)

1   $C = [\ ]$ // List of cycles
2   $m = k$ // Maximum number of tasks in a cycle, defined by user
3   $O' = [\ ]$ // Updated List of Observations
4   $S = [\ ]$ // List of lists of tasks that have been replaced with cycle pointers
5   **for** $o \in O$
6       $o, S, C = $ MAGIC-ASSISTANT(o, S, m, C)
7   O'.append(o)
8   $T = $ CALCULATE-TRANSITIONS(O', S)
9   **return** T, S

CONTAINS(o, s)

1   **if** $\exists_{0 \leq i \leq j \leq |o|} \, o[i..j] \cap s! = \emptyset$ // Does o contain s, sequentially?
2   **return** i, j // If so, return the start and end points in o.
3   **return** NIL

MAGIC-ASSISTANT(o, S, m, C)

1   $t = \emptyset$ // List of repeated tasks
2   **for** $c \in C$
3   **for** $j = 0$ **to** $|o| - (|c| + 1)$
4           $s, e = $ CONTAINS(o, c)
5   **if** $s, e \neq \emptyset$
6               $o[s..e] = c$ // Replace the list of tasks with a pointer to the cycle in the cycle list
7   S.append$(o[s..e])$ // Add list of repeated tasks to list for transition calculations
8   **while** $m > 2$
9   **for** $i = 0$ **to** $|o| - (m + 1)$
10          $j = i + m - 1$
11          $t = o[i..j]$ // Set of contiguous tasks taken from the observation
12          $s, e = $ CONTAINS(o, t)
13   **if** $s, e \neq \emptyset$
14   **if** $\neg \exists_{c \in C} \, t \subseteq c$ // If t is not a subset of an old cycle
15   C.append(t)
16              $o[s..e] = t$ // Replace the list of tasks with a pointer to the appropriate cycle
17   S.append$(o[s..e])$ // Add list of repeated tasks to list for transition calculations
18      $m = m - 1$
19 **return** o, S, C

Fig. 2. The MAGIC algorithm. The CONTAINS procedure tells us if the list of observations o contains the set of tasks t anywhere within it, but contiguously. The MAGIC-ASSISTANT procedure identifies cycles, checks if they are subsets of existing cycles, and records any new cycles found.

they appear twice, even if in different order: the first time as t_3, t_4, t_5 and the second time as t_3, t_5, t_4. This match is performed by the CONTAINS procedure, shown in Fig. 2, which tells us if the list of observations o contains the set of tasks t anywhere within it, contiguously, and then returns the indexes i, j within o that mark the start and end of the set of tasks t, or NIL if they are not contained in o.

The MAGIC-ASSISTANT procedure takes as input a single observation o, the list of tasks S that have been replaced by a cycle, the current list of cycles found C, and an integer m which is the maximum number of tasks that we will allow in a cycle. MAGIC-ASSISTANT first checks to see if o contains any cycles that are already in the cycle list C, as seen in lines 6–7. If any are found, then it modifies o so that tasks that we recognized as belonging to c are replaced with a pointer to c in C (see line 6). The list of tasks that have been replaced is appended to S, so that the transition probabilities within the cycle can also be calculated.

MAGIC-ASSISTANT then steps through the observation sequence (see lines 8–18) selecting the maximum number of tasks in a cycle, converting them to a set s where $s = o[i..|s| - 1]$ and using the CONTAINS helper function to check for repetitions of that set of tasks in the same observation, that is, checking for a cycle. If a new cycle is found, we determine if it is a subset of one of the cycles that is already on the cycle list C. If the cycle is not yet on the list, it is added to C. The cycle is then replaced in the observation o with a reference to its location on the cycle list C. Finally, MAGIC-ASSISTANT returns the new modified observation o and the list of tasks S that have been replaced by a cycle $c \in C$.

The MAGIC procedure repeatedly calls MAGIC-ASSISTANT for each observation o and appends the new modified observations to O'. Finally, it calculates the transition probabilities T using the new O' and the list S by adding how many times a state follows another one and using the proportions as probabilities. In other words, if state s_6 appears right after s_2 in $1/3$ of the observations where we see s_2, then we set $T(s_2, 1/3, s_6)$.

As an illustration of the way that the MAGIC algorithm functions, consider the set of observations in Fig. 3, which simulates the attempt to play fetch with a dog who doesn't seem to understand the concept of giving the ball back. Since the length of the maximum observation is 8, we know the longest possible cycle will be 3, because the start and end states cannot be in a cycle. Thus, we set $m = 3$ in MAGIC. However, there are no cycles 3 tasks in length. The first and only cycle found is $c = (throw\text{-}ball, chase\text{-}dog)$, which also matches the set $(chase\text{-}dog, throw\text{-}ball.)$ Each time c is found, the list of tasks that are replaced by the pointer to c in the list of cycles C is added to the list of lists of tasks S, to be used in transition calculations inside of the cycle. An illustration of the SCMDP produced by MAGIC is shown in Fig. 4. At the decision point the agent needs the external knowledge of whether or not it has the ball, and whether or not the dog wants to play. If the agent has the ball, it can throw the ball. If not, it must chase the dog to get the ball. If the dog doesn't want to play any longer, the agent will go inside. Going outside is always the first event in the sequence, and going back inside is always the last event.

> *go-out, throw-ball, chase-dog, throw-ball, chase-dog, throw-ball, chase-dog, go-in*
> *go-out, throw-ball, chase-dog, throw-ball, chase-dog, go-in*
> *go-out, throw-ball, go-in*
> *go-out, throw-ball, chase-dog, throw-ball, chase-dog, throw-ball, chase-dog, go-in*
> *go-out, throw-ball, chase-dog, chase-dog, go-in*
> *go-out, chase-dog, throw-ball, throw-ball, chase-dog, throw-ball, chase-dog, go-in*
> *go-out, throw-ball, chase-dog, throw-ball, chase-dog, throw-ball, go-in*
> *go-out, throw-ball, chase-dog, throw-ball, chase-dog, throw-ball, chase-dog, go-in*

Fig. 3. Example input data for MAGIC algorithm.

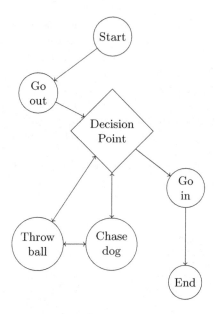

Fig. 4. Example SCMDP produced using MAGIC algorithm

The cycle created by our decision point ensures that, after completing the tasks of throwing the ball and chasing the dog, the agent returns to the decision point to once again make a decision based upon who has the ball, and whether or not the dog wants to play. This allows behavior that is based upon the human behavior pattern, but does not necessarily repeat one particular logged observation. For instance, if the agent goes outside and the dog does not want to play, the agent will go inside again. Likewise, the agent would continue playing fetch with the dog for more than three cycles if the dog still wants to play.

The modeler and the domain expert must choose the specific external inputs needed at the decision nodes. In this simple case, it is easy to determine that the input is simply whether or not the dog wants to play. In the case of a more complex model, however, the domain expert may need to tell the modeler what the agent would need to know in order to proceed. Well-named tasks in the logged data make this process simpler, so it is important for trained observers who are logging behavior to be as accurate and clear as possible in naming tasks. It is likewise important that they remain consistent. If the same task is given two different names by observers, it will appear as different tasks in the final model.

4   Validation Using Synthetic Data

In order to test how well MAGIC can extract cycles from raw data, we performed a test in which we created a synthetic model of a simple agent from which we could generate observational sequences. We then used the MAGIC algorithm to attempt to recover the original model from the observations.

The SCMDP we created mimics a player's movements in a first-person shooter "capture the flag" game. The agent has a single decision point called *Idle*. At this point, the agent needs to know if it is injured, needs ammunition, sees its opponent, or is at the checkpoint that must be seized in order to win the game. There are two possible initial actions: crouch or duck, and there are two possible final stages: win or die. The SCMDP used for this test is shown in Fig. 5.

We used a Python script to generate 10,000 strings from the SCMDP and fed these as input 10 times to the MAGIC algorithm, for a total of 100,000

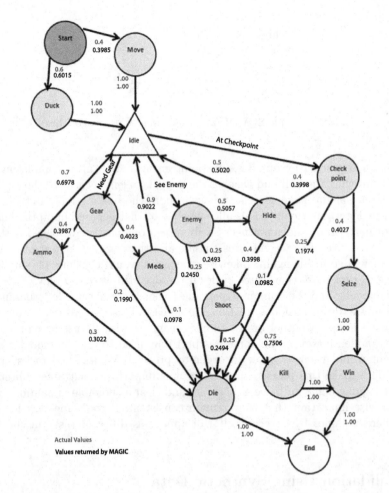

Fig. 5. SCMDP used for testing the MAGIC algorithm. The numbers in red (above) are the original transition probabilities in the SCMDP. The numbers in black (below) are the probabilities found by MAGIC (Color figure online).

randomly generated strings. The resulting SCMDP mirrored the original's pattern, providing an appropriate decision graph for an agent in a first-person shooter "capture the flag" game. The transition probabilities found by MAGIC were, on average, within 0.19 percent of the ones in the original SCDMDP, with a variance of 0.08 percent, as shown by the black numbers (below) in Fig. 5.

Our results show that, with the use of 10,000 strings, we are able to closely approximate the original pattern with minimal deviation between individual test runs. The low error rate in transition values indicated that, by adding enough data, we were able to overcome the disadvantage of unusual behavior patterns, allowing us to recover the correct pattern of behavior using the MAGIC algorithm. The identification of task cycles enabled us to determine the location of the decision point, indicating that the *Idle* state is a state where the agent would require further information before making a decision, rather than simply relying upon a percentage chance of a transition.

We then performed further tests on this SCMDP by adding Gaussian white noise with 1 % variance to the input data, meant to simulate the type of errors we might encounter in data gathering and subject observation. The addition of this noise did not disrupt the location of the identification of the decision point. It did cause a minimal error in transition values, which was easily correctable by removing transitions that had less than one percent chance of occurring. This slight adjustment to transition calculations also enabled better compensation for occasional unusual behavior patterns.

4.1   Validation with Real-World Data

A pilot study of the nurse medication administration process was conducted in a hospital setting [7,8,13]. In this study, over a 6 week period of time, nurses were shadowed by trained observers, and their activities were recorded using an iPad application. The actions used by the observers were chosen by domain experts. Observation data from 6 of the 17 observed nurses were used for the study, and the resulting files were combined into a CSV file. The start and end of each observation sequence was determined by when a nurse entered and exited a room, as evidenced by the room number in the log files. In total, there were 10,391 tasks recorded which together comprised 313 observations.

An example of a subset of the data used is shown in Table 1.

Despite the limited amount of sample data, we were able to achieve some success using the MAGIC algorithm. We were able to identify 12 decision points needing external information, such as the number of medications the patient required, or whether or not the patient needed special medication. Some of these were less obvious in nature, such as whether or not the nurse needed to wear gloves, whether or not the patient needed the medication explained, or whether the patient refused to take the medication.

The nursing study was particularly interesting because the nurses had two distinct approaches to patient care, as identified by domain experts (clinicians, in this case). We have referred to these approaches as bundled and unbundled. Nurses that took the unbundled approach visited a patient's room to administer

Table 1. Example of nursing data.

Room number	Behavior
628	enter_room
628	greet_patient
628	scan_patient_id
628	review_patient_computer_record
628	review_patient_med_box
628	scan_patient_meds
628	document_med_admin
628	scan_patient_meds
628	scan_patient_meds
628	document_med_admin
628	scan_patient_meds
628	document_med_admin
628	review_patient_med_box
628	scan_patient_meds
628	prepare_meds_for_admin
628	administer_meds
628	prepare_meds_for_admin
628	setup_for_med_admin
628	administer_meds
628	other_care

medication, and then returned later to perform any other necessary tasks, while nurses that took the bundled approach performed all required tasks during the same visit. The SCMDP we obtained from the test data reflected the fact that it contained both methods, as indicated by the decision point that requires knowledge of whether or not the patient requires other care than simply administering medications. While this pilot data set provided us with the location of the appropriate decision points, because of the difference in approaches to patient care, it will be necessary to have a greater number of observations to ensure the correct transition values.

Despite the smaller size of the data set, by using this format, we were able to create simulations using both NetLogo and the Unity3D game engine that can read the text file and use it as a logic controller for the nurse agent's behavior, as seen in Fig. 6. This allowed the nurse domain experts to visualize current medication administration processes.

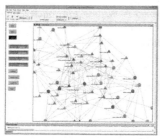

Fig. 6. The MAGICBAG Tool (left) and the NurseView simulation (right). Simulation video at http://youtu.be/JH94PolDhZQ

5 Summary

As cognitive modeling is difficult, imitation is a viable alternative to achieve believable human behavior in simulation. Statistical analysis of observed data allows us to achieve a pattern of human actions, essentially simulating human behavior by mimicking human behavior.

While building behavior models by hand can be complex and time-consuming, there is a better alternative. We have shown that it is possible to derive an agent decision process using the MAGIC algorithm which encapsulates the observational data in a small behavior model (SCMDP) that responds to external input, provided there is sufficient data, and tasks are labelled consistently.

Even with an automatically generated decision process, it will be necessary for an expert in the area that is being modeled to review the results. The process, however, will be less complex and time-consuming than making all of the necessary calculations by hand. The simple, standardized output format used in this study is easy to parse, allowing adjustments to be made quickly, and making it easy to load in a wide variety of simulation environments. Therefore, as part of our ongoing work, we have created a NetLogo tool, called MAGICBAG (MAGIC Behavior Adjustment Graph), which allows modelers to adjust the graph in a more visual and intuitive manner. We are continuing to refine this tool, and to test the MAGIC algorithm in different domains in order to further confirm its capability to work as a generic tool, rather than being domain-specific. We are also developing methods to determine decision points that are not cycle-specific in order to alleviate more of the modifications to the model that must be made by the domain expert, thereby further reducing modeling time.

References

1. Bentivegna, D.C., Atkenson, C.G., Cheng, G.: Learning tasks from observation and practice. Robot. Auton. Syst. **47**(2), 163–169 (2004)
2. Cook, D.J., Youngblood, M., Heierman III, E.O., Gopalratnam, K., Rao, S., Litvin, A., Khawaja, F.: Mavhome: an agent-based smart home. In: Proceedings of the First IEEE International Conference on Pervasive Computing and Communications, pp. 521–524 (2003)

3. Floyd, M.W., Esfandiari, B., Lam, K.: A case-based reasoning approach to imitating RoboCup players. In: Proceedings of the 21st International Florida Artificial Intelligence Research Society Conference, pp. 251–256 (2008)

4. Gigerenzer, G., Gaissmaier, W.: Heuristic decision making. Annu. Rev. Psychol. **62**, 451–482 (2011)

5. Guillory, A., Nguyen, H., Balch, T., Charles Lee Isbell, J.: Learning executable agent behaviors from observation. In: Proceedings of the Fifth International Joint Conference on Autonomous Agents and Multiagent Systems, pp. 795–797. ACM (2006)

6. Guralnik, V., Haigh, K.Z.: Learning models of human behaviour with sequential patterns. In: Proceedings of the AAAI-02 Workshop "Automation as Caregiver", pp. 24–30 (2002)

7. Huynh, N., Snyder, R., Vidal, J.M., Tavakoli, A.S., Cai, B.: Application of computer simulation modeling to medication administration process redesign. J. Healthcare Eng. **3**(4), 649–662 (2012). http://jmvidal.cse.sc.edu/papers/huynh12c.pdf

8. Huynh, N., Snyder, R., Vidal, J.M., Tavakoli, A.S., Cai, B.: Application of computer simulation modeling to medication administration process redesign. In: Chyu, M.C. (ed.) Advances in Engineering for Healthcare Safety, pp. 129–142. Multi-Science Publishing, Brentwood (2013)

9. Kaiser, P., Lewis, M., Petrick, R.P.A., Asfour, T., Steedman, M.: Extracting common sense knowledge from text for robot planning. In: IEEE International Conference on Robotics and Automation (ICRA) (2014)

10. Leon, E., Clarke, G., Callaghan, V., Doctor, F.: Affect-aware behaviour modelling and control inside an intelligent environment. Perv. Mobile Comput. **6**(5), 559–574 (2010)

11. Papadimitriou, C.H., Tsitsiklis, J.N.: The complexity of Markov decision processes. Math. Oper. Res. **12**(3), 441–450 (1987)

12. Schrum, J., Karpov, I.V., Miikkulainen, R.: Ut^2: human-like behavior via neuroevolution of combat behavior and replay of human traces. In: IEEE Conference on Computational Intelligence and Games, pp. 329–336 (2011)

13. Snyder, R., Huynh, N., Cai, B., Vidal, J., Bennett, K.: Effective healthcare process redesign through and interdisciplinary team approach. In: Studies in Healthcare Technology and Informatics, vol. 192. MEDINFO 2013 (2013), http://jmvidal.cse.sc.edu/papers/snyder13a.pdf

Data Analysis of Social Simulations Outputs - Interpreting the Dispersion of Variables

Christophe Sibertin-Blanc[1](✉) and Nathalie Villa-Vialaneix[2,3]

[1] IRIT, Université de Toulouse, Manufacture des Tabacs, 21 Allées de Brienne,
31042 Toulouse, France
sibertin@ut-capitole.fr
[2] SAMM, Université Paris 1 Panthéon-Sorbonne, 90 Rue de Tolbiac,
75634 Paris Cedex 13, France
nathalie.villa@toulouse.inra.fr
[3] INRA, Unité MIAT, BP 52627, 31326 Castanet Tolosan Cedex, France

Abstract. In the domain of social simulation, there are very few papers reporting on the statistical analysis of simulation results, while it is very common in empirical social sciences. The paper advocates the recourse to the statistical analysis of social simulation outputs, as a very efficient way to improve the interpretation of simulation results and so the understanding of the system that is the model's target. This is illustrated by the study of a simulation model designed to analyze a real case regarding the management of a river in South West of France. Several standard statistics methods are used to shed light on the possible outcomes of the debate between the stakeholders.

Keywords: Agent-based modeling · Social simulation · Statistical analysis

1 Introduction

The standard way to build a social simulation model may be sketched as this: you are concerned by or interested in a phenomenon that occurs in some system of reference which, according to the classification of [5], may be either a particular *"empirical space-time circumscribed"* case, the application of a *"theoretical construct intended to investigate some properties that apply to a wide range of empirical phenomena"* or *"focus[es] on general social phenomena"*, or stylized fact. This phenomenon of interest is characterized by *indexes*, which allow to measure various features of each occurrence of the phenomenon and whose value is either directly measured, given by an expert, collected in any way or resulting of a treatment of these. Then, the simulation model is built to produce *outputs*, also issued directly or resulting from additional treatments, which values are as close as possible to the indexes when it is run in the appropriate conditions.

To validate the model and to ensure that the mechanisms it embeds are able to reproduce the phenomenon of interest, the model building process includes the use

© Springer International Publishing Switzerland 2015
F. Grimaldo and E. Norling (Eds.): MABS 2014, LNAI 9002, pp. 133–150, 2015.
DOI: 10.1007/978-3-319-14627-0_10

of statistics to identify the model's parameters whose initial values influence the model's surface response (sensitivity analysis) and to give to each parameter the most suitable value (calibration). The simulation model is run many times, and optimization techniques are used to calibrate the parameters in such a way that the (mainly univariate) statistical properties of each output variable (i.e., mean, standard deviation or distribution, auto-correlation if the variable is distributed in space or time, ...) are as close as possible, (i.e., with a reasonable confidence interval) to the properties of the corresponding index in the system of reference. The same holds when statistics is used for the replication of a model as e.g., [15].

In simulation models designed for the study of systems such as the customer waiting times of a queuing system, bottleneck in a mass transit system during rush hour, the throughput of a production workshop or the mean time to failure of a machine, it is very common to perform statistical analyses for operation research regarding the system performances (duration of the start-up phase, steady-state analysis, confidence intervals, ...). In these engineering cases, the model is analyzed to know its own internal control logic, not in order to improve its mirroring (or whatever relationship between the model and its target) of a system of reference; see [11] or [1] or [10] as instances of many papers on this topic at the Winter Simulation Conference.

Many authors advocate the systematic analysis of simulation models in accordance with [3] and [9]. The need for engineering principles and tools to improve the practice of Multi-Agent Based Simulation and enhance the knowledge obtained in this way is increasingly recognized; see for instance [12,13] regarding the Design of Experiments. In this line, we claim that this kind of statistical analysis is beneficial for the study of social simulation models as well. While the system of reference (SR) is most often observed only once, since experimentation in social affairs are rarely feasible, the simulation model is run many times (at least thirty times or more) and thus we can proceed to a statistical analysis of the data produced by these runs as if we had thirty exemplars of the system of reference. In fact, a statistical analysis is very common in empirical social sciences for the analysis of questionnaire surveys, data collected from archival records or dataset pick up in whatever way.

Then, the question is no longer to compare the unique value of each index observed in the SR with the mean value of the corresponding simulation output; it is to consider each run as an observation of a SR's numeric analog and to proceed to a statistical analysis of this dataset. Beyond the matching between the SR indexes and the simulation outcomes, the purpose of the analysis is to uncover structural or behavioral patterns that could be buried into the dataset [8]. This knowledge comes from the operating mode of the simulation model under various circumstances (instantiated by the series of random values for each run) and thus it bears on its deep characteristics, features which can not be identified in the course of a single observation.

Then, three cases can occur:

- the feature is already identified and well known by the experts of the SR, so that the data analysis brings a new piece to the validation of the model;

– the feature is in contradiction with what the experts know about the SR, so that the data analysis questions, more or less severely, the validity of the model;
– the feature is not a fact known by the experts of the SR but it is consistent with their actual understanding, so that the data analysis is likely to bring a new piece of knowledge about the SR, to the extent that the relationships between the SR and the model are well-defined.

We guess there is no uniform way to conduct the statistical analysis of any simulation model results, because the methods likely to provide interesting findings depend on the very nature of the SR and the hypotheses that the model is aiming to test. Moreover, statistics is a quickly growing discipline and new analysis techniques are continuously developed to tackle specific questions.

So, in the following of this paper, we will just illustrate how statistical analysis techniques can be exploited to enhance the knowledge about social simulation models, and in this way the knowledge about the system of references under consideration. The model and the simulation outputs have been produced using a social simulation platform, SocLab[1], designed for analyzing power and collaboration relationships within social organizations. This platform allows the user to edit models of organizations, to study the properties of models with analytic tools, and to compute by simulation the behaviors that the members of the organization could adopt each other.

The remaining of the paper is as follows. We first present the SocLab modeling framework, the main features of an organization it allows to consider and the questions it intends to address. Section 3 presents our real-world case study related to water management in a French area and the simulation outputs. The following sections show how quite simple statistic analyses bring answers to a number of questions about social features of the system. A discussion and a conclusion are finally provided in Sect. 7.

2   The SocLab Modelling of Social Organizations

The SocLab framework formalizes and slightly extends the Sociology of Organized Action (SOA), introduced by [6]. For space limitation we just outline the syntax and semantics of SocLab models, a comprehensive presentation of this framework and its use may be found in [17].

Roughly speaking, SOA proposes to explain why people behave as they do, especially when they do not behave as they are supposed to, with regard to the organization's rules. An organization is defined as a set of *actors* and a set of relationships based on the access to *resources*. Each actor has some goals, which are a mix of his own objectives and his organizational roles, and he needs some resources to reach these goals. On the other hand, each actor controls the access to some resources, and so determines to what extent those needing

---

[1] http://soclabproject.wordpress.com.

these resources have the means to achieve their goals. Actors are reciprocally dependent on each other.

Actors are assumed to be rational, that is to say their behavior is driven by their beliefs on the best way to achieve their goals. So, each actor cooperates with others in the management of resources under its control to get from them access to the resources it needs. We call the process, by which they mutually adjust their behaviors with respect to others, the *social actor game*. The well-known regulation phenomenon results from this process: the adjustments drive actors to exhibit quite steady behaviors as if they obey to external rules. So, SocLab proposes to shed light to the regulation of organizations, how and why they occur, with what shape.

Figure 1 shows the SocLab metamodel of the structure of organizations. Accordingly, the model of an organization includes:

- the list of the *actors*;
- the list of the *resources*: each resource is controlled (or managed) by one actor[2]. This actor behaves in a more or less cooperative way and the *state* of a resource measures (on a scale of -10 to 10) how much he tends (or not) to cooperate with others by favoring (or hindering) accesses to the resource;
- the *stake* of every actor on every resource: this quantity measures the importance of the resource for the actor; a not null stake means that the actor actually depends on the resource. The more a resource is needed to achieve an actor's important goal, the higher the corresponding stake (on a scale of zero to ten; the sum of the stakes for every actor sums to ten);
- the *effect function* of a resource on an actor who has a not null stake on this resource: this function quantifies how well the actor can use the resource to achieve his goals, depending on the state of the resource;
- the *solidarities* of every actor towards each of the others.

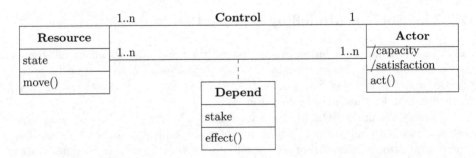

Fig. 1. The SocLab metamodel of organizations as a UML class diagram

---

[2] SocLab allows resources to be controlled by several actors but, from the social point of view, each one is the unique performer of his own behavior.

A *configuration* (or state) of the organization is defined as the vector of the resource states. Thus, a configuration is characterized by the level of cooperation of each actor with regard to others. In any configuration of an organization, every actor gets from others some capacity to access the resources it needs to achieve his objectives. This *capability* of an actor a when the organization is in a configuration $s = (s_r)_{r \in R}$ is calculated as the sum on the resources of the values of effect functions weighted by the actor's stakes:

$$\text{capability}(a, s) = \sum_{r \in R} \left(\text{stake}(a, r) \times \text{effect}_r(a, s_r) \right).$$

This raw capability is weighted by the solidarities between actors, so that the important output we will consider is the *satisfaction* of actors, where:

$$\text{satisfaction}(a, s) = \sum_{b \in A} \left[\text{solidarity}(a, b) \times \sum_{r \in R} \left(\text{stake}(b, r) \times \text{effect}_r(b, s_r) \right) \right].$$

(1)

To compute the configurations that are likely to be issued by the regulation process within an organization, the SocLab platform includes a simulation engine which implements the social game and so computes which behavior each actor is likely to adopt [7,16]. To this end, a multi-agent implementation of the model of an organization provides the actors with rationality for playing the social actor game. Social actor agents try, as a meta-goal, to get a high level of satisfaction, *i.e.*, to have the means needed to achieve their concrete goals. However, according to the bounded rationality assumption [19], they just look for a "satisficing" level of satisfaction, not an illusory optimal one. So, within a trial-error reinforcement learning process, each actor maintains a dynamic level of aspiration, and a simulation terminates when a stationary state is reached because every actor has a satisfaction that is over his *level of aspiration*. A state is stationary if actors manage the resources they control in such a way that every one accepts his level of satisfaction: then, the organization can work in this way, a regulated configuration has been found. The length of a simulation, *i.e.*, the number of steps necessary to reach a stationary state, indicates how difficult it is for the actors to jointly find how to cooperate.

3   The Management of the Touch River

The simulation model to which we will apply statistical tools concerns the management of a river called Touch. A detailed presentation of the case is given in [17,18], including the empirical and theoretical dimensions of the system of reference and a detailed presentation of the SocLab model.

Touch is a tributary of the Garonne in which it flows downstream of Toulouse, an agglomeration of one million inhabitants in the South West of France. Its catchment area covers 60 municipalities and its course crosses 29 municipalities. Three fourth of these municipalities stand upstream and are mainly agricultural villages or small towns. Other municipalities, located downstream, form a dense urban area of the Toulouse agglomeration. Downstream municipalities have had to deal with several episodes of flooding during the past decades. They have tried to protect themselves by building dikes that, even if expensive, are not sufficient to eliminate the flooding risks, and they consider that upstream municipalities do not cooperate enough. On the contrary, upstream municipalities, strongly influenced by farmers, consider that they have done their best for preventing flooding by letting some land lying uncultivated in order to absorb the excess of water in case of flooding.

Since 1995, the French water policy requires the elaboration of a flood risk prevention plan (FRPP) for each river, and this obligation was reinforced by the European Water Framework Directive (WFD 2000/60/EC), transposed into the French law as the Law on Water and Aquatic Ecosystems (LEMA, Law of 30 December 2006). On the occasion of the establishment of the PRPP of the Touch, B. Baldet [4] studied the difficulties to reach an agreement that combines the views of all the field stakeholders and administrative authorities. He analyzed the field observations to the light of several sociological theories. The SocLab model, whose simulation results are analyzed in this paper, describes the system of organized action devoted to the elaboration of a new Touch's FRPP. It has been designed in order to formally confirm (or infirm) the empirical findings of the sociological study and the possibility of hypotheses about the future management of the Touch.

The simulation model includes 10 actors which are involved in the management of the river and so are interested in the definition and the application of the FRPP. In this model, each actor controls a single resource that synthesizes its means of actions:

- *actor 1: Departmental Territory Direction (DDT)* acts as the State representative and will instruct the new FRPP; it controls the **Validation** resource;
- *actor 2: National Office for Water and Aquatic Ecosystem (ONEMA)* is the reference agency for the monitoring of water and aquatic environment; it controls the **Expertise** resource;
- *actor 3: Adour-Garonne Water Agency (AEAG)* is the operational authority in charge of strategic plans at the basin level. Accounting for the requirements of the various water uses and of the protection of aquatic ecosystems, it defines, supervises and funds the water policy; it controls the **Funding** resource;
- *actor 4: a citizen organization* of riparian farmers in the upstream area. They own floodplain lands and, as riparian, they have the right to use the river and must maintain the banks; it controls the **Lobbying** resource;
- *actor 5: the group of 25 upstream municipalities* that have 21,000 inhabitants; it controls the **Control of flow** resource;
- *actor 6: the group of 4 downstream municipalities* (75,000 inhabitants) that are incriminated at each occurrence of a natural catastrophe. Due to flooding threats, they must prohibit any building on a portion of their territory; it controls the **Self funding** resource;

- *actor 7: the inter-communal association for water civil engineering (SIAH)*, in charge of the management of Touch[3]. It has to maintain the river bed and banks and is funded by actor 3. It includes representatives of the 29 riparian municipalities and is managed by an active technician who favors the cooperation among municipalities while worrying about the Good Ecological Status of the river; it controls the **River management** resource;
- *actors 8* and *9: political authorities*, the regional and departmental councils, respectively. They can bring additional financial support to civil engineering measures; each one controls an **Additional funding** resource;
- *actor 10: an engineering consulting firm*, specialized in water, energy and environment, in charge of technical studies. It controls the **Studies** resource;

The actors who are the most engaged in the negotiation are actors 6, 4 and 5 from the population point of view, and actors 7, 3 and 9 from the institutional point of view. All these actors are strongly concerned by both the elaboration and the further implementation of the FRPP. Actors 1, 2, 8 and 10 are less concerned. In this model, each actor controls a single resource that summarizes its means to influence the discussion. We skip a technical presentation of the SocLab model resulting from the sociological analysis - it is useless for the following of this paper - and all details may be found in [18].

The analysis of the debates, notably within the SIAH, shows three main options for the Touch management, each one supported by committed actors:

(O1) : protecting the downstream towns against floods, and defending the interests of these municipalities (supported by actor 6);

(O2) : protecting the daily life of upstream villages, and especially supporting agricultural activities (supported by actors 4 and 5);

(O3) : ensuring a good ecological state of the aquatic environment, that is viewing the river as a component of an ecological system (the hydromorphological view) and not just as a water pipe (the hydrological view) (supported by actors 2 and 3).

Upstream and downstream municipalities are interdependent, though their respective interests are different or even conflicting. So the elaboration of the FRPP includes a fourth option which is probably the main issue of the discussions:

(O4) : finding a solution which is a compromise acceptable to the population and its representatives (sought by actors 7, 3, 1, 8 and 9 by order of influence, according to their respective status). This issue is essential because, whatever the chosen solution for the Touch management, it will not be effectively implemented if it is not agreed by the operational actors.

The SocLab platform provides tools for the analytical investigation of (the model of) organizations. For instance, it computes indexes about structural or

---

[3] Literally "Syndicat Intercommunal d'Aménagement Hydraulique" of the Touch river. It is entrusted by the State with the maintenance of the river for the sake of the riparian proprietors, which own the bank and the bed of the river. See http://www.siah-du-touch.org for more details.

state-dependent properties of an organization and allows to interactively explore the space of the configurations by computing, *e.g.*, the configurations which optimize or minimize the satisfaction of a given actor or the Nash equilibria. These analytical results frame the context where the regulation process takes place. They contribute to the interpretation of simulation results by placing what actually happens in the range of what could happen.

The dataset we examine contains the outputs of 100 simulation experiments with the same initial values: the resources are put in the neutral state (*i.e.*, the value 0, and runs with different values give same results). Thus, experiments vary just by the seed of the random numbers generator. The output variables are the number of steps to reach convergence (a stationary configuration), the state of the 10 resources and the resulting satisfaction of actors at the end of the simulation. The higher the state of a relation, the more cooperative the controlling actor is. The level of cooperation of a resource is evaluated as the total satisfaction it provides, accounting for the fact that most relations are conflictive: most states provide a positive satisfaction to some of the (dependent) actors and a negative satisfaction to others.

The satisfaction of each actor, *i.e.*, its capability to reach its goals, is determined according to Eq. (1) by its solidarities, the state of the resources he depends on, its stakes and the effect functions of the resources it depends on. A quick sensitivity analysis of these parameters (without checking interactions) shows that the model's response is not sensible to a variation of 15 % of their values. Each actors put 3 or 4 stake points on the relation it controls so that its satisfaction depends on about one third of its own behavior. The range of values of actors' satisfactions are quite dispersed, from 90 (actor 2) to 195 (actor 6). The lower bounds (the worst configuration for each of them) range from −25 (actor 2) to −85 (actor 6) and the upper bounds (the best configuration) from 60 (actor 8) to 110 (actor 6). The dataset may be found in [20] together with some other results[4].

4   Univariate Statistical Analysis

A quick overview of the variables distributions is provided in Fig. 2. The number of steps is strongly skewed with a small number of simulations having a very large number of steps; so, the mean or median are not a good summary of the distribution.

Most resource states (except for "Self funding", "River management" and "Additional funding") also have a skewed distribution, with several outliers having small values. The scattering of the state variables is very varied: some variables have a very small dispersion, like "Validation" (which is frequently equal to 10, its maximum possible value) or "Additional funding 2" which is almost always equal to 6 (also its upper bound value). For these resources, as well as for "Lobbying", "Control of flow" and "River management" (but to a lesser extent),

---

[4] See also http://www.nathalievilla.org/soclab.html.

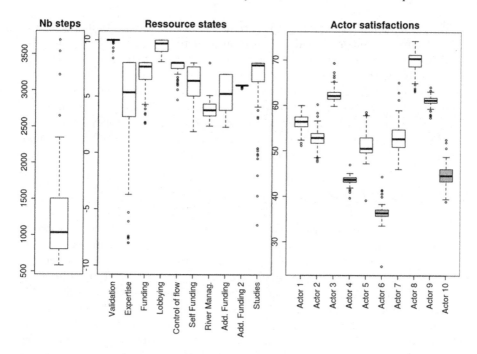

Fig. 2. Boxplots for the number of steps before the simulations converge (left), the resource states (middle) and the actor satisfactions (right, grey boxplots indicate a median satisfaction below 50).

the management of these resources seem almost fixed in advance by organizational constraints that strongly determine the behavior of the controller actors. On the contrary, "Expertise", or even "Self funding" and "Additional funding" are resources that have a larger dispersion (for "Expertise" the values spread on the whole range from −8 to 8): the actors which control these resources are less constrained by the organization and a deeper analysis is necessary to decide whether they hesitate between quite equivalent attitudes or whether they have enough power to strategically adapt their behavior to the context.

The satisfactions of actors are given in value, but they could be considered in proportion to account for the disparity of their respective range of values. Most of them are approximately symmetric, but with a small variability regarding their range. Actors 3, 8 and 9 are the most satisfied in almost all simulations (actor 8 appears the most satisfied, but it is less committed in the game), while actors 4, 6 and 10 are frequently poorly satisfied. As actor 6 has a low satisfaction, the option (**O1**) will probably not prevail. The same holds for actors 4 and 5 and the option (**O2**), but to a lesser extent. As the satisfaction of actors 2 and 3 is slightly better, the option (**O3**) seems to be the most likely. As the satisfaction of actor 7 is medium, it seems that a compromise that would be acceptable by most actors is possible (**O4**), and this is compliant with the fact that none of the options (**O1**), (**O2**) or (**O3**) strongly prevails upon the others.

The dispersion of the actors' satisfactions shows that the position of actors 4, 9, 6 and 3 are well settled, while the positions of actors 5 and 7 are more precarious. Regarding the respective range of values, the actor satisfactions are globally more steady (with smaller dispersions) than the resource states: the variation coefficients of actor satisfactions have a range of 0.02 to 0.06, whereas those of resource states have a range of 0.06 to 0.98 (except for "Additional Funding 2"). This fact might be interpreted as a form of fairness among actors ensured by a complex system effect: actors compensate a decrease of accessibility to a needed resource by a better access to other ones.

5   Correlation Analysis

Figure 3 shows a graphical representation of the correlation coefficients between all pairs of variables. The number of steps has a slight negative influence on all actors (and resources), except for upstream actors 4 and 5. This is a general and meaningful property of the simulation algorithm: long simulations indicate that actors struggle to find a configuration that provides each of them with an acceptable level of satisfaction, and this difficulty to cooperate entails lower levels of satisfaction for most actors. Here, Actors 4 and 5 are the beneficiaries of delay in convergence, and their conflict with the remaining of the organization will be confirmed by further analysis in the following section.

The correlations between the actors' satisfactions show two groups of strongly related actors: actors 1, 2 and 3; actors 8 and 9. Actors 1, 2 and 3 are organizations that represent the State and carry out public policies. The positive correlation between their satisfactions means that their main interests are consistent and that these three domains of the State policy strengthen one another. Moreover, actor 7, instituted by actor 1 and funded by actor 3, is shown to be in accordance with the State services. Actors 8 and 9 are political institutions and it is satisfactory that they have similar interests on topics such as the river management, despite their political divergence. Moreover, the correlation between the two groups is positive: there is no conflict between the State representatives and the local authorities.

As for actors 4, 5 and 6, the most concerned with the river functioning, they have to be regarded in conjunction with actor 7, which is the place where they can build a compromise together. Actor 5 seems careful; surprisingly, it does not support the farmer association nor is it in conflict with downstream municipalities. The case of actor 4 requires a specific attention: it is in conflict with actors 6 and 7, and also with most of other actors. It is responsible for long-lasting simulations but we will see that it is not powerful enough to make its interests to prevail (this is because the effect functions of the relation it controls have a small amplitude). The satisfaction of actor 7 is positively correlated with those of actors 5 and 6, also in addition to those of the state representatives group: these actors support the options (O1), (O2) or (O3). This fact confirms the possibility of a compromise (O4), which has already been pointed out in the analysis of the actor satisfactions.

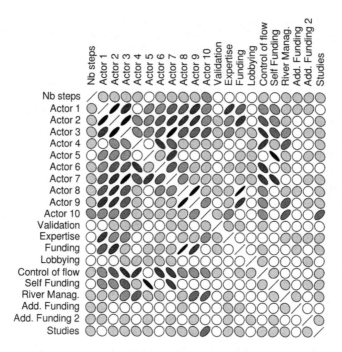

Fig. 3. Graphical representation of the correlation coefficients between pairs of variables: the thinner the ellipse, the larger the absolute value of the correlation coefficient (see [14], implemented in the R package **ellipse**). The grey level matches the absolute value of the correlation coefficient (darker colors are used for larger values).

Regarding the correlation between actors and resources, let us recall that, through the effect of solidarities (see Eq. (1)), each actor depends more or less on most resources. Table 1 shows the global influence of each resource on actors. Some actor satisfactions are strongly correlated with the state of a specific resource: "Expertise" conditions the satisfaction of Actor 1, in accordance with its strong concern with ecological issues that are important in the management of this resource. The satisfaction of Actors 8 and 9 is strongly correlated with "Funding" because a higher financial engagement from Actor 3 means a lesser need for their financial effort; moreover, we have seen that the commitment of Actor 3 on ecological issues meets the concerns of Actors 8 and 9. "Control of flow" is the most influential resource on actors, in value and in proportion regarding its small dispersion (see Fig. 1): it is positively correlated with the satisfaction of Actor 4 and strongly negatively correlated with the satisfaction of all other actors, except Actor 5: a low level of this resource means a stronger control on the river and thus a higher decision power for Actors 2, 3, 6 and 7. "Self funding" is strongly negatively correlated with the satisfactions of Actors 5 and 7: a high level for this resource means a higher decision power for Actor 6 which reduces the decision power of actors 5 and 7. Finally, "Lobbying" is not

Table 1. The influences of each relation as: the (absolute in case of the "Absolute Influence") sum of the values of its correlations with actors' satisfactions); its correlation with the satisfaction of its controlling actor; its relevance (as the sum of the stakes actors put on it).

	Absolute Influence	Effective Influence	Influence on the Controlling Actor	Relevance
Validation	1.30	1.25	0.45	13
Expertise	2.04	1.83	0.41	5
Funding	3.52	3.52	0.24	12.5
Lobbying	0.54	0.22	0.03	9
Control of flow	4.00	−2.41	0.11	14
Self funding	3.24	−2.83	0.15	10
River management	2.42	0.24	−0.25	21.5
Add. funding CR	1.18	−0.01	0.27	4.5
Add. funding DR	1.13	−0.51	0.27	4.5
Studies	1.62	0.58	0.81	5.5

very influential on the actors' satisfaction and thus, while actor 4 is in conflict with others, it does not have the means to make its point of view to prevail.

These results show that, despite its analytical structure, the behavior-selecting processes of actors make the model strongly non-linear: the column "Influence on the controlling actor" of Table 1 shows that the satisfaction of most actors is not so much correlated with the resource it controls and, as expected, actors compensate losses due to their concessions by a better access to others' resources. As an other conclusion, the correlation between the "Absolute Influence" and "Relevance" columns is 0.47: if the control of an highly relevant resource is, of course an advantage for an actor, that does not ensure to him with a high influence; to this end the actor must also properly use this resource and their capability[5] to do that varies from 0.06 (actor 4) to 0.41 (actor 2). There is no remarkable correlation between any pair of relations. Despite the significant correlations between their satisfactions, actors behave independently one another. There is no coordination or coalition within a subgroup of actors, no actor seems to influence the behavior of another one; in other words, each actor is autonomous with regard to others. A Principal Component Analysis of the resources' states confirms this fact since the first two components explain just 29.7 percent of the variance: no relation plays a preponderant role.

Regarding actors, the first two components of the Principal Component Analysis explain 69 percent of the variance and confirm the analysis of pairwise

---

[5] The cleverness of actors in the SocLab model is not in question since each of them applies the same learning algorithm to select the state of the resource it controls. The difference in capability of actors results from their constraints to obtain a good level of satisfaction.

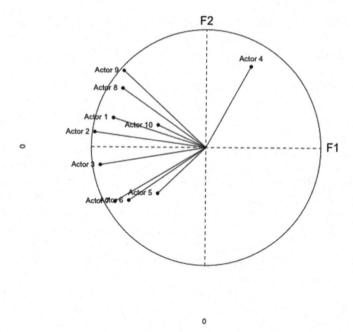

Fig. 4. The position of each actor shows its relative contribution to the variance of actors' satisfactions. Actor 4 is in clear opposition with all others, mainly Actors 5, 6, 7 and 3.

correlations between actors' satisfactions (see Fig. 4). Actors 10 and 5 are not very influential; actor 4 is in conflict with all others, especially 5, 6 and 7; actors 8 and 9 are on their side; actors 1, 2 and 3 also go together. Finally, the position of actor 7 is very noticeable, since it is the key actor for the option (**O4**): being very close to actors 5 and 6 and not so far from actor 3, it seems to have the means to promote this option.

6   The Modes of Simulations' Outputs

According to SOA, simulations may include runs whose outputs are quite far from the actual observations of the system of reference: they correspond to "potentialities", possible ways of operating of the organization, to configurations which do not actually occur but might be observed in the future. Indeed, the regulated behavior exhibited by a social system is the result of past events, occasional opportunities or constraints, random choices made at bifurcation points or whatever contingent circumstance while, to the extent of its adaptability and latent variety [2], the organization could as well operate in another way under other circumstances. A tight matching between simulation outputs and the indexes of the organization is just interpreted as a structural property of the organization: a strong regulation which prevents actors to depart from a normative behavior. When simulation results are dispersed, the simulation algorithm can exhibit runs which are either widely scattered corresponding to an organization that is little regulated or are clustered corresponding to alternative functionings and possible futures. Regarding our case study, it is of first importance to know whether runs are uniformly distributed or whether there are modes in correspondence with the possible options **(O1)** to **(O4)**. In the latter case, their respective frequencies may serve as a forecast of the possible issues in the debate.

This requires that the analysis does no longer focus on the variables but on the vector provided by each simulation run as a whole. To this end, we use the hierarchical clustering method which seeks to build clusters containing similar simulations. Pairwise distance between simulations are computed using the Euclidean distance of the vectors of scaled variables (*i.e.*, variables are centered and reduced to unit variance) containing all satisfactions, all resources and the number of steps (so that observations in the same cluster are alike for all these values) and a bottom up approach is used to hierarchically aggregate the simulations into clusters in a greedy way. A linkage criterion specifies the dissimilarity between clusters: we used the Ward's method which minimizes the total within-cluster variance at each step of the hierarchy. The number of clusters is chosen classically by cutting the hierarchical tree at the smallest height that corresponds to a large increase in within-cluster variance. The result of this analysis is shown in Fig. 5 where four clusters can be identified.

Then, for each cluster, the mean value of the actors and resources scaled variables can be calculated for this class, as shown in Fig. 6. For instance, regarding the resource plot, the state of the "River Management" resource decreases from cluster 2 to cluster 3. Using the same method as for the constitution of the 4 clusters, the resources are compared regarding their values in the clusters, resulting in the dendrogram at the top of the panel. According to this super-classification, the "Studies" and "Validation" resources are very close; the same holds for the "River Management" and "Add. Funding 2" resources, which are also close to "Add. Funding 1". The smallest the length of the dendrogram path between two resources, the most similar values these resources have among the four clusters. Similarly, the dendrogram at the left side of each plot shows the similarity between the clusters regarding the values of the resources or the actors. This display of the clustering should be completed by boxplots gathered either by clusters or by elements.

From these figures, the following conclusions can be made:

- It appears that the upstream municipalities are rather in opposition with the other actors of the organization since actor 4 is the most far from other actors and the "Control of flow" resource (controlled by actor 5) is the most far from other resources.
- The hierarchical clustering identifies four clusters that can be related to the four options emerging from the empirical analysis.
- Cluster 2 corresponds to reaching the best compromise in the process of elaborating the new public policy of Touch **(O4)**; simulations are shorter (857 steps

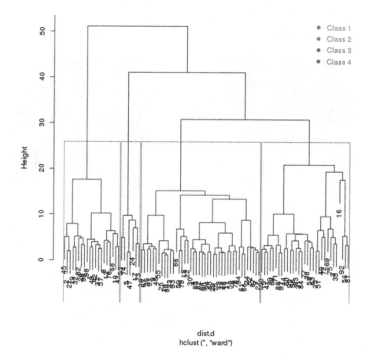

Fig. 5. Hierarchical clustering. Experiments are partitioned into 4 clusters (numbered from 1 (at left) to 4 (at right)) as represented by the colored rectangles. An outlier (simulation number 16) can also be identified (at the right hand side of the figure).

instead of about 1300 for other clusters) and the average satisfaction of actors is higher (56 instead of about 52.7). Unfortunately, it is not the most likely outcome, since the cluster includes only 7 % of simulations, but it is a possible outcome.

- Cluster 1 (containing 20 simulations) contains simulations that are almost the opposite of cluster 2: in this cluster, all actors except actor 4 have a lower satisfaction than in other cases (51.6). In these simulations, the state of "Control of flow" is high and the state of "Funding" and "Expertise" is low. These simulations correspond to the success of option **(O2)** over the other options: actors 4 and 5 succeed in making their interest prevails over other actors' interests.
- Clusters 3 and 4 (respectively, 42 and 31 simulations) are the closest clusters (see Fig. 5 and the left side dendrogram of Fig. 6) with mostly average values, where most actor satisfactions and resource states take an intermediate value between those of clusters 1 and 2. These clusters gather 75 % of the simulations and thus correspond to the most likely outcome of the negotiation process.
- Cluster 3 is characterized by a stable low satisfaction for actors 5 and 7 and by a high state for "Self funding". These simulations are rather in favor of option **(O1)**. In cluster 4, actors 4 and 5 are more satisfied than in the other clusters

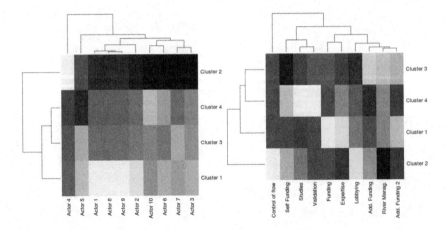

Fig. 6. Mean scaled satisfactions of actors (left) and states of resources (right) in the 4 clusters (darker colors correspond to higher values). As the values are scaled values by variable (actors, resources), the colors should be compared by columns, not by rows.

and the state of "Self funding" and "Studies" is low. These simulations are rather in favor of option **(O2)**.

7   Conclusion and Discussion

The paper has given an example of the benefice of the statistical analysis of simulation outputs distributions to reveal causality patterns and improve the understanding the operating mode of the system of reference. Mostly, the relevance of the model of the considered organizational setting has been confirmed as well as the likelihood of the behavior-selecting learning process of actors. In addition, some unexpected, but consistent facts have been revealed such as the singularity of upstream municipalities with regard to the whole organization.

When a simulation model is an abstraction of a phenomenon modeled as a "stylized fact", the purpose is to propose a mechanism, as simple as possible, able to generate the phenomenon as an emergence from the interactions between the system's components. In this case, the study of the simulation outputs aims mainly to verify whether outputs are steadily focused with a small standard deviation, since their dispersion means that the proposed mechanism is not a good explanation for the phenomenon.

When the simulation model refers to a concrete system as the case considered in this paper, a "good fit" between the system of reference indexes and the simulations outputs must also be checked first to confirm the relevance of the model. In this case, the model includes a wider heterogeneity of agents, with a variety of individual features and goals, and so a larger number of properties are to be investigated. Then, further data analyses of simulation outputs can bring new knowledge and a much deeper understanding of structural and behavioral properties of the model. These model's properties may then be interpreted in terms of properties of the system of reference to the extent the matching between the elements of the model and the system of reference is well defined. The nature of the properties of interest straight depends on the questions that motivate the elaboration of the model. Thus, there is no method that could be applied in a systematic way and, among the huge number of tools and derived data that could be calculated, it is to the designer of the model to find the ones allowing to shed light on the question he considers.

References

1. Alexopoulos, C., Kim, S.: Output data analysis for simulations. In: Yücesan, E., Chen, C., Snowdon, J., Charnes, J. (eds.) Proceedings of the 2002 IEEE Winter Simulation Conference (2002)
2. Ashby, W.: Principles of self-organizing systems. In: von Foerster, H., Zopf Jr., G.W. (eds.) Principles of Self-organization, pp. 255–257. Pergamon Press, London (1962). http://csis.pace.edu/~marchese/CS396x/Computing/Ashby.pdf
3. Axelrod, R.: Advancing the art of simulation in the social sciences. In: Conte, R., Hegselmann, R., Terna, P. (eds.) Simulating Social Phenomena. Lecture Notes in Economics and Mathematical System, pp. 21–40. Springer, Heidelberg (1997)
4. Baldet, B.: Gérer la rivière ou la crue? Le gouvernement du risque d'inondation entre enjeux localisés et approche instrumentée. Le cas de la vallée du Touch en Haute-Garonne. Ph.D thesis (Sociology), Université de Toulouse, 26th June 2012
5. Boero, R., Squazzoni, F.: Does empirical embeddedness matter? Methodological issues on agent-based models for analytical social science. J. Artif. Soc. Soc. Simul. 8(4), 6 (2005). http://jasss.soc.surrey.ac.uk/8/4/6.html
6. Crozier, M., Friedberg, E.: Actors and Systems. The Politics of Collective Action. University of Chicago Press, Chicago (1980)
7. El Gemayel, J., Chapron, P., Adreit, F., Sibertin-Blanc, C.: Quand et comment les acteurs sociaux peuvent-ils coopérer? un algorithme de simulation pour la négociation de leurs comportement. Revue d'Intelligence Artificielle 25(1), 43–67 (2011)
8. Evans, A., Heppenstall, A., Birkin, M.: Chapter 9: Understanding simulation results. In: Simulating Social Complexity, Understanding Complex Systems. Springer, Heidelberg (2013)
9. Gilbert, N., Troitzsch, K.: Simulation for the Social Scientist. Open University Press, Maidenhead (2005)
10. Law, A.: Statistical analysis of simulation output data: the practical state of the art. In: Johansson, B., Jain, S., Montoya-Torres, J., Hugan, J., Yücesan, E. (eds.) Proceedings of the 2010 IEEE Winter Simulation Conference (2010)
11. Law, A.: Simulation Modeling and Analysis, 5th edn. Law, A.M., Tucson (2014)
12. Lorscheid, I., Bernd-Oliver, H., Meyer, M.: Opening the 'black box' of simulations: increased transparency and effective communication through the systematic design of experiments. Comput. Math. Org. Theory 18(1), 22–62 (2012)
13. Lorscheid, I., Meyer, M., Hocke, S.: Simulation model and data analysis: Where are we and where should we go? In: Proceedings of ESSA 2013 Conference, Warsaw, Poland, pp. 10–16, September 2013
14. Murdoch, D., Chow, E.: A graphical display of large correlation matrices. Am. Stat. 50, 178–180 (1996)

15. Radax, W., Rengs, B.: Prospects and pitfalls of statistical testing: insights from replicating the demographic prisoner's dilemma. J. Artif. Soc. Soc. Simul. **13**(4), 1 (2010). http://jasss.soc.surrey.ac.uk/13/4/1.html
16. Sibertin-Blanc, C., El Gemayel, J.: Boundedly rational agents playing the social actors game - How to reach cooperation? In: Raghavan, V. (ed.) Proceeding of IEEE Intelligent Agent Technology. IEEE, Atlanta (2013)
17. Sibertin-Blanc, C., Roggero, P., Adreit, F., Baldet, B., Chapron, P., El Gemayel, J., Mailliard, M., Sandri, S.: Soclab: a framework for the modelling, simulation and analysis of power in social organizations. J. Artif. Soc. Soc. Simul. **16**(4), 8 (2013). http://jasss.soc.surrey.ac.uk/16/4/8.html
18. Sibertin-Blanc, C., Roggero, P., Baldet, B.: Interplay between stakeholders of the management of a river. In: CoMSES, Computational Model Library (2013). http://www.openabm.org/model/3760, it gives an extensive presentation of the case and the model
19. Simon, H.: A behavioral model of rational choice. Q. J. Econ. **69**(1), 99–118 (1955)
20. Villa-Vialaneix, N., Sibertin-Blanc, C., Roggero, P.: Statistical exploratory analysis of agent-based simulations in a social context. Case Stud. Bus. Ind. Gov. Stat. **5**(2), 132–149 (2014). http://publications-sfds.fr/index.php/csbigs/article/view/223

Reproducing and Exploring Past Events Using Agent-Based Geo-Historical Models

Nasser Gasmi[2,4], Arnaud Grignard[2], Alexis Drogoul[2],
Benoit Gaudou[1]([✉]), Patrick Taillandier[3],
Olivier Tessier[4], and Vo Duc An[2]

[1] UMR 5505 IRIT, CNRS, University of Toulouse, Toulouse, France
`benoit.gaudou@ut-capitole.fr`
[2] UMI 209 UMMISCO, IRD, UPMC, Hanoi, Vietnam
[3] UMR 6266 IDEES, CNRS, University of Rouen, Rouen, France
[4] French School of Asian Studies, EFEO, Hanoi, Vietnam

Abstract. The field of "digital humanities" is about using the latest digital methodologies in order to tackle humanities disciplines and social sciences questions. The ARCHIVES project belongs to this new research area. It proposes a methodology to build agent-based models of historical events, in particular crisis events, in order to answer new questions about them or explore them in new ways. In this paper, we present the first implementation of ARCHIVES on the case study of the management of floods in Hà Nội (Việt Nam) in 1926. We show how we collected, digitized and indexed numerous historical documents from various sources, built a historical geographic information system to represent the environment and flooding events and finally designed an agent-based model of human activities in this reconstructed environment. We then show how this model helped us understanding the decisions made by the different actors during this event, testing multiple scenarios and answering several questions concerning the management of the flooding events.

Keywords: Agent-based model · Historical geographic information systems · Historical event simulation · Crisis management

1 Introduction

It is now widely accepted that the adaptation of human communities to natural hazards is partly based on a better understanding of similar past events and of the measures undertaken by impacted groups to adapt to them. This "living memory" has the potential to improve their perception of the risks associated to these hazards and, hopefully, to increase their resilience to them. However, it requires that: (1) data related to these hazards are accessible; (2) relevant information can be extracted from it; (3) "narratives" can be reconstructed from these information; (4) they can be easily shared and transmitted. This is classically the task of archivists and historians to make sure that these conditions are fulfilled. However, these last years, the new area of research of Digital Humanities

© Springer International Publishing Switzerland 2015
F. Grimaldo and E. Norling (Eds.): MABS 2014, LNAI 9002, pp. 151–163, 2015.
DOI: 10.1007/978-3-319-14627-0_11

that consists in integrating computer technology into the activities of humanities scholars, has brought innovative approaches and methods to fulfill these tasks.

The ARCHIVES project is part of this new research area. It has for goal to propose a methodology that would enable to support the work of the historians, in a systematic and automated way, from the analysis of documents to the design of realistic geo-historical computer models. Our aim is that, using these models, users can both visualize *what happened* and explore *what could have happened* in alternative "what-if" scenarios. Our claim is that this tangible, albeit virtual, approach to historical "fictions" will provide researchers with a novel methodology for synthesizing large corpuses of documents and, at the same time, become a vector for transmitting lessons from past disasters to a contemporary audience. In addition, it is an attempt to give an experimental approach to History [6]. Previous works have used agent-based modeling and simulation to tackle historical and archeological questions, e.g. [1] tested possible causes of the disappearance of the Kayenti Anasazi and [5] investigated the resilience of the ancient Maya civilization. But such projects simulate a whole civilization over hundreds years, whereas we focus on a short event (a crisis) at a very low level (individual human beings), with (often) a large amount of detailed documents.

In this paper, we present a first implementation of ARCHIVES concerning the study of the floods in Hà Nội (Việt Nam) at the beginning of the 20th century. The aim of this study is to better understand decisions that have been taken during those exceptional events and especially to understand the role of the political actors implied in the decision process. This case study is particularly interesting as the problem of floods in Hà Nội is still topical. Moreover, a lot of period documents have been written and stored concerning these events.

This paper is organized as follow: Sect. 2 presents the historical context of the case study. Section 3 is dedicated to the presentation of the methodology that has been carried out. Section 4 presents the final model that has been developed. Section 5 exposes the results and proposes a discussion about them. At last Sect. 6 concludes and proposes some perspectives.

2   Historical Context

2.1   Việt Nam and Floods: A Thousand Years Story

Due to its climatic and geographical location, and in particular to the fact it is structured around two huge deltas (the Red River delta in the north and the Mekong River in the south), Việt Nam has faced devastating floods all along its history [7,8]. Opposite strategies have been used in the two deltas that structure the country: while the north has emphasized the construction of dykes to stem the Red River, the south has adapted by digging a dense network of canals in the Mekong River delta. And, despite the political upheavals undergone by the country in the last centuries, and more recently during the Nguyễn dynasty (1802–1945), the French colonization (1865–1954), the independence (1955) or the reform policy (đổi mới, 1986), these strategies have remained virtually unchanged.

In this study we focus on the Red River delta. In this area both in the past and today, effects of floods are often devastating both for the population and for economy and agriculture, because the area is very populous and produces a huge amount of rice. Even in 1930, 6,5 millions inhabitants lived in the delta (with a density very high of 430 people par km2) and cultivated 1,1 millions ha of rice fields.

Works to build dykes on the Red River began in 1099. All over history, speed and progress of works have followed the strength and wealth of the government. In particular in the XIIIth century, with the reinforcement of the power the Trần dynasty, huge works have been done from the source of the river to the sea. Gourou in [3] considered that the embanking of the whole river has been achieved at the eve of the French colonial period (1865), with about 4000 km of dykes.

2.2   Political and Social Context in Việt Nam in 1926

In 1926, the north (Tonkin) and the center (Annam) of the Việt Nam were under a French protectorate, whereas the south (Cochinchina) was a French colony. They were all part of the French Indochina, a federation that also included Cambodia and Laos protectorates.

The fact that the Tonkin was at that time a protectorate (and not a colony) had several consequences in terms of governance. In particular indigenous institutions, from the emperor and his ministries to local authorities, were maintained. The country was divided into provinces, provinces into districts and districts into commune. Each of these levels was managed by local authorities hierarchically organized. The French authority was limited to the Resident Superior of Tonkin that managed all the area and one Resident of France per province. There was no French authority in sub-levels. In addition to authorities (Residents), the French organization also included technical services (public works, hydraulic...).

It is important to note that officially, there is no hierarchical relationship between the French organization and the Vietnamese one. As illustrated in the Fig. 1, the Resident of France in Bắc Ninh (the province on which we focus for the floods, on the east of Hà Nội on the other side of the Red River) could only request intervention to his Vietnamese homolog, but cannot order anything.

2.3   Floods in Hà Nội in 1926

This study focuses on the particular case of floods in Hà Nội during the summer 1926 (from the 25th of July until November when the last breach have been plugged). We can distinguish two main parts in the disaster management. In the sequel we will focus on the first one.

The first period, from the 25th of July to the 30th of July, corresponds to the increase of the water level and the breaches in dykes. The first priority was to protect the dykes and in particular to avoid water submersion, which is the main reason of dyke breaches. The best (and the only) way to do it is to increase their height by building small dykes on top of them using anything available

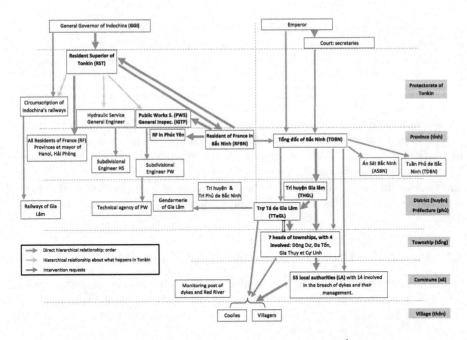

Fig. 1. Hierarchical organization of the Tonkin and the Bắc Ninh province

(e.g. ground of the dyke itself). So the main task of the authorities was to go from commune to commune to order the construction of small dykes and to supervise works. Even with these works, in the 28th and 29th of July, dykes were broken in three main locations: Gia Quất, Ái Mộ and Lâm Du (Fig. 2).

From the 31st of July to November, French authorities began large works to plug the three breaches. Technical services called up thousands of Vietnamese workers and provided a large amount of materials (e.g. sandbags or bamboos) to plug the three main breaches, which took months for the Lâm Du's one. The authorities had also to deal with thousands of victims: they provided foods and raw materials to build shelters. They also tried to determine responsibilities: an inquiry has concluded to the guilt of the vice-chief of the district where the three breaches occurred (Gia Lâm). Thanks to this inquiry, a lot of written documents and reports have survived until now in the Vietnamese archives.

3   Methodology and Tools

3.1   General Methodology

In order to achieve our goal, we propose a methodology composed of 3 steps:

1. Building of a comprehensive and navigable corpus from the heterogeneous set of archives.
2. Representation of this corpus in its multiple (spatial, temporal, social) dimensions so that it can be manipulated and explored freely by users.

3. Building of models of the reality depicted by the corpus so that they can offer an account of what happened but also become the objects of experiments.

The first step consists in building the corpus. Indeed, the memory of a past event is preserved by society and state through testimony or records, materialized by various documents from heterogeneous sources that offer a fragmented vision, sometimes contradictory, of reality. The goal of this step is to collect all the documents that are relevant for the studied event and to digitize them.

The second step consists in enriching and contextualizing this textual corpus. It requires linking it to a geospatial representation. Maps are essential in disaster preparedness as they provide information of paramount importance: communities know where impacts have been the greatest in past events or where infrastructures are likely to be weaker which gives a chance to adapt more quickly and thoroughly to a new disaster. Spatializing this corpus also represents a great opportunity for historians to establish relationships between events distant in time.

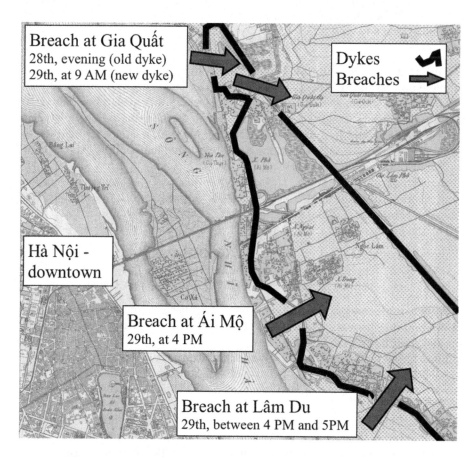

Fig. 2. Summary of the three main breaches during the floods of 1926

The last steps consists in deriving *geo-historical models* from *geo-historical representations*. Indeed, the corpus and its associated multidimensional representation carry a linear causality, which can prevent users to gain an empirical understanding of the decisions taken by the actors in their context. The course of the event and the decisions are all *inputs* of this representation, while an experimental approach based on hypothetical reasoning ("what would have happened if ...", "what effect this decision could have had on ...") would require some of them to become *outputs* as well, so as to enable the exploration of alternative paths or the assessment of hypotheses.

In the next sections, we detail the three steps and their implementation for the Hà Nội floods of 1926.

3.2   Step 1: Building of the Corpus

The first step consists in building the corpus. This step requires to:

– define the event to study and the questions that the model should answer,
– identify the possible sources of data,
– delimit the study area,
– delimit the calendar.

Note that these delimitations could be modified at any moment during the complete process (our methodology follows the Agile trend). Thus, the goal here is to define area and calendar delimitations big enough in order to be sure not to miss documents that could be important later. It is the same for the questions that the model would have to answer. During this step, it is not mandatory to have precise questions: some questions could be deleted and modified throughout the complete process if necessary.

Concerning our case study, the main question that we wanted to answer about floods in Hà Nội in 1926 is: *what were the impacts of the decisions that have been taken during this event?*

For the sources of data, we identified 3 main sources:

– The National Archives Center #1 (Hà Nội, Việt Nam),
– The French mapping agency - IGN (Paris, France),
– The French School of Asian Studies - EFEO (Hà Nội, Việt Nam).

After a quick analysis of the documents, we proposed a first area delimitation: Hà Nội and its surrounding. Concerning the calendar delimitation, we choose to consider months around July 1926.

Once these required elements defined, the next sub-step consists in collecting, digitizing and indexing all the available data in the identified sources that have a link with the study question and that are consistent with the area and calendar delimitations. In our case study, we collected topographic maps of Hà Nội (and its surroundings) of 1925. In addition, we collected documents about the management of these floods. We got qualitative data about the water level and qualitative data about exchanges and communication between actors. More precisely, we used:

- The report of the Resident of France in Bắc Ninh (RFBN) with the chronology of events and the causes and responsibilities of each breach.
- The report of the Vietnamese Head of the district of Gia Lâm to the RFBN with the events, decision chains and dysfunctioning in order execution.
- The report of the inquiry of the province judge about responsibilities of local actors in dyke breaches (in particular the district Vice-Head's responsibility).

Note that in our context, the collection process was complicated by the linguistic diversity of the documents, written in hán nôm (Sino-Vietnamese), French or quốc ngữ (romanized script). And, despite progresses in digitization, analyzing and indexing documents remains a largely manual and tedious task.

3.3   Step 2: Representation of the Corpus

This step concerns the representation of the corpus. It is composed of two sub-steps: the first one is to create accurate GIS data from the disparate maps available in the corpus; resorting to recent sources (Digital Elevation Models, satellite imagery, etc.) if necessary. The second is to integrate temporal information and to offer the same querying and navigation facilities in time than the ones existing for 2D and 3D spatial data.

In the context of our case study, we build a GIS (see Fig. 3) composed of following layers:

- buildings, source: vectorisation of the 1925 Hà Nội map (IGN),
- Red River, source: vectorisation of the 1925 Hà Nội map (IGN),
- lakes, vectorisation of the 1925 Hà Nội map (IGN),
- dykes, source: vectorisation of a map from National Archives Center #1,
- DEM (resolution of 10 m), source: vectorisation of the 1925 Hà Nội map - contour lines (IGN).

The creation of GIS has required an important work of digitization and calibration of the data (in particular, for the dykes).

Concerning the second sub-step, we have developed a web-mapping application (Fig. 4), based on Geoserver, allowing navigation through a web interface in time and space. This work required georeferencing all the documents in time and space and transforming these information into a GIS layer.

3.4   Step 3: Development of Models

This step consists in developing a model according to the corpus that will answer the questions identified in Step 1. This model will rely on Agent-Based Modeling (ABM) as its core technology. ABM has been used over the last twenty years in a growing number of disciplines, including social sciences. This approach has now become the paradigm of choice to couple models from different domains into a same integrated model: in the case of flooding, for instance, hydrodynamic models representing the dynamics of the event itself need to be coupled with the models used to simulate human decision-making, taking into account the fact

Fig. 3. GIS built from historical data and maps

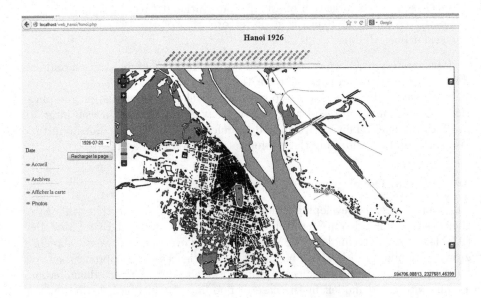

Fig. 4. Snapshot of the web-mapping application

that each model can change the boundary conditions under which other models operate. A key issue of this step is to couple the GIS data with historical data and then to integrate them into the model to produce new knowledge. It is also very important that historians participate to this step. Indeed, our claim is that their implication and their understanding of the models produced is mandatory for the success of the modeling process. In this context the use of graphical formalisms like UML is very interesting as they are easily understandable by all.

In our case study, a difficulty comes from the representation of the various decision-making processes, as they rely on information on management and adaptation measures undertaken by the social actors before, during and after the event considered. This has implied the ability to identify these actors, to understand their individual roles and inter-individual relationships and to build models of their decision-making and communication processes. To this purpose, we relied on existing Artificial Intelligence techniques (such as the FIPA communication language [2]). The challenge was to extract from the transcript of decisions and communications, the information related to the management and adaptation measures undertaken by the social actors.

4   Model

4.1   Purpose of the Model

The model developed has for main purpose to study the decisions made by the different actors during the Hà Nội floods of 1926 and their impacts in terms of flooded area and causality.

4.2   Entities

To this purpose we have defined two kinds of entities: physical entities and actors. All these entities (with their attributes) are summarized in a UML diagram presented in Fig. 5.

We have defined **physical entities** in our model that can be divided in 3 groups:

- Space entities: cells. A cell represents a partition of the space that is homogenous in terms of altitude and water level.
- Hydrological entities: rivers and lakes.
- Obstacle entities: buildings and dykes.

From data collected in the previous step, we have been able to identify all the individual **actors** involved in the floods management, i.e. all the actors mentioned in the (French) archives (cf. Fig. 1). Among all these actors, we identify three main groups, with different roles in the flood management:

- Decision-makers, who include the French administration, Resident of France in Tonkin and in Bắc Ninh province, and central technical services. These actors are the senders of about 86 % of all the messages.

– Order transmitters, i.e. actors involved in the Vietnamese hierarchy from the province to the commune level.
– Order executors, i.e. the manpower that practically execute the orders.

This distinction has driven our modeling of actors. As we focus on the management of the event during the crisis, i.e. the reaction to it, we do not need to model high-level decision-makers, as they are mostly involved in planning phases. Among order transmitters, we simplify by considering only one actor at each level (province, district and township, denoted as local authorities). Finally, we choose to introduce a kind of agent "commune" that will gather the local authority, its manpower and the dykes the local authority is responsible of. In addition this kind of agent will be an intermediate between actors and the hydraulic part of the model. This modeling choice is based of several hypotheses that we made on this model: we do not represent each coolie and villager individually; in particular we consider they do not have an autonomous behavior (they cannot disobey). In addition, we consider that manpower is not a blocking resource, so we do not represent it explicitly. These hypotheses are of course strong, they will be discussed in conclusion.

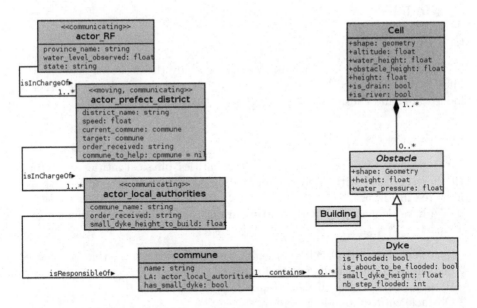

Fig. 5. UML class diagram of the model

4.3   Processes

Hydrological Process. Due to the lack of precise data concerning the Red River at the study period (flow, cross section...), we chose to use a simple flowing model based on a grid (the cell entities). Another advantage of this type of models is to be more easily understood by historians.

Each cell represents an area which has homogenous altitude and water level. In addition, it has a height variable that corresponds to the sum of its altitude, water level and max height of its obstacles. At each simulation step that represents 2 h, all the cells are sorted by height. Then, from the lowest to the highest, each cell that contains water (water level >0) diffuses its water to the lower cells (in terms of height) in its (Moore) neighborhood. This diffusion works as follow: the cell sorts by height all its neighbor cells that are lower than it. Then, from the lowest to the highest, it diffuses to this cell a quantity of water that corresponds to the difference of height between the two cells.

We also implemented a dyke destruction process: if the water level on the cell containing the dyke is not null (meaning that there is water above the dyke) for at least 12 consecutive simulation steps, the dyke breaks (the dyke agent dies).

Crisis Management. Given the hydraulic model presented above, we introduce a model dealing with the crisis management including the actors introduced above. This model will mainly represent the way actors fight against floods (in particular against the water level increase) and the way orders and information are transmitted through the actor network. We thus aim at investigating how orders and information transmissions induce the building of small dykes.

To this purpose, the main process we consider is the top-down order chain. Basically, when the Red River water level is higher than a given threshold, the Head of the province will order to Heads of district to build small dykes. Heads of districts will thus move to meet local authorities actors, order them to build small dykes (with a given height) and supervise works that will be performed by villagers or coolies. Then the Head of districts will move to another commune and so on. This pattern has been (manually for the moment) identified in several exchanges in archives.

4.4 Implementation of the Model

The model was implemented with the GAMA platform[1] [4]. This generic modeling and simulation platform is particularly well-suited to our application context as it allows to simply integrate GIS data and offers the possibility to use FIPA-ACL [2] for agent communication. In addition, its integrated agent-based modeling language (the GAML), which is easy to understand, has allowed to ease the exchange between the different participants of the project.

The implemented model offers a realistic rendering of the city of Hà Nội in 1926 (Fig. 6). It allows users to interact with the simulation at runtime to see the impact of a dyke breaking. In addition, it provides a multi scale online analysis of the flow of messages occurring during the flood event. Messages coming from different parts of the administrative hierarchy is represented as a new layer on the already existing representation of the city as shown in Fig. 6 where aggregated and instantaneous graph are displayed on top of Hà Nội map.

---

[1] http://code.google.com/p/gama-platform/.

5   Results and Discussion

First results are very encouraging: we are able to reproduce in a realistic way from historical documents both the physical phenomenon (the floods) and its management by authorities (in a given time scale). They tend to show that, even in an ideal situation from a social point of view, without disobeying villagers or local authorities who do not execute orders, submersion of dykes could not have been avoided. This reinforces conclusions of some of the people involved in the crisis management that there is no human responsibility in the set of breaches in the dykes during these floods in contrary to the French inquiry conclusions.

Fig. 6. Snapshot of the model implemented in GAMA

A very important outcome of this work were the reflections it generates about the role and the interest of simulation for historical research and Digital Humanities in general. It is important to notice that we have not exactly reproduced the events occurred in 1926 (in particular in terms of location of dyke breaches). We built possible and realistic histories that have been produced by the processes that occurred during the actual History. Reproducing exactly the film of the actual events can have an interest to visualize in a 3D realistic environment what happened, but this would be possible only by scripting the simulation. From our point of view, this holds very little interest because this precludes us from testing various hypotheses on the model and the effects they could have had.

6   Conclusion

In this paper, we presented the ARCHIVES project that has for goal to propose a methodology to model historical events to better understand them. ARCHIVES aims at providing historians with new tools allowing them to not only replay historical events, but also to explore *what could have happened* in alternative "what-if" scenarios.

We already carried out a first implementation of ARCHIVES for the floods of Hà Nội (Việt Nam) in 1926 that were particularly destructive. The model built has allowed us to test several scenarios concerning the chain of commands (ideal situation vs actual one) and to extract knowledge from it. The next step of ARCHIVES will be to generalize this case-study in order to provide historians with generic tools allowing them to carry out this modeling work by themselves. In this context, we propose first to work on digitization tools to support the historical document collection and indexation. We propose then to work on the integration of graphical modeling features inside GAMA. The goal is to allow historians - that have most of the time no programming skills - to develop the models by themselves (or at least the main part of the models).

Acknowledgements. The ARCHIVES Project is funded by the University of Science and Technology of Hà Nội and has been supported by the summer university "Les Journées de Tam Dao". Authors would like to thank institutions that have provided the historical and geographical documents: the National Archives Center #1 (Hà Nội, Việt Nam), the French mapping agency, IGN (Paris, France) and the French School of Asian Studies, EFEO (Hà Nội, Việt Nam).

References

1. Dean, J.S., Gumerman, G.J., Epstein, J.M., Axtell, R.L., Swedlund, A.C., Parker, M.T., McCarroll, S.: Understanding Anasazi culture change through agent-based modeling. In: Kohler, T.A., Gummerman, G.J. (eds.) Dynamics in Human and Primate Societies, pp. 179–205. Oxford University Press, New York (2000)
2. Foundation for Intelligent Physical Agents. FIPA Communicative Act Library Specification (2002). http://www.fipa.org/repository/aclspecs.html
3. Gourou, P.: Les paysans du delta tonkinois. Publications de l'Ecole Française d'Extrême Orient, Les Editions d'art et d'histoire, Paris (1936)
4. Grignard, A., Taillandier, P., Gaudou, B., Vo, D.A., Huynh, N.Q., Drogoul, A.: GAMA 1.6: advancing the art of complex agent-based modeling and simulation. In: Boella, G., Elkind, E., Savarimuthu, B.T.R., Dignum, F., Purvis, M.K. (eds.) PRIMA 2013. LNCS, vol. 8291, pp. 117–131. Springer, Heidelberg (2013)
5. Heckbert, S.: MayaSim: an agent-based model of the ancient maya social-ecological system. J. Artif. Soc. Soc. Simul. **16**(4), 11 (2013)
6. Moss, S., Edmonds, B.: Towards good social science. J. Artif. Soc. Soc. Simul. **8**(4), 13 (2005)
7. Tessier, O.: Outline of the process of red river hydraulics development during the nguyen dynasty. Environ. Change Agric. Sustain. Econ. Dev. Mekong Delta **45**, 45–68 (2011)
8. Tessier, O.: Hydrological development of the red river delta: a historical perspective of the role of the imperial then colonial state (From the XIIth century to the first half of the XXth century). In: Lagrée, S. (ed.) Water and its Many Issues. Methods and Cross-cutting Analysis, Regional Social Sciences Summer University, chapter 1.6, pp. 130–154. Journées de Tam Dao (2013)

Applications

TENDENKO: Agent-Based Evacuation Drill and Emergency Planning System

Toshinori Niwa, Masaru Okaya, and Tomoichi Takahashi$^{(\boxtimes)}$

Meijo University, 1-501 Shiogamaguchi, Tempaku, Nagoya, 468-8502, Japan
{e0930064,m0930007}@ccalumni.meijo-u.ac.jp, ttaka@meijo-u.ac.jp

Abstract. Evacuation drills are conducted periodically to practice smooth evacuations from buildings and rescue operations at emergency sites. An agent-based evacuation simulation provides a platform for simulating human evacuation behavior during emergencies, which can be affected by various social and human factors. These factors include agent characteristics, societal behavior codes, evacuation guidance, and so on. These factors make it difficult to conduct evacuation drills and develop prevention plans for unexpected emergencies. TENDENKO aims to simulate evacuation drills at buildings where real drills cannot be conducted, and to improve evacuation planning for the building to save more lives during future emergencies.

1 Introduction

During emergencies, it is extremely important to safely exit buildings and perform rescue operations quickly. Evacuation drills are conducted periodically at schools and shopping malls to practice smooth evacuations and effective rescue operations. The drills are used to estimate the time taken to exit buildings (exit time) and improve prevention plans for predictable emergencies. However, it is difficult to conduct drills involving many people in various scenarios in real environments.

Disaster reports have provided crucial lessons on reducing human casualties. One key lesson is that people tend to respond individually during emergencies. Emergency information is usually announced through speakers or circulated as people communicate with each other. The rapidity with which people respond to announcements and the behavior people demonstrate can influence their own lives and those of the people around them. Evacuation announcements significantly influence human behavior during emergencies.

In a study on a 1965 Denver flood, Drabek found that most behavioral responses could be classified into four categories, namely appeals to authority, appeals to peers, observational confirmation, and latent confirmation [1]. Documents held by the National Institute of Standards and Technology (NIST) related to the World Trade Center attacks on September 11, 2001, and reports from the cabinet office of Japan on evacuations during the Great East Japan Earthquake (GEJE) and resulting tsunami on March 11, 2011, reveal similar

© Springer International Publishing Switzerland 2015
F. Grimaldo and E. Norling (Eds.): MABS 2014, LNAI 9002, pp. 167–179, 2015.
DOI: 10.1007/978-3-319-14627-0_12

evacuation behavior patterns and individual responses over the past 50 years, despite changes in the way people communicate [2,3].

To evaluate the effectiveness of evacuation drills, it is necessary to analyze human evacuation behaviors from two perspectives: the perspective of the evacuee and the perspective of the rescue responder. The evacuee perspective is concerned with how quickly and safely they can evacuate buildings. Conversely, rescuers are concerned mainly with how smoothly and efficiently they can reach target points and begin rescue operations. TENDENKO[1] provides three features in simulating the evacuation of a crowd of heterogeneous agents (i.e., evacuees and rescuers) in realistic situations. First, emergency information is announced to agents; agents then communicate information about the evacuation via various methods. Second, agents have social and personal relationships between them and behave according to their roles within these relationships. Third, some rescue agents move against the flow of evacuee agents, thus introducing perception-driven behaviors at the reactive level.

The remainder of this article is organized as follows. Section 2 describes the background and provides a review of the literature. In Sect. 3, features in the emergency planning fields are described. Evacuation scenarios and simulation results are discussed in Sect. 4, and a summary is provided in Sect. 5.

2   Background and Literature Review

2.1   Emergency Behaviors and Lessons

The International Organization for Standardization (ISO) published a technical report providing information on evacuees' behavior during evacuations in fire emergencies, and evaluated the impact on aspects contributing to securing human lives [4]. They divided evacuation time into several stages:

t_{pred} : The interval before the actual emergency occurs.

t_{warn} : The interval between emergency occurrence and the time authorities initiate alarms or warnings to individuals.

t_{evac} : The time it takes individuals to reach safe locations after hearing the alarms. It is comprised of pre-travel activity time (PTAT) and the time individuals require to move to safe locations.

Table 1 illustrates the time sequence for information dissemination during the GEJE. There were approximately 45 min before the tsunami's full impact. This period comprised two stages: t_{warn}, from 14:46 to 14:49, and t_{evac}, from 14:49 to 15:15. According to the GEJE report, only 40 % of evacuees heard the loudspeaker emergency alert warning. Of those that heard the warning, 80 % recognized the urgent need for evacuation, while the other 20 % did not understand the announcement because of noise and confusion.

For the World Trade Center (WTC) attack, the NIST report indicates that, when the planes crashed into the buildings, evacuation messages were announced

---

[1] Named after a Japanese tradition of saving lives from tsunamis.

Table 1. Event sequence for the GEJE (March 11, 2011)

Time	Events
14:46	Emergency earthquake alert system
	Earthquake bulletins broadcasted
	The earthquake continued for about 6 min
14:49	Tsunami warnings were issued:
	"A big tsunami will hit at around 15:10"
15:15	Aftershocks occurred
15:00–15:25	An initial, relatively small, tsunami struck
15:25–15:40	A much larger tsunami arrived

in buildings following guidelines provided in a manual. Individuals in both buildings (WTC1 and WTC2) began to evacuate when WTC1 was attacked. When WTC2 was attacked 17 min later, approximately 83 % of WTC1 survivors remained inside the tower. Approximately 60 % of survivors remained inside WTC2. WTC1 and WTC2 were similar in size and layout, and nearly an equal number of individuals were present in both buildings during the attacks. The NIST report identified dissimilarities in evacuation percentage fluctuations between the two buildings. The differences originated from interactive and social factors related to leadership or evacuation guidance announcements.

Drabek pointed out similar factors in sections of his study entitled "But not everyone responds the same" and "Confirmation: a likely action" [1]. People typically attempt to confirm the information in warning messages in numerous ways.

These disaster reports share common lessons:

- Some individuals evacuated immediately when the disasters occurred. However, others failed to evacuate, even though they heard the emergency alarms sounded by the authorities.
- The latter category included individuals with family members located in remote areas, those who attempted to contact their families by phone, and others who continued to work because they believed they were safe.
- Once individuals understood their situation and received emergency information and building layouts, and were able to address concerns about their families' safety, they implemented the announcement information. They also benefitted from communication with other individuals.

2.2 Evacuation Simulation Systems

During emergencies, the behavior of humans differs from their usual behavior. People's mental condition affects their behavior. For example, when people fear for their physical safety, they tend to think of only themselves, and flee a building without considering anything or anyone else. However, when no anxiety is experienced, people tend to consider others and evacuate together. Based on the empirical findings of their study, Perry et al. summarized these human relationship factors in the decision-making process [5].

Agent-based simulation (ABS) provides a platform for the development of computing behavior related to interactive and social issues [6]. Through ABS, Pelechano et al. illustrated that communication among people improved evacuation rates [7]. They devised a scenario focusing on two types of agents: (1) leaders who help others and explore new routes; and (2) agents who might panic during emergencies that occur in unknown environments. Tsai et al. developed ESCAPES, a multi-agent evacuation simulation system incorporating four key features: (1) different types of agents; (2) emotional interactions; (3) informational interactions; and (4) behavioral interactions [8]. Using a multi-agent system, Prikh et al. simulated human behavior in the aftermath of a hypothetical, large-scale, human-initiated crisis in the center of Washington D.C. using a multi-agent system [9]. Okaya et al. proposed an information dissemination model among people during evacuation and presented simulation results using a large number of people [10]. These key features have been used to estimate evacuation times during building design processes or to develop prevention plans that might minimize damage and loss of human lives.

Hui et al. developed a network information diffusion model [11], and Abbas investigated how local preferences affected the network development [12]. These studies focused on information diffusion in human relationship networks.

3   Agent-Based Evacuation Drills and Planning

3.1   Agent States Transitions from Hearing Information to Evacuation

The sounding of alarms and subsequent guidance provided by authorities changed the behavior of individuals during emergencies. PTAT in t_{evac} represents the elapsed time between the moments individuals first heard warnings until the time they began to evacuate. PTAT involves two stages, namely recognition of the emergency and responding to it. Agent behavior during these two stages plays a critical role in the speed of the evacuation.

Figure 1 illustrates how individuals internally process authorities' guidance information and transfer this information to others. Individuals obtain information by experiencing the emergency as it unfolds around them: They hear authorities' announcements or exchange emergency information with each other by communicating (these actions are represented by solid black arrows in Fig. 1). Once they have received the information, individuals attempt to comprehend it by comparing it with their own knowledge and/or experiences. Next, they plan their subsequent actions based on their comprehension (these actions are represented by dotted blue arrows in Fig. 1).

The authorities, as one component of the environment, serve as an information source. Messages sent to individuals comprise warnings related to predictable emergencies or guidance that provides evacuation instructions. Individuals select

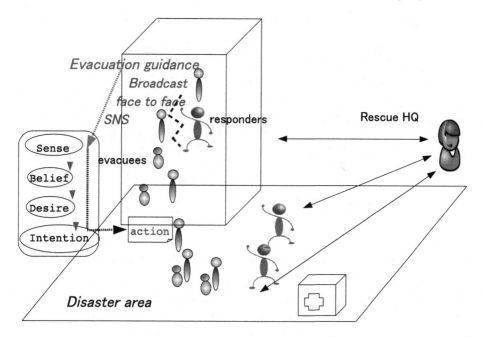

Fig. 1. Information diffusion model and agent behavior (Color figure online)

their actions based on their own knowledge and experiences, and their roles in the community. The Belief-Desire-Intention (BDI) model represents individuals' internal selection processes. Mental biases are represented by the filtering functions that operate from sensing data to the set of belief, from the belief to desire, and the desire to the set of intention.

3.2 Guidance Information Transfer During Emergencies and Evacuation

Noise can affect the dissemination of information during emergencies and can prevent individuals from selecting appropriate strategies that could help them evacuate safely and quickly. The first stage involves individuals' abilities to sense environmental data. Some individuals miss announcements or misunderstand messages. The second stage involves individuals' action choices based on their personal databases, including personal relationships comprised of data compiled by their senses.

The choice of actions during the second stage can be reviewed according to Weaver's levels in Shannon's communication model [13]:

Level A: How accurately can the symbols of communication be transmitted? (The technical problem)

Level B: How precisely do the transmitted symbols convey the desired meaning? (The semantic problem)

Table 2. Communication methods used to communicate emergencies to others.

types	broadcast	face-to-face	SNS
range	entire building	surrounding	no range
number	large	small	middle
trust	low	middle	high

Level C: How effectively does the received meaning affect conduct in the desired way? (The effectiveness problem)

During emergencies, it is assumed that individuals hear evacuation warnings or guidance (Level A). This level is related to the type of communication devices employed. After hearing the messages, people transfer the message content to others. Some contents may be missed because of the "broken telephone" effect and new information added to messages by recognizing dangers involved in the situation outlined in the announcement (Level B). In a situation where the speaker desires people to seek refuge in a safe location, the intent of the speaker is completed when people start evacuating to safe locations (Level C). The dotted red arrow in Fig. 1 illustrates communication that occurs at Levels B and C.

Information passed on to people during emergencies is usually announced through speakers or shared by people communicating with each other. As soon as individuals hear announcements by the authorities or receive phone calls from others, they tend to perform the following actions: transfer the information to others; confirm the information with people nearby; or evacuate. How quickly a person responds to announcements or calls depends on how trustworthy they regard the source. Three different types of communications are modeled, namely broadcast (announcement), face-to-face (word of mouth), and social network (e-mails) (Table 2).

Broadcast: Announcements by authorities are broadcast to the general public through a PA system.

Face-to-Face: People speak to others in their vicinity. The communicator may be a stranger to the receivers. The area the voice reaches(range) is limited, and the message is disseminated following the "broken telephone" pattern, which often results in changes to the message.

Social network: SNS provides simultaneous communication transmission methods using the Internet. In numerous instances, receivers receive messages from friends and therefore tend to trust them.

3.3   Reactive-Level Behavior from Perception of Agents' Roles

People swerve when nearly colliding with each other. When people see responders approaching, they automatically make way for them to pass. While these two behaviors are similar, they do differ at a conscious level. The motions in the latter scenario are reactive-level behaviors. Our system categorizes the agents around an agent into three groups to take into account the unwritten behavior codes of the agent's community:

G_g: normal agents, agents around the agent make no special considerations for the agent and the agent expects that no considerations would be made for itself.

G_h: agents with high priority, the agent gives them special consideration.

G_l: agents with low priority, the agent expects that special considerations are expected from them.

The normal agent unintentionally makes way for rescuers and the disabled, who are categorized as G_h agents. For occupants, a rescue responder is a G_h agent, whereas, for the other responders, the responder is categorized as a G_g agent by other responders.

4   Simulations for Evacuation Drills and Planning

4.1   TENDENKO: Simulation Platform

During emergencies, the behavior of humans differs from their usual behavior. Social relationships among people, their emotions, and other factors are also different from individual to individual. TENDENKO consists of an authority setting mode and an evacuation simulation mode. The evacuation simulation mode can simulate the behavior of people during emergencies, while considering people's social and psychological factors [10]. The main components of the simulation system are described below.

Agents: The number, location, role, and type of agent are set in the authority mode according to the drill scenarios. Agent roles are rescuers, security officers, and evacuees. The different agent types specify their actions upon hearing the alarm: some people evacuate immediately; others do not, despite hearing the announcements sounded by authorities. Agents' behaviors are represented in the BDI models [14].

Environments: The environments are 3D CAD models of buildings with different communication model parameters. Three different types of communication models are implemented in the current version. Table 2 lists three types of parameters: broadcast (announcements), face-to-face (word of mouth), and social network (e-mails).

Dynamic Model: The motions of an agent are simulated based on the forces determined by Helbing's social force model. The force comprises two forces: motions to go to the place of the agent's targets and interaction forces to avoid collision with other agents and walls around the agent. The difference in the categories of other agents is considered when calculating the interaction force of reactive-level motions.

4.2   Examples of Evacuation Drill Scenarios

Followings are examples of evacuation drill simulations.

Subterranean shopping mall evacuation. Many people visit malls. Figure 2 (a) illustrates a subterranean mall in our city, Nagoya. The mall has approximately 90 shops distributed into three rows; there are two main walkways between the rows. Exits to the ground level are located every 50 m. A total of 4,039 people were randomly positioned throughout the mall. After reviewing TENDENKO's simulation, the management company of this subterranean mall prepared emergency manuals, and periodically conducts drills based on these manuals.

Building evacuation and rescue operations. Many people work in buildings. During emergencies, rescue teams enter the building to conduct rescue operations as the building occupants evacuate the building. Figure 2 (b) shows the facade of a five-story library building and an image of the agents' behavior on the second floor. The scenario depicted is of 1,000 occupants (200 occupants on each floor) evacuating the building at the same time, during which a rescue team enters the building to implement rescue operations.

4.3   Results of Evacuation Simulation

Evacuation at a Subterranean Shopping Mall. Evacuation scenarios at the shopping mall were as follow: Fire alarms were set off to communicate the need to move to safe locations to people. Evacuation guidance was simulated through three communication styles.

Scenario 1: At the start of the emergency, all agents were taken through the evacuation guidance once.

Scenario 2: The PA system was assumed to be disabled during the emergency. Therefore, emergency news were transmitted through face-to-face communication. People within 10 m of the speaker were able to hear the guidance.

Scenario 3: People exchanged information through their mobile-phones or SNS. A Facebook social circle was used as an example of such networks [15]. Figure 3 indicates the distributions of nodes in the network used in the simulation.

The graphs in Fig. 4 indicate how agents evacuated the mall (evacuation rate: the left vertical axis) and the number of agents who heard the announcement (diffusion rate: the right vertical axis). As indicated in Sect. 3.2, various factors influence agents' decisions to begin evacuating during an emergency. For example, how precisely the information is transferred to others and whether they start action. In TENDENKO, the factors are treated as a parameter of p that agents

(a) Image depicting the mall interiors and the initial position of 4,039 agents. (Arrows point to agents who communicate emergencies face-to-face or via social networking services (SNS).)

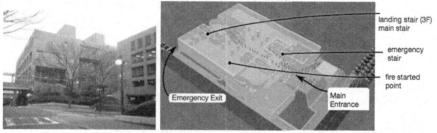

(b) Library facade (left) and image of agent behavior on the second floor (right).

Fig. 2. Evacuation drill places and simulations.

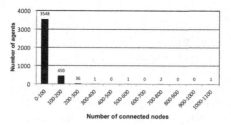

Fig. 3. Distribution of node degress in the SNS Network.

process sensing data. This parameter represents the rate at which an agent initiates actions after receiving guidance or calls along the flow as a dotted red arrow in Fig. 1.

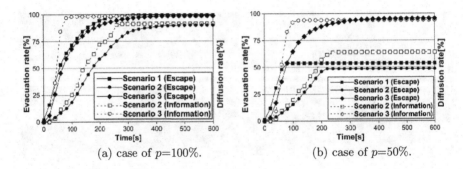

(a) case of $p=100\%$.   (b) case of $p=50\%$.

Fig. 4. Evacuation rates and diffusion rates based on three communication styles. (a) All people evacuate instantly when they hear alarm announcement. (b) Half people evacuate instantly and others continue shopping.

Scenario 1 in Fig. 4 (a) is an ideal scenario because all people instantly started evacuating upon hearing the announcement (rate $p = 100\%$). In Scenarios 2 and 3, an agent (pointed by an arrow in Fig. 3) spoke first to others around him/her or sent mails to SNS friends. Half the number of receivers evacuated instantly, while others continued shopping (rate $p = 50\%$) as shown in Fig. 4 (b). Figure 5 are snapshots of evacuation simulation. The following can be deduced from the graphs:

1. The evacuation rate is proportional to the diffusion rate. Broadcast rates were limited to a certain rate and the rates of other types of communication over time.
2. Communication via the SNS network among agents leads them to carry out quick evacuation.
   (a) At $p = 100\%$, the evacuation rate with SNS (scenario 3) is nearly equal to the evacuation rate with guidance (scenario 1).
   (b) At $p = 50\%$, the evacuation and diffusion rates with SNS (scenario 3) increase as per the progression of steps, becoming nearly 100%. This is because people who received messages from SNS friends multiple times had more prompts to start evacuating than others who heard the messages only form people around them.

These results indicate that the provision of accurate information is a crucial factor in guiding evacuations during emergencies. In addition, while broadcast communication among agents is ideal, this does not guarantee the dissemination of information to all people during an emergency.

4.4   Evacuation from Building and Rescue Operations

Figures 6 (a) and (b) illustrate the counterflow of occupants and fire responders at the main entrance. The occupants (light-colored body with dark arrow) exit from left to right and the responders (black body with white arrow) enter the

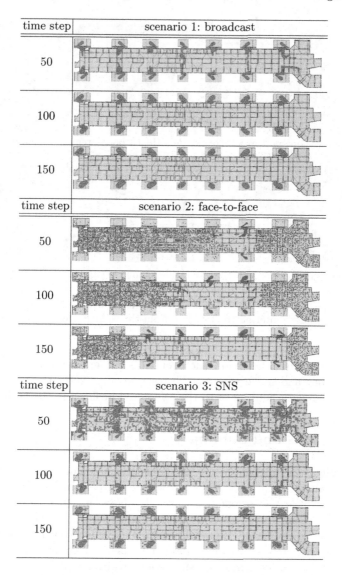

Fig. 5. Snapshots of evacuations at steps 50, 100 and 150.

building from right. The triangles on their heads indicate the directions of their movements. Figures 6 (a) and (b) are snapshots of occupants without and with perception-driven behavior respectively. The time-sequence is ordered from left to right. The simulation time steps are 40, 45 and 50 respectively. In the case of occupants without perception-driven behavior, the rescue team cannot enter the building against the flow of evacuating occupants. In the case of occupants

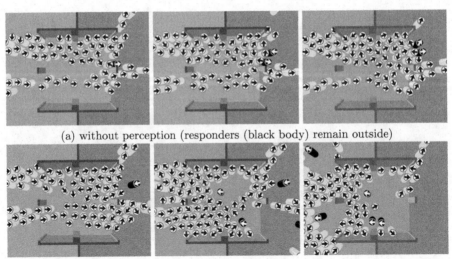

(a) without perception (responders (black body) remain outside)

(b) with perception (responders move inside against occupants (light color body))

Fig. 6. Building evacuation simulation: Snapshots of counter-flows between occupants and rescue responders entering the building from the right (Color figure online).

with perception-driven behavior, the occupants recognize the rescue agents in the G_h category and make way for the responders to enter the building. The rescue team can enter and move to the appointed position in the building.

5   Discussions and Summary

During emergencies, emergency information is crucial in ensuring that all people are safely evacuated from buildings and that rescue operations can be conducted quickly. Today, nearly everyone has a mobile phone, and people communicate with each other using SNS. This type of communication has increased the number of people who can be alerted of ongoing emergencies, and thus has the potential to assist in the instant evacuation of many more people than previously possible. In addition, SNS can help improve emergency prevention plans.

TENDENKO supports communication among agents by providing evacuation guidance to agents via face-to-face and SNS communication models in addition to the traditional broadcast announcements using PA systems. The differences in communication methods, the content of such communication, and the source of announcements can yield different simulation results. The simulation results we obtained indicate that, to plan for real situations, TENDENKO can evaluate existing emergency planning systems and improve the effect of such planning in buildings and areas where evacuation drills cannot be conducted.

This work was supported by JSPS KAKEN Grant Number 24500186.

References

1. Drabek, T.E.: The Human Side of Disaster, 2nd edn. CRC Press, Boca Raton (2013)
2. Averill, J.D., Mileti, D.S., Peacock, R.D., Kuligowski, E.D., Groner, N.E.: Occupant behavior, egress, and emergency communications (NIST NCSTAR 1-7). Technical report. National Institute of Standards and Technology, Gaitherburg (2005)
3. C.O.G. of Japan. Prevention Disaster Conference, the Great West Japan Earthquake and Tsunami. Report on evacuation behavior of people, 21 January 2014. (in Japanese) http://www.bousai.go.jp/kaigirep/chousakai/tohokukyokun/7/index.html
4. ISO:TR16738:2009. Fire-safety engineering - technical information on methods for evaluating behaviour and movement of people
5. Perry, R.W., Mushkatel, A. (eds.): Disaster Management: Warning Response and Cummunity Relocation. Quorum Books, Westport (1984)
6. Thalmann, D., Musse, S.R.: Crowd Simulation. Springer, London (2007)
7. Pelechano, N., Badler, N.I.: Modeling crowd and trained leader behavior during building evacuation. IEEE Comput. Graph. Appl. 26(6), 80–86 (2006)
8. Tsai, J., Fridman, N., Bowring, E., Brown, M., Epstein, S., Kaminka, G., Marsella, S., Ogden, A., Rika, I., Sheel, A., Taylor, M.E., Wang, X., Zilka, A., Tambe, M.: Escapes: evacuation simulation with children, authorities, parents, emotions, and social comparison. In: The 10th International Conference on Autonomous Agents and Multiagent Systems, AAMAS 2011, vol. 2, pp. 457–464. International Foundation for Autonomous Agents and Multiagent Systems, Richland (2011)
9. Parikh, N., Swarup, S., Stretz, P.E., Rivers, C.M., Bryan, M.V.M., Lewis, L., Eubank, S.G., Barrett, C.L., Lum, K., Chungbaek, Y.: Modeling human behavior in the aftermath of a hypothetical improvised nuclear detonation. In: International Conference on Autonomous Agents and Multiagent Systems, AAMAS 2013, pp. 949–956 (2013)
10. Okaya, M., Southern, M., Takahashi, T.: Dynamic information transfer and sharing model in agent based evacuation simulations. In: International Conference on Autonomous Agents and Multiagent Systems, AAMAS 2013, pp. 1295–1296 (2013)
11. Hui, C., Golberg, M., Mogdon-Ismail, M., Wallace, W.A.: Simulating the diffusion of information: an agent-based modeling approach. Int. J. Agent Technol. Syst. 2(3), 31–47 (2010)
12. Abbas, S.M.A.: Homophily, popularity and randomness: modelling growth of online socail network. In: International Conference on Autonomous Agents and Multiagent Systems, AAMAS 2013, pp. 135–142 (2013)
13. Weaver, W., Shannon, C.E.: The Mathematical Theory of Communication. University of Illinois Press, Champaign (1949)
14. Okaya, M., Takahashi, T.: Effect of guidance information and human relations among agents on crowd evacuation behavior. In: Weidmann, U.K.U., Schreckenberg, M. (eds.) Pedestrian and Evacuation Dynamics 2012, pp. 231–243. Springer, New York (2014)
15. Snap, 30 September 2013. http://snap.stanford.edu/data/egonets-Facebook.html

Analysing the Apprenticeship System in the Maghribi Traders Coalition

Christopher Frantz[1]([⊠]), Martin K. Purvis[1], Mariusz Nowostawski[2], and Bastin Tony Roy Savarimuthu[1]

[1] Department of Information Science, University of Otago, Dunedin, New Zealand
christopher.frantz@otago.ac.nz

[2] Faculty of Computer Science and Media Technology, Gjøvik University College, Gjøvik, Norway

Abstract. In this work we further the investigation into the functioning of the Maghribi Traders Coalition – a historically significant traders collective that operated along the North African coast between the 10th and 13th centuries. They acted as a closed group whose interactions were governed by informal institutions (i.e. norms). Historical accounts point to an apprenticeship system that was in force in this society. In this work we propose an agent-based model of the society with the apprenticeship mechanism and analyse the role the mechanism may have played in the removal of cheaters from their trade relationship networks.

Keywords: Maghribi Traders Coalition · Apprenticeship system · Institutions · Norms · Social simulation · Agent-based modelling

1 Introduction

The area of New Institutional Economics [24], with its quest to delineate the extent to which institutions based on norms and rules could have made the difference for the development of societies we observe today, is of increasing interest in the context of computational sociology and economics (e.g. [17]). Equilibria-based game-theoretic approaches, such as Greif [17], have shown compelling results and provide a structured formal backing that is felt to be desirable for comprehensive modelling. However, in order to explore the emergent characteristics of individual-based interactions in the context of an institutional setting, the wider scope of agent-based modelling offers an approach that does not limit the diversity of individuals, can reveal emerging social structures that supersede individuals' influences, and can allow relaxation of the rationality assumption associated with game-theoretical approaches.

In this work we review an important example from comparative historical analysis, namely the Maghribi Traders Coalition, a term coined by Greif [17] with respect to a traders collective that relied on informal enforcement of cooperation based on norms to facilitate the group's long-distance trade operations along the North African coast between the 10th and 13th centuries. Its importance

F. Grimaldo and E. Norling (Eds.): MABS 2014, LNAI 9002, pp. 180–196, 2015.
DOI: 10.1007/978-3-319-14627-0_13

for institutional research lies in its nature as an early documented example of multi-party long-distance trading, which offers us a useful source of empirical information concerning the rise of institutional mechanisms to govern networks of interacting agents.

Prior research [14,15,17] into the reasons for stable institutional equilibria that facilitated cooperation without relying on formal institutional instruments, such as contracts and commercial courts, has generally been based on the assumption of a closed group in which cultural bonds and the interlinked nature of the Maghribis' reciprocity relationships led to an environment of trust that would reassure proactive reporting of non-cooperators.[1] From the perspective of the social science domain of Institutional Analysis, the Maghribi Traders Coalition is a primary historic example of how cooperative behaviour could be achieved based on informal means, i.e. without the reliance of laws or other explicit rules, but merely based on normative principles.

In the present work we address some aspects of the coalition's activities that, though documented in historical records, have not been explored computationally to understand and relax some of the assumptions mentioned above, such as the cultural embeddedness of cooperative behaviour. In particular we are looking at the systematic grooming of new traders in an apprenticeship system in which established 'full' traders employed inexperienced young society members, often sons of fellow traders ('associates') [13], to train, and eventually mentor their progressive integration into the wider trader relationship network. The mentees eventually became established as full traders, or, if considered disloyal or ineffective, were permanently excluded from the network's trade operations.

Central contributions of this work include the conception of the Maghribi Traders Coalition in its entirety as a structure (aṣḥābunā) that emerged from interlinked elementary tightly knit groups (aṣḥābs) that still maintained some degree of openness in order to facilitate the shift of active traders over time (which is in contrast to the coalition's understanding as a unified well-defined and integrated entity). Based on this we analyse the impact of the apprenticeship concept on the collective's ability to identify and exclude non-cooperators.

In the following section (Sect. 2) we provide an overview of the characteristics of the Maghribi Traders Coalition that are of relevance to this work. Then, in Sect. 3, we carve out an agent-based model that captures the aspects of interest, namely the apprenticeship network, and explore results for given parameter sets (Sect. 4). We finish with a discussion of the results and their implications on the interpretation of the institution 'apprenticeship system', and finally reintegrate it with the literature context (Sect. 5).

2   Maghribi Traders Coalition

The 'Maghribis' (historically referred to as "Maghrebis" [9]), were named after their geographic situation with respect to the Fatimid Empire's world view

---

[1] This would contrast with Southern European societies such as the Italian city states of Genoa and Venice that operated based on formal institutions.

centred in Fustat (nowadays: 'Old Cairo'), and largely derived from the Jewish communities of the two cities Qayrawān and al-Mahdiyya (both located in what is nowadays Tunisia). This group had moved from Baghdad and settled in the Western part of the Mediterranean Basin, integrating into the Muslim environment by adopting a wide range of customs and norms, while maintaining their identity based on their own religion and descent as well as the shared experience of occasional discrimination. The Maghribis used this strong in-group bond to their advantage as it enabled them to assure cooperation by members based on possible social consequences of communicated misconduct (along with a strong emphasis on gossip) and family reputation within their tightly knit cultural group. As a consequence, they developed a trader network that spanned across and beyond the Northern African coast, expanding to al-Andalus (nowadays Spain) in the West and the Indian Ocean in the East. For their trade operations, traders relied on individual (personal) trader relationships that had formal rituals of initiation (face-to-face meetings) and termination (termination under witnesses).[2] Based on this institutional instrument[3] traders formed their personal network of associates, their 'aṣḥāb', upon which individual traders drew to extend their trading activities by means of delegation. This associate network created the backbone of a long-distance trader's success as it allowed one's economic presence at multiple widely distributed trading locations and to benefit from varying market prices, an aspect that would have not been achievable by personal travel. This system of associates inherently relied on a high level of trust between associates that performed trade-related services for each other (such as storing goods, selling them, etc.). To reassure trust and to monitor compliance with instructions Maghribi traders communicated extensively via letters whose delivery was often delegated to fellow traders, overlaying the trade network with a second, not necessarily symmetric information transmission network. The receipt of such letters can be considered guaranteed, both by sending those redundantly, but also by expecting the acknowledgement of their receipt in future correspondence [12]. As part of those letters, traders dealt with their business operations as well as more general gossip that included information about markets and prices as well as conduct of fellow traders.[4] Those letters are in fact the primary source of information historians such as Goitein [9], Udovitch [23], Greif [14,15,17], Ackerman-Lieberman [1] and Goldberg [10,11,13] used to reconstruct the lives of medieval Jews in the Fatimid Empire.

From the different individual aṣḥābs, i.e. the non-transitive personal relationship networks individual traders maintained, emerged the construct of the aṣḥābunā ('our colleagues'), which represented the Maghribi network in its totality. Performing agency services, i.e. selling each others' goods and returning

---

[2] These rituals describe the suḥba relationship whose interpretation has been subject of more recent discussion (see [7,11,13]).

[3] A more in-depth overview of different institutional instruments available to and employed by the Maghribi traders can be found in [13,15].

[4] Goldberg's statistical analysis [11] allocates the fraction of gossip in letter content at around 20 %.

incurred profits, occurred without direct remuneration, as payment was considered slave-like and would have questioned the courteous nature in which trade was pursued [13]. Instead in suḥba relationships, services were 'paid' by gaining reciprocal favours against the other party. Furthermore, money was not handled on a transactional basis, but instead traders managed accounts for each other, increasing the mutual leverage should a party be observed to defect, or only be suspected of shirking profits. The practically closed nature of the group, the dependency on reciprocal favours and the delayed clearing of accounts all assured, or at least motivated, compliance throughout one's aṣḥāb.

As refined and integrated as the methods that assured compliance appear, the establishment of relationships did not simply occur at random but underlay a further filtering feature: an individual's $jāh$, his[5] 'standing' or 'reputation' [11]. Based on the perceived jāh differences (and obviously the trade interest in general, such as the traded goods) an individual could decide whether he would engage in long-lasting relationships.

To analyse the jāh's effect one can consider the jāh as a means to help traders consider whom to enter a trade relationship with, and whom to avoid. Agency services in the context of the suḥba were not monetarily rewarded. However, a merchant's gain (the one performing services on behalf of another) to his investor (the one that delegates the sales to a merchant) was proportional to the jāh difference of both parties, with one of higher jāh being able to demand more services such as multiple different operations or higher volume sales [11]. On the other hand, one could consider dealings with traders of lesser jāh to be unattractive, because of the impact their lower standing could have on one's own jāh. Even more importantly, considering that a trader with lower jāh faced lesser cost (i.e. loss in absolute reputation) when detected as a cheater, his incentives to engage in cheating could be considered higher. We thus believe that traders had an interest in concentrating their relationships on the traders that had not necessarily the same but similar jāh levels.[6] We make this assumption a central concern when modelling the aṣḥābunā network in an agent-based manner.

The second aspect central to this contribution is to investigate the extent to which the Maghribi apprenticeship system could have made a difference in removing potential cheaters from the trader network. Long-distance trading was considered to be a profession that required a carefully developed skill set and a mentor that would be an initial business partner for newcomers striving to become 'full traders'. Given the common sociocultural background, traders often inherited the profession from their parents, who sent their child to a fellow

---

[5] It is safe to use the male form. The trader community was of patriarchal nature, with men performing trade operations, while their (potentially multiple) wives managed their different homesteads and warehouses. The geographic spread of marriages in principle allowed the development of extensive trade operations across the Mediterranean [1,13].

[6] Note that the proposition of partner choice based on status similarity is compatible with the principles proposed by Podolny [20] in the context of organisational studies. He suggests that in the face of market uncertainty organisations choose partners they had *previous experience* with and which are of *similar status*.

associate who was then considered responsible for their livelihood in exchange for unremunerated trade-related services by those young apprentices [13]. Over time, those apprentices' activities could expand beyond the dealings with their mentors and establish their own relationships. However, given their inferior standing, the apprentices' operations carried strict monitoring, not only to assure their loyalty (which could ultimately affect their own family's reputation) but also to assess their acquired ability before opening access to other trade connections. Those apprenticeships were by no means short-lasting as they could take more than a decade and bore the option for failure [13]. This refined mechanism existed in stark contrast to Southern European traders that (a) operated in one-off transactions, (b) applied strict role stratification into investors and merchants, and (c) potentially employed opportunists to manage one-off business dealings that were formally regulated based on contracts but also private-order enforcement [17].

This background presented here provides the grounds for our basic model for representing the development of the aṣḥābunā as an emergent property of 1:1 agent relationships established based on a conceptualisation of reputation grounded on jāh levels. Using this base model, we can examine the extent to which the Maghribi apprenticeship system could have restrained cheating levels. Both those aspects did not find consideration in previous research. Exploring those, we can relax the high-level assumption that cooperation based on informal means was intrinsic to the collectivistic culture. We do not challenge this assumption as such, but wish to offer a more refined analysis of previously neglected factors that may have contributed to the cooperative outcome.

3   Simulation Model

At this stage, we want to propose an agent-based model that incorporates selected aspects discussed above. Our model aims at increasing the level of understanding of the Maghribi trader collective, and does not aim at accurate reproduction, given that this is challenged by a lack of sufficiently detailed historical data. More importantly, we think it is important to develop an understanding of used institutional mechanisms, such as the jāh as a regulative artefact for the number of connections an agent would engage in and how this would affect the performance of the overall society. We thus use a generative model to represent the aṣḥābunā, as opposed to using global thresholds (e.g. for the setup and size of trader networks) to drive controlled emergence.

In the following we describe an agent's proactive execution cycle (Algorithm 1) as well as his reactions (Algorithm 2) to other agents' requests. During each execution round, each agent acts from the perspective of the merchant, i.e. the one seeking employment by an investor (who delegates its business dealings to merchants). It randomly picks another agent to offer oneself as a potential merchant. If the agent has not been previously employed it will need to offer its services as an apprentice looking for initial employment. If the apprenticeship employment request is accepted, the agent commits to its employer for a randomly picked number of rounds between $apprenticeshipDuration_{min}$

and *apprenticeshipDuration_{max}*. During this period the apprentice agent does not seek further employment relationships and only deals with 'its' mentoring investor. Alternatively, if the merchant had been previously employed, it checks whether the randomly picked agent's jāh lies within an acceptable range of its own jāh, the lower threshold being jāh - jāh * *lowerJahDifference* and the upper threshold being jāh + jāh * *upperJahDifference*, with *lowerJahDifference* and *upperJahDifference* being values between 0.0 and 1.0.

Following this, the agent trades with a fixed fraction (*tradeQ*) of agents it enjoys employment relationships with. Every successful trade results in an absolute jāh increase of *jahIncrement* for both participating traders. The announcement of cheaters likewise leads to a jāh increase for the announcing agent.

Beyond trading, agents involve themselves in the observation of other agents. To do so agents randomly pick a fraction of all agents (*observationQ*). The random choice of observation targets may appear unrealistic at first. However, note that agents did not necessarily need to maintain trade relationships with observed agents, but potentially operated in the same market places and thus were potential targets for the observation of conduct. Observers would inform their aṣḥāb not only about known but likewise about unknown peers as the individual aṣḥābs were a non-transitive private matter; observers could not make assumptions about their partners' other trade relationships, an uncertainty aspect that, we believe, motivated compliance in the first place. Likewise, the observer may not be able to observe its own trading-partner agents' conduct. However, for apprenticeship relationships we consider more frequent closed-loop interactions, such as small-scale deals or services, that would allow the determination of his conduct in any case.

To represent the proactive reporting norm of announcing trading-partner cheating, observing agents notify their entire network of trade relationships (their respective aṣḥābs) about any observation. We believe that this modelling intuition is realistic as traders used different means for letter exchange (such as land-based couriers in contrast to sea-based sending of goods), sent them redundantly, mutually acknowledged their receipt, and often read them in public to demonstrate compliance [12].

Agents age and die with a probability of $p_{deathBelowExpectedAge}$ if *age* $\leq$ *expectedAge* at the end of each round. If older, they die with a probability of $p_{deathBeyondExpectedAge}$. This mechanism allows us to incorporate the unexpected death of agents. In order to keep the number of agents stable while modelling the change of traders over time, for each dying trader a new agent is introduced, who will need to pass the apprenticeship phase prior to full employment.

In our algorithms, an individual agent's jāh levels continuously increase as a reflection of 'standing' and experience in a society. The ageing mechanism provides a natural boundary to jāh levels. Also, when cheating, counter-intuitively, the jāh levels of the cheater are not adjusted (e.g. reduced). A more refined representation would use the notion of endorsements [2][7] in which the individual's jāh would be exogenous to the individual and be derived from its social

---

[7] This suggestion was raised by one of the anonymous reviewers.

environment, i.e. what others think about the individual. However, we opted for a more primitive endogenous jāh model, primarily to isolate the effect of exclusion from employment based on announcement of cheaters from the effect of dropping jāh levels of cheaters. For this iteration the primary focus lies on cheater propagation as the institutional cornerstone, as opposed to preventing re-employment based on increasing jāh differences.

Beyond its own execution cycle an agent reacts to incoming requests, which include requests for engagement in trading relationships (employment) and receiving goods in order to realise the actual trade. As a final aspect agents react to incoming cheater notifications by remembering them as well as sharing cheater information with all agents they have trade relationships with (except the original sender). This models the cascading effect of cheater notifications in the Maghribi society.

Algorithms 1 and 2 show the pseudocode representation of agents' execution cycle and reactions.

Algorithm 1. Agent Execution Cycle

Agent picks random other agent;
if *unemployed and not previously employed* **then**
    Offer oneself as apprentice;
    if *accepted* **then**
        Commit to apprenticeship for random duration between
            $apprenticeshipDuration_{min}$ and $apprenticeshipDuration_{max}$ rounds;
else
    if *randomly picked agent is within acceptable range of own* jāh **then**
        Offer oneself as employee;
end
Trade with *tradeQ* of employed agents;
Increase own jāh by *jahIncrement* for each trade;
Randomly choose *observationQ* number of agents from all agents (incl. eventual apprentice);
foreach *agent in observed agents* **do**
    Check if agent has cheated;
    if *agent has cheated* **then**
        Announce to other agents in own aṣḥāb;
        Increase own jāh by *jahIncrement*;
end
Increment *age* each round;
if *age* $\leq$ *expectedAge* **then**
    Check for death with probability $p_{deathBelowExpectedAge}$;
else
    Check for death with probability $p_{deathBeyondExpectedAge}$;
end

We parametrize agents with an initial unified jāh level and define whether an agent cheats, and if so, assign a fixed cheating probability ($p_{cheating}$). Table 1 summarizes the base parameter set used in our simulations, the intuitions of which we will discuss in more depth.

In the simulation we model 'rounds' in a rough equivalence to years, with one year being represented by 10 simulation rounds. As soon as traders enter the simulation they participate in trade, either entering an apprenticeship or (in the control case without the apprenticeship system) by directly engaging in trade relationships.[8] An expected trader lifespan is around 40 years, an assumption

---

[8] We ignore any lifespan before or following active tradership.

Algorithm 2. Agent Reactions

---

if *receiving employment request* **then**
    if *requester seeks initial employment and receiver has no other apprentice at current stage* **then**
        Employ irrespective of jāh difference;
    else
        if *requester within* jāh *range and not known as cheater* **then**
            Employ requester;
        else
            Reject request;
        end
    end
if *receiving trade request* **then**
    if *cheater* **then**
        Decide whether to cheat or to trade fair;
    Trade;
    Increase own jāh by *jahIncrement*;
if *receiving cheater notification by others* **then**
    Share with own aṣḥāb (excluding agent who sent cheater announcement);
    Increase own jāh by *jahIncrement*;

Table 1. Simulation parameters

Parameter	Value	Variation in section
Number of agents	400	Sect. 4.4
Fraction of cheaters	0.4	
$p_{cheating}$	0.5	Sect. 4.2
$expectedAge$	400 rounds	
$apprenticeshipDuration_{min}$	50 rounds	
$apprenticeshipDuration_{max}$	100 rounds	
$lowerJahDifference$	0.2	Sects. 4.1–4.4
$upperJahDifference$	1	Sect. 4.1
$tradeQ$	0.5	Sect. 4.4
$jahIncrement$	1	
$observationQ$	0.025	Sects. 4.3 and 4.4
$p_{deathBelowExpectedAge}$	0.0001	
$p_{deathBeyondExpectedAge}$	0.001	

we base on documented evidence of a long-lasting suḥba relationship between Nahray Ibn Nissīm and one of his associates [13]. Instead of removing a trader at the expected end of his life, we introduce the more realistic notion of changing death probabilities ($p_{deathBelowExpectedAge}$ and $p_{deathBeyondExpectedAge}$) to smoothen the generational transition without total loss of cheater knowledge. As indicated in Sect. 2, apprenticeships last for up to a decade, with the minimal value being five years, the equivalence of which is represented in the round values for $apprenticeshipDuration_{min}$ and $apprenticeshipDuration_{max}$. We further assume six trade interactions with the apprentice during each year of apprenticeship. We will vary this value for the later set of simulations.

Initially, the number of agents is parametrised at 400. Historical evidence offers widely varying information, examples ranging from 330 [16], up to 550 [18]. However, note that those values are derived from subsets of the actual Geniza corpus, with future research likely to offer more realistic (possibly higher) values. In this light, the chosen value represents a rough middle ground between documented values, while being computationally tractable.[9] This aspect showcases an example of the problems when building models based on anecdotal accounts, which we can balance with the flexibility of agent-based modelling. Instead of arguing precise values, the central evaluation implication is to perform experimental parameter variation to analyse the impact on simulation results.

Most other parameter values (the ones related to cheating, jāh differences as well as trading and observation quotas) do not rely on specific evidence, which makes their experimental variation important, an aspect that is explored in the following section.

4   Results

To recall, our central question is whether the apprenticeship system employed by Maghribis could have had a filtering function by improving the society's resilience to cheaters. To measure this effect, we use *the number of cheating traders who maintain relationships with non-cheaters* as an indicator for the institution's performance. We operationalise this as the mean number of cheaters that maintain relationships with non-cheaters across all simulation rounds.[10] For this evaluation one simulation run consists of 20,000 rounds.

To evaluate the model with respect to the measure of interest we performed parameter sweeping based on the initial parameter set by systematically varying two parameters each for a given simulation run. Given the large amount of possible combinations, we focused on parameters of central interest, namely the ones related to the traders' jāh, and used those to guide further analysis.

4.1   Upper and Lower Jāh Differences

Given the importance of jāh differences to constrain partner choice, we initially concentrated on the interaction between permissible *lowerJahDifference* and *upperJahDifference* for trade partner choice – to recall, the maximum acceptable jāh difference for traders of lower status to engage with ones of higher status (*upperJahDifference*), and the maximum acceptable jāh difference for traders of higher status to engage with ones of lower status (*lowerJahDifference*).

We instantiated simulations covering the parameter range from 0.1 (implying a permissive relative difference of 10 %) to 1 (implying any difference in jāh) in

---

[9] A representative set of simulation runs for one parameter sweep takes about three weeks on current hardware (Intel i7 8-core with 12 GB RAM).

[10] We use 'round' to describe a simulation step, as opposed to 'run' that describes a complete simulation execution over the parametrised number of rounds.

steps of 0.1. The results are shown in the form of a surface plot (see Fig. 1). Simulation runs with enabled apprenticeship system are represented in green colour, the control variant without apprenticeship system is plotted in red colour. To provide a better overview of the relative differences in results of both configurations and to isolate those from trends, a further surface (in light blue colour) plots the inverted absolute value difference (i.e. reduction of cheaters by the apprenticeship system). Interactive versions of this and all further result charts, including variants that show the relative difference for each data point, are provided in [6].

Looking at the overall effect of introducing the apprenticeship model, for nearly the entire parameter space (with the exception of trade-engagement acceptance for all jāh levels, i.e. lower jāh = 1.0), we can observe a significant drop in cheating levels. This is driven by the comprehensive observation of an apprentice by his mentor and the proactive exclusion from trade and notification of the mentor's aṣḥāb, should the mentee decide to cheat.

The model displays very high numbers of cheaters with relationships to non-cheaters, which is based on our pessimistic parameter settings. However, this aspect is secondary, given that our interest lies in the understanding of the institution, as opposed to an accurate representation of historical reality.

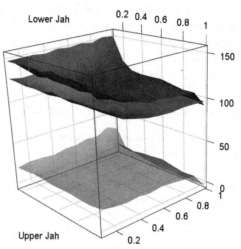

Fig. 1. Number of cheaters with relationship to non-cheater for varied upper and lower jāh differences (red surface: without apprenticeships; green surface: with apprenticeship system; blue surface: inverted absolute cheater reduction by apprenticeship) (Color figure online)

For the specific jāh level-related parameter combinations we can observe the correlation of lower parameter values with larger numbers of socially embedded cheaters. The reason lies in the nature of jāh levels to control the establishment of new relationships. Limiting the access for newcomers and constraining their willingness to enter relationships with higher-status traders segregates the traders into groups of relatively homogeneous jāh levels. Overall, the apprenticeship system nearly consistently fares better at limiting cheater embeddedness with a relatively constant reduction of around 15 % for lower jāh levels below 1.0. (max. reduction: 0.216, min: −0.056, mean: 0.127, σ: 0.054). However, for high lower jāh levels we can observe a performance breakdown of the apprenticeship system (it produces around 5.6 % *more* economically embedded cheaters).

The reason for this lies in the interaction frequency. Immediate admission to full tradership without an initial apprenticeship phase results in a higher trade frequency and observations of those newcomers, which are then discovered more rapidly, which, in consequence, leads to a lower mean. In this case the apprenticeship-free system achieves around 5 % fewer connections. This is an important finding, inasmuch as it reveals under which conditions the apprenticeship system achieves better results despite fewer interactions with cheaters (which, as apprentices, exclusively deal with their mentors).

Varying higher jāh differences, in contrast, hardly showed any effect on the relative performance (shown as blue surface). For further simulations, we thus fix it to the value of 1.0. Instead we consider the lower jāh difference as pivotal for the institution's performance as it determines how receptive established traders are towards newcomers, which affects the filtering effect of the apprenticeship system. The further exploration thus concentrates on the effect of *lowerJahDifference* in conjunction with the cheating probability of traders ($p_{cheating}$), and beyond this, the impact of the observation quota (*observationQ*).

4.2   Cheating Probability and Jāh Difference

A consequent choice is the analysis of the varying cheating probability, given its likeliness to affect detection of cheating. Figure 2 shows results for the parameter variation of $p_{cheating}$ in combination with *lowerJahDifference*. Both variables have been systematically varied across the range from 0.1 to 1.0 (step size: 0.1).

In absolute numbers, we can observe that the cheating probability has an impact on the number of potential cheaters with relationships to non-cheaters, which decreases with increasing cheating probability because of the earlier detection of cheaters (max. reduction: 0.186, min.: −0.082, mean: 0.119, σ: 0.062). However, the cheating probability has little impact on the performance of the apprenticeship system (in comparison to the apprenticeship-free variant). Again, the impact of lower jāh values is of greater significance as immediate admission of newcomers overrules the apprenticeship system's effect.

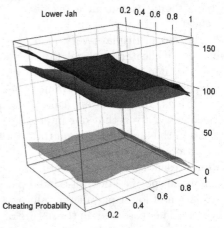

Fig. 2. Number of cheaters with relationship to non-cheater for different cheating probabilities and jāh differences

4.3   Observation Quota and Jāh Difference

Another interesting question is how much of a difference could the extent of observation, or monitoring, have made in maintaining a compliant trader society. To examine this, we fix the cheating probability at 0.5 and look at the impact of different observation quotas. For this purpose, we analyse the interaction between the lower jāh difference and the fraction of all traders an individual monitors (*observationQ*). We concentrate on a range from 0.025 to 0.3 (step size 0.025) for pragmatic reasons, as the assumption that agents could observe as much as 0.3 of *all* agents seems unrealistic. The results are shown in Fig. 3. As is intuitively retraceable, an increasing observation quota leads to an increasing exclusion of cheaters, reaching the point of reducing cheaters with relationships to non-cheaters (in the apprenticeship variant) to around 60 agents for an observation quota of 0.3 (max. reduction: 0.203, min.: −0.257, mean: 0.023, σ: 0.097). As with the previous case, a more liberal attitude towards newcomers (i.e. greater acceptance of lower jāh values) leads to improved identification of cheaters. However, closer inspection of the simulation outcome for both configurations (i.e. with apprenticeship model and without an initial apprenticeship employment) reveals insights about the apprenticeship system's actual purpose as part of the informal institution employed by the Maghribis.

For higher values of jāh difference and observation quota, one can observe a better performance for the model that operates *without* apprenticeship relationships (more than 20 % fewer connections for an observation quota of 0.3 and lower jāh difference of 1.0 as compared to the apprenticeship-based model). Note the lower number of potential cheaters with relationships to non-cheaters shown by the red surface (no apprentices) in Fig. 3, which dominates the apprenticeship-based model for lower jāh values ≥ 0.4 when paired with higher observation quota levels (especially for values ≥ 0.2); in such cases the apprenticeship model permits up to 26 % more cheater connections.

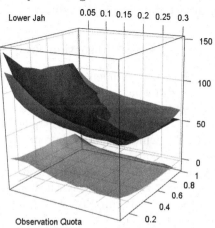

Fig. 3. Number of cheaters with relationship to non-cheater for different observation quotas and jāh differences

The reason for this lies in the greater probability of both attracting cheaters as employees (greater permissible jāh difference), and also a greater likelihood of identifying cheaters enabled by the greater observation coverage. At first one could conclude a limited or different purpose of an apprenticeship system under those circumstances. However, one should take into account the differentiated characteristic of the informal institution when considering higher acceptance of jāh differences and observation quota. For higher values, the function of identifying cheaters (and thus the cost in terms of lost profit associated with it) is born by the collective of all traders. Thus all traders have to expect potential cheating for trade encounters, which, if addressed, leads to fast identification of newly introduced cheaters. In contrast, relying on the apprenticeship system concentrates the uncertainty associated with introducing new traders into the system exclusively with the apprentices' mentors, who bear the full risk and cost of cheating (since all trade with newcomers concentrates on their mentors) but who may also benefit from unremunerated cheap services, should the apprentice turn out to act reliably truthful. The apprenticeship system thus concentrated the risk of introducing cheaters and converted it into a potential investment on the part of established traders. In an environment with an explicit use of the apprenticeship system, the risk of cheating, which includes both the loss of profits associated with the individual transaction and the loss of trust in the institution, could be minimized for the collective, as cheaters could often be identified before becoming fully established members of the trader community. Beyond this, particularly for lower, and probably more realistic levels of observation quota and acceptance of lower jāh values, the apprenticeship system bears a clear benefit (more than 20 % increase in undesirable connections for the apprenticeship-free system for observation quota of 0.05 and lower jāh difference of 0.1) in reducing cheater relationships, particularly if traders have limited interest in dealing with agents of lesser status (jāh differences < 0.4).

4.4   Reducing Interaction Frequency

To extend the argument that the apprenticeship system bears a clear benefit for scenarios in which monitoring opportunities are limited or costly, we explore the effect of reducing the interaction frequency.

We do so by reducing the trade frequency, which is indirectly represented in the trade quota ($tradeQ$), the fraction of all partners from his aṣḥāb a trader trades with during each round. Initially we set a high value of 0.5, which we reduced to 0.1. For the apprenticeships we reduced the assumed trade interactions from initial 6 per apprenticeship year to 1. In both cases, reducing the number of interactions likewise reduces the chance to observe and detect cheaters. Figure 4 shows the experimental results. Those show a significantly higher performance of the apprenticeship system, in particular for higher parameter settings[11] (max: 0.192, min: −0.121, mean: 0.079, σ: 0.069), which supports its purposefulness for cooperation scenarios in which observation opportunities are limited by fewer interactions.

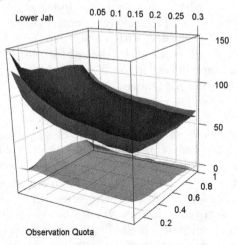

Fig. 4. Number of cheaters with relationship to non-cheater for different observation quotas and jāh differences for low trade frequencies

---

[11] This includes the borderline case of *lowerJahDifference* = 1.0, which nevertheless still performs worse compared to the apprenticeship-free variant.

To address a last concern, the model's robustness with respect to population variation, we tested the previous scenario against a variant with 200 agents. The results reveal a difference between the respective performance means of around 0.006.[12] This offers the suggestion that the trade network structure had a low sensitivity to changing trader numbers and strong scalability characteristics. However, this aspect demands further investigation in future research.

5   Discussion

This work investigates an existing scenario from the area of comparative economics, the Maghribi Traders Coalition, and analyses the apprenticeship network Maghribi traders employed to establish a professional trader community by informal means.

The presented model analyses the function of a systematic apprenticeship mechanism on the functioning of the 'rather closed' trader society (highlighted by Greif [17]) but relaxes some of its more rigid assumptions and explores the potential function of the apprenticeship system, which has been described in more depth by historians such as Goldberg [13]. Exploring the apprenticeship system not only extends the detail of analysis, but more so, it can possibly be considered a necessary element to sustain trust in an institution that facilitated cooperation by informal means and lasted over multiple trader generations.[13] The closed system assumption used in previous approaches cannot capture this generational aspect.

Beyond the quantitative aspect (minimisation of cheaters with relationships to non-cheaters) the interpretation of the results offers us further insight into the apprenticeship system's institutional function of reducing uncertainty [19]. For the Maghribis, the apprenticeship system converted the task of identifying cheaters into a potentially profitable endeavour by diverting the uncertainty towards self-selected more risk-affine traders. Those could expect a benefit if they employed honest apprentices to further their trade operations for a considerable time. However, identifying a cheating newcomer comes at a cost for the risk-taking mentor, who would share this information gain with his community to maintain his reputation and thus save the collective from identifying the observed mentee as a cheater, but would bear the consequences incurred by his cheating apprentice. By effectively 'privatising' the uncertainty associated with cheater detection, risk-averse traders, in contrast, could rely on a comparatively cheater-free cooperative trader network. Furthermore, besides the increasing benefit of apprenticeship systems for 'more closed' societies, limiting monitoring opportunities (here represented by reduced trade interactions) contributed to (in our case consistently) better performance of the apprenticeship system, compared to the apprenticeship-free variant.

---

[12] Max. difference: $\sim$0.042; min. diff.: $\sim$0.025; σ: 0.0067. See [6] for the resulting graphs.

[13] The Geniza letters considered by Goldberg [13] cover the period from 990 until the early 13th century.

These results support the idea that, whether intentional or not, the Maghribian apprenticeship system could have been an important part of the overall informal institutional setup (beyond its obvious function to train newcomers) that allowed the Maghribis to operate compliantly over multiple centuries.

The model proposed here is by no means a complete or accurate model of the trader scenario, but extracts relevant aspects and concentrates on the extensive exploration of selected model properties. The approach taken is a prototypical example for the KIDS modelling approach [5], in which anecdotal or weak evidence is permissible to support a poor information base to reflect aspects that would otherwise not find consideration at all. However, this increases the demand for a systematic exploration of the model's parameter space (jāh differences, etc.) and testing of parameter settings which are based on uncertain information (here: number of agents).

Beyond the concrete historical case, the principle of apprenticeship relationships is commonly adopted in the area of skilled labour but likewise in knowledge-based occupations, such as scientific research. Following the analogy of the Maghribian apprenticeship, emerging researchers are continuously tested for their compliance to scientific standards (e.g. plagiarism as cheating), but also the quality of their work (e.g. significance), while giving them the opportunity to develop their own standing. The risk of failure lies in part with the grooming institution and the supervisor, while promising the benefit of furthering one's research and consequently academic jāh.

Other characteristics of the historical trader society are also compatible with contemporary findings from the area of social control. This includes the central role of norm communication in conjunction with material sanctioning as explored by Andrighetto et al. [3]. Giardini and Conte [8] provide an overview of the related research field and offer a set of examples from the area of ethnography that showcase gossip as a means of social control.

As alluded to earlier, a potential refinement is a more realistic development of reputation, as done in Alam et al.'s work [2]. They apply the concept of endorsements as an exogenous determinant of reputation, which we avoided in this set of experiments as it would have challenged the differentiation of cheater exclusion based on notification and loss of jāh. However, by including a refined representation of reputation, our approach would be more aligned with a systematic construction of network relationships by shifting from an initial random selection (as done here) to a trust-based partner selection (see e.g. [4,22]).

A further limitation concerns the assumption of perfect memory; in this model agents do not have a notion of 'forgetfulness' and retain all cheater information until their death.[14] Constraining the number of memory entries (as done in [7]) would reflect individuals' bounded rationality [21].[15]

Gaps in historical records restrict the establishment of a fully grounded model of the Maghribis' apprenticeship system as described by Goldberg [13]. However, we believe the model proposed here can foster the understanding of the function

---

[14] Note: This effectively represents intergenerational 'forgetfulness' on the social level.

[15] In this context we wish to thank the anonymous reviewers for their contribution.

of the specific institution 'apprenticeship system' in the Maghribi Traders Coalition, a phenomenon not addressed elsewhere as far as we are aware.

References

1. Ackerman-Lieberman, P.I.: The Business of Identity. Stanford University Press, Stanford (2014)
2. Alam, S.J., Geller, A., Meyer, R., Werth, B.: Modelling contextualized reasoning in complex societies with "endorsements". J. Artif. Soc. Soc. Simul. **13**(4), 6 (2010)
3. Andrighetto, G., Brandts, J., Conte, R., Sabater-Mir, J., Solaz, H., Villatoro, D.: Punish and voice: punishment enhances cooperation when combined with norm-signalling. PLOS ONE **8**(6), e64941 (2013)
4. Bravo, G., Squazzoni, F., Boero, R.: Trust and partner selection in social networks: an experimentally grounded model. Soc. Netw. **34**(4), 481–492 (2012)
5. Edmonds, B., Moss, S.: From KISS to KIDS – An 'Anti-simplistic' Modelling Approach. In: Davidsson, P., Logan, B., Takadama, K. (eds.) MABS 2004. LNCS (LNAI), vol. 3415, pp. 130–144. Springer, Heidelberg (2005)
6. Frantz, C.: Interactive versions of the apprenticeship model result plots. http://papers.christopherfrantz.org (2014). Accessed 6 July 2014
7. Frantz, C., Purvis, M.K., Nowostawski, M.: Agent-based modeling of information transmission in early historic trading. Soc. Sci. Comput. Rev. **32**(3), 393–416 (2014)
8. Giardini, F., Conte, R.: Gossip for social control in natural and artificial societies. Simulation **88**(1), 18–32 (2012)
9. Goitein, S.D.: A Mediterranean Society: The Jewish Communities of the Arab World as Portrayed in the Documents of the Cairo Geniza, 6 vols., University of California Press, Berkeley (1967–2000)
10. Goldberg, J.L.: On reading Goitein's A Mediterranean Society: a view from economic history. Mediterr. Hist. Rev. **26**(2), 171–186 (2011)
11. Goldberg, J.L.: Choosing and enforcing business relationships in the eleventh century mediterranean: reassessing the 'Maghribī Traders'. Past Present **216**(1), 3–40 (2012)
12. Goldberg, J.L.: The use and abuse of commercial letters from the Cairo Geniza. J. Medieval Hist. **38**(2), 127–154 (2012)
13. Goldberg, J.L.: Trade and Institutions in the Medieval Mediterranean: The Geniza Merchants and their Business World. Cambridge University Press, Cambridge (2012)
14. Greif, A.: Reputation and coalitions in medieval trade: evidence on the Maghribi traders. J. Econ. Hist. **49**(4), 857–882 (1989)
15. Greif, A.: Contract enforceability and economic institution in early trade: the Maghribi traders' coalition. Am. Econ. Rev. **83**(3), 525–548 (1993)
16. Greif, A.: Cultural beliefs and the organization of society: a historical and theoretical reflection on collectivist and individualist societies. J. Polit. Econ. **102**(5), 912–950 (1994)
17. Greif, A.: Institutions and the Path to the Modern Economy. Cambridge University Press, New York (2006)
18. Greif, A.: The Maghribi traders: a reappraisal? Econ. Hist. Rev. **65**(2), 445–469 (2012)
19. North, D.C.: Institutions. J. Econ. Perspect. **5**(1), 97–112 (1991)

20. Podolny, J.M.: Market uncertainty and the social character of economic exchange. Adm. Sci. Q. **39**(3), 458–483 (1994)
21. Simon, H.A.: A behavioral model of rational choice. Q. J. Econ. **69**, 99–118 (1955)
22. Skyrms, B., Pemantle, R.: A dynamic model of social network formation. Proc. Natl. Acad. Sci. U.S.A. **97**(16), 9340–9346 (2000)
23. Udovitch, A.: At the origin of the Western commanda: Muslim, Israel. Byzantium. Speculum **37**, 198–207 (1962)
24. Williamson, O.: The Economic Institutions of Capitalism. Free Press, New York (1975)

Spatial Modeling of Agent-Based Prediction Markets: Role of Individuals

Bin-Tzong Chie[1] and Shu-Heng Chen[2(✉)]

[1] Department of Industrial Economics, Tamkang University,
Tamshui, New Taipei City 251, Taiwan
chie@mail.tku.edu.tw
[2] Department of Economics, AIECON Research Center,
National Chengchi University, Taipei 116, Taiwan
chen.shuheng@gmail.com

Abstract. In this paper, we extend the spatial agent-based prediction market proposed by Yu and Chen at MABS 2011 into a spatial model in which agents choose their community (neighbors) by following Schelling's proximity model. This extended model generalizes the spatial configuration of the original model and enables us to examine the validity of the Hayek hypothesis when the information distribution is determined by clusters of agents with heterogeneous identities. Specifically, we examine the role of the toleration capacity, the key parameter in the Schelling model, which generates the clusters of agents with different sizes, and the role of exploration capacity which determines how well an agent is informed about his local surroundings. We find that after taking into account market activity and price volatility, both the toleration capacity and exploration capacity have a positive effect on the prediction accuracy and enhance information polling and the information aggregation of markets. The results obtained in this agent-based simulation, therefore, add a qualification to the well-known Hayek hypothesis and point to the significance of individuals in information aggregation.

1 Motivation and Introduction

How accurately the prediction market can predict, up to the present, is basically an empirical issue. However, empirical studies per se cannot articulate why sometimes the market for some events performed extremely well and sometimes it did not [2]. While there are a number of studies trying to identify the factors contributing to its successes or failures, the explanations supporting the found causal links remain very verbal and informal, and a rigorous mechanism has not been explicitly spelled out. This is partially due to the limited analytical tractability of the prediction markets which operate in practice. In this article, we argue that, the spatial configuration, i.e., the distribution of information over agents, situated in different places, can matter for the prediction accuracy of the prediction markets. However, since the usual analytical model cannot effectively deal with these geographical variables, an agent-based spatial model of prediction markets is proposed to address the geographical significance. To begin with

© Springer International Publishing Switzerland 2015
F. Grimaldo and E. Norling (Eds.): MABS 2014, LNAI 9002, pp. 197–212, 2015.
DOI: 10.1007/978-3-319-14627-0_14

this line of research, our model is tailored to the future events related to political elections only, normally known as the *political futures*. In other words, we shall show how geographical factors can be part of the functioning of the prediction accuracy of the political futures markets.

The rest of the paper is organized as follows. Section 2 introduces our proposed spatial agent-based prediction markets and the two essential ingredients in the model, namely, toleration capacity and exploration capacity. Section 3 discusses the design of our simulation and shows the simulation results. Section 4 gives the concluding remarks.

2   The Model

2.1   The Market

Network-Based Formation of Expectations and Reservation Prices. Our first step is to make the social network explicit (Sect. 2.2). Through the given social network, agents disseminate and acquire the information and form their expectations of the future election outcomes, upon which their decisions on bids and asks are based. We assume that, to form an expectation regarding the election outcome, all agents use the sample average as the estimate, and the sample available for each agent is identical to the set of all his connecting agents (to be defined later). In other words, by using the sample proportion of the connecting agents supporting each political candidate, the agent forms his expectations about the share of the vote of each candidate. This estimated share becomes the *reservation price* held by the agents. To make this point precise, let $\hat{p}_{i,j}$ be the subjective estimation of agent i regarding the share of the votes attributed to candidate j, and $b_{i,j}$ be the reservation price that agent i holds for the futures related to the vote share of candidate j. Then

$$b_{i,j} = \hat{p}_{i,j} = \frac{\#\{k : k \in N_i \cap V_j\}}{\#N_i}, \quad i = 1, 2, ..., N, \quad j = 1, ..., m, \qquad (1)$$

where N_i is the set of agent i's connecting agents (to be defined later), and V_j is the set of voters who support candidate j. By (1), if the estimated share of the votes of Candidate A is 60 %, then the reservation price of the future contract for the share of votes of Candidate A is 60 cents. With this reservation price, the agent would not accept any bids which are lower than 60 or any asks which are higher than 60.

Bidding and Asking Strategy. In fact, following most agent-based prediction markets [5,9], we assume that all agents are *zero-intelligent agents* (the entropy-maximizing agent) in the sense that the agent will bid or ask randomly with the constraint of making no expected loss [1,4]. Therefore, his bid $p_{b,i,j}$ will be uniformly sampled from the interval between the floor, which is zero cents, and the reservation price $b_{i,j}$, and his ask $p_{a,i,j}$ will be uniformly sampled from the

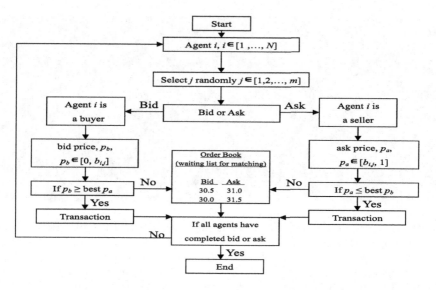

Fig. 1. The flowchart of the order-book driven prediction market

interval between his reservation price and the ceiling, which is one dollar, as shown in Eq. (2).

$$p_{b,i,j} \sim U[0, b_{i,j}], \quad p_{a,i,j} \sim U[b_{i,j}, 1], \quad i = 1, 2, ..., N, \quad j = 1, 2, ..., m. \quad (2)$$

Trading Mechanism. The trading mechanism adopted to run the market is continuous double-auction, the one frequently used in experimental economics to test the Hayek hypothesis [7]. As shown in Fig. 1, our agent-based prediction market starts from a random draw of the agents. Each agent shall be drawn exactly once; in other words, the draw proceeds in a sampling-without-replacement manner. When agent i is drawn, he will be randomly placed into one of the m markets and will be equally likely to be assigned either a buyer position or a seller position. He will then submit a bid if he is a buyer and submit an ask if he is a seller. His bid or ask will be placed in the order book. A match happens if either his bid ($p_{b,i,j}$) is greater than the remaining lowest ask (bestp_a) in the order book or his ask ($p_{a,i,j}$) is lower than the remaining highest bid (bestp_b). The transaction price will then be determined as bestp_a if the former applies or as bestp_b if the latter applies.

2.2 Geographical Distribution of Agents

The social networks considered in this paper are generated from the *Schelling segregation model* [6], in which the location of agents is determined by their *toleration capacity* for agents with different political identities. In other words, we replace the ethnic heterogeneity of agents in the original Schelling model with

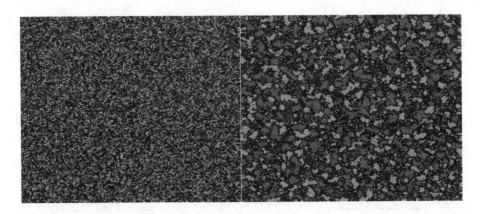

Fig. 2. Geographical distribution of voters and their political identity. Both panels are the converged configurations using $v_1 = 45.63\%$ (green), $v_2 = 51.60\%$ (blue), $v_3 = 2.77\%$ (orange), $N = 13,454$, and G (number of grids) $= 193 \times 193$. The black grids denote the unoccupied cells, and the colored grids denote the occupied cells. The number of occupied cells and the number of unoccupied cells are determined in such a way that the resultant population density is close to 36% (see Table 1). The two panels differ in terms of the toleration capacity: on the left, $s = 0.75$, and, on the right, $s = 0.25$. (Color figure online)

their *political identity* $(j = 1, 2, ..., m)$. Agents tend to reside in the place which is surrounded by neighbors with the same political identity. Their toleration of neighbors with different political identities is characterized by the parameter, *toleration capacity* (s). If the ratio of neighbors with different political identities is larger than this threshold s, they tend to move to a close place which their toleration capacity can handle. This migration process will be iterated until it converges to a fixed configuration. We then use the resultant configuration to represent the geographical distribution of residents with different political identities.

Apart from the toleration capacity, an additional parameter of Schelling's segregation model is the demographical structure characterized by the percentage of agents of various political identities. Denote them by v_j $(j = 1, 2, ..., m)$.

$$v_j = \frac{\#(V_j)}{N}, j = 1, 2, ..., m, \tag{3}$$

where N is the total number of agents.

Figure 2 demonstrates a geographical distribution of political identities. In this specific example, there are a total of 13,454 agents, distributed on a checkerboard with 193×193 grids, i.e., with a population density of 36.12%, and $m = 3$ (three candidates or three political parties): $v_1 = 45.63\%$, $v_2 = 51.60\%$, and $v_3 = 2.77\%$. Agents with the three political identities are denoted by the green

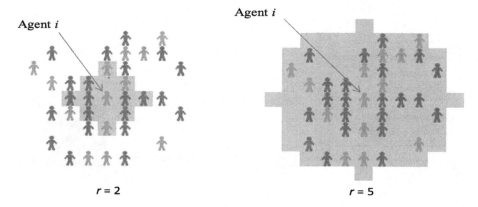

Fig. 3. The von Neumann Neighborhood with a radius of 2 (left) and 5 (right). The above figures show the von Neumann neighborhood of agent i, as pointed to by an arrow. The left panel is a neighborhood with a radius of 2, whereas the right panel is a neighborhood with a radius of 5. (Color figure online)

($j = 1$), blue ($j = 2$), and the orange color ($j = 3$), respectively.[1] What is demonstrated in Fig. 2 are, therefore, two of the converged configurations of agents who followed the Schelling rule of migration. The one on the left is the one corresponding to a toleration capacity of 0.75, and the one on the right is the one corresponding to a toleration capacity of 0.25.

2.3   Exploration Capacity

For each agent, his information supplier, i.e., his set of connecting agents, is determined by a von Neumann neighborhood with a given radius (r). This is shown in Fig. 3. As shown in Eq. (1), agents are assumed to know the political identities of all of their connecting agents in the neighborhood (agents in the gray area), and they use this sample (local information) to estimate the share of the votes for each candidate. The radius, r, can be interpreted as the information exploration capacity of the agent. The larger the radius the larger the sample, and hence the less biased and the better the estimation. In this article, we assume that agents are homogeneous with respect to this capacity but would like to examine how this parameter may affect the emergent market performance.

2.4   Programming with NetLogo

The above-mentioned spatial agent-based prediction market is programmed with NetLogo 5.0.3 and is available from the OpenABM website[2]. Figure 4 shows a familiar NetLogo display of running this program.

---

[1] These parameter values are based on the 2012 Presidential Election in Taiwan. Based on the 2012 Presidential election outcome, the DPP candidate (colored in green) won a share of 45.63 % of the vote, the KMT candidate (colored in blue) won a share of 51.60 %, and the PFP candidate (colored in orange) won a share of 2.77 %.

[2] http://www.openabm.org/model/3764/.

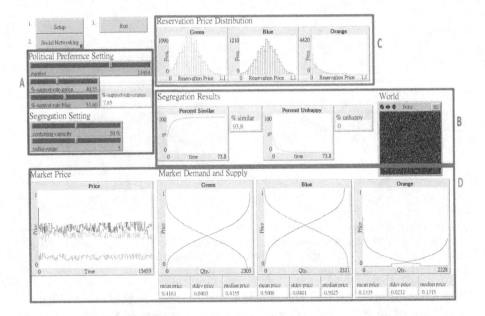

Fig. 4. Display of the NetLogo program (Color figure online).

In Fig. 4, the upper left panel (panel A) gives the user-supplied control parameters: $N = 13,454$, $v_1 = 40.55\%$ (green), $v_2 = 51.60\%$ (blue), $v_3 = 7.85\%$ (orange), $s = 0.50$ (50%) and $r = 5$. The diagram shown in the right middle panel (panel B) is the converged configuration using the Schelling rule with $s = 0.5$. With a radius of 5, we can have the price expectations (reservation prices) of all three futures for all agents, i.e., $b_{i,j}$ ($i = 1, ..., 13454$, and $j = 1, 2, 3$). What is shown in the right upper panel (panel C) of the figure are the three histograms of the reservation prices corresponding to the green, blue and orange party, respectively. The basic statistics, including the mean, the median and the standard deviation, are shown in the very bottom of the figure (panel D). There we can see that the mean and median for the green candidate are 0.4163 and 0.4155, which is a one-point upward bias away from the true value of 0.4055. In addition, for the blue candidate, these two statistics are 0.5008 and 0.5025, which is a one-point downward bias away from the true value of 0.5160. Maybe the worst case is the market for the orange candidate. The two corresponding statistics are 0.1335 and 0.1315, almost two times larger than the true value of 0.0785. Our research question is then, to what extent, this specific network topology may affect the accuracy of the prediction market or the political futures market in our case.

From the histogram, we can further derive the aggregate willingness to buy (when the price is below the reservation price)

$$Q_j^D(p) = \#\{i : b_{i,j} > p\}, \tag{4}$$

and the aggregate willingness to sell (when the price is above the reservation price)

$$Q_j^S(p) = \#\{i : b_{i,j} < p\} \tag{5}$$

i.e., the demand curve (Q_j^D) and the supply curve (Q_j^S).

The demand and supply curves of the three markets are shown in the lower middle and right panels (panel D). Then through the random draws of the agents and their reservation price, the order book for each market is formed, and the corresponding transaction price is generated as the time series shown in the lower left panel of the figure.

3 Simulation

3.1 Simulation Design

The main focus of this paper is to understand how the information aggregation can be affected by how it is distributed through the two control parameters, namely, toleration capacity (s) and exploration capacity (r). In fact, we believe that these two parameters, to some extent, characterize the quality of voters, their cultural backgrounds, sociability, and openness. None of these attributes has been mentioned in the original article of the Hayek hypothesis [3]. Presumably, they are all irrelevant or insignificant. This paper is purported to revisit this hypothesis from a cultural and social-psychological aspect.

Given this focus, most parameters should be held constant throughout the simulation, and include N, m, d, and G (Table 1). Nonetheless, to make the choice of these parameters not entirely arbitrary and to clothe them with some empirical flavor, we use the real data from Taiwan to suggest some reasonable values of these parameters. According to the 2010 demographic census data in Taiwan, the number of qualified voters in the 2012 presidential election was 13,453,305. By scaling down the number of people by 1,000 times, there are 13,454 agents. Hence, N is set to 13,454. In addition, by considering the population density of Taiwan, d is set to 36.12%, which implies that we need to have a grid size of 193×193.[3] Hence, G is also determined. As to the number of candidates, in the most recent Presidential election in Taiwan, held in the year 2012, there were three major political parties and hence three major candidates. Hence, m is set to 3. This finishes the description of constant parameters in Table 1.

The rest of the prediction market is characterized by four major parameters, s, r, v_1, and v_3. We first give a range for each of these parameters; each design can be regarded as a three-tuple randomly selected from this range. For s, we consider a range from a low toleration capacity (0.26) to a high toleration capacity (0.75), with an increment of 0.01. The exploration capacity (r), it starts with a minimum of 2, and ends with a maximum of 6. Finally, for v_i, considering the practice of Taiwan politics, we fix the share of the votes for the small party, i.e., 3%, and

---

[3] Taiwan's population density is around 630 people per square kilometer. If we only consider the number of qualified voters, and not the entire population size, then the population density is approximately 372 per square kilometer. By assuming that one square kilometer is roughly equal to 32×32 grids, we can then figure out the required d (36.12%) and the number of grids (193×193).

Table 1. Tableau of control parameters

Parameter	Description	Value
m	The number of candidates	3
s	Containing capacity	0.25, 0.26, ..., 0.75
r	Exploration capacity (Radius)	2, 3, ..., 6
v_1	Vote share of Green candidate	18, 19, ..., 47
v_2	Vote share of Blue candidate	100 - v_1 - 3
v_3	Vote share of Orange candidate	3
N	Number of agents	13,454
d	Population density	36.12 %
G	Grid size	193 × 193
R	Simulation runs	50

then allow the other two major parties to vary in opposite directions. Again, from an empirical consideration, the range of v_1 is set from 18 to 47, and then v_2 takes the rest. We then randomly generate 1,000 designs, and each design is run 50 times. To sum up, we have

$$Design_k \equiv \{s_k, r_k, v_{1,k}\}, k = 1, 2, ..., 1000, \tag{6}$$

where

$$s_k \sim U[0.26, 0.75], r_k \sim U[2, 3, 4, 5, 6], v_{1,k} \sim U[19, 47]. \tag{7}$$

The random design described above allows us to have enough observations to examine the effect of these two parameters on the emergent market performance.

3.2 Basic Results

Table 2 shows that the results for each design look like. Notice that we do not present all of them; otherwise, the table would be 1,000 rows long, since we have a total of 1,000 designs. Each row starts with parameters characterizing the design, namely, s, r, v_1, v_2, and v_3, followed by the key summary statistics of each design, including the mean price, trading volume, and volatility (standard deviation of the price) of each future. Since each design has been run 50 times, all these statistics are the averages taken over 50 runs. For the mean price, we first take the average of the price series for each run (Eq. 9), and take the average of the average over these 50 runs (Eq. 8).

$$\bar{p}_j = \frac{\sum_{l=1}^{50} \bar{p}_{j,l}}{50}, \quad j = 1, 2, 3, \quad l = 1, 2, ..., 50, \tag{8}$$

where

$$\bar{p}_{j,l} = \frac{\sum_{t_{j,l}=1}^{T_{j,l}} p_{j,l}(t_{j,l})}{T_{j,l}}, j = 1, 2, 3, \quad l = 1, 2, ..., 50, \tag{9}$$

Table 2. Simulation input and output table

s	r	v_1	v_2	v_3	$\bar{p}_1$	$\bar{p}_2$	$\bar{p}_3$	Vol_1	Vol_2	Vol_3	σ_1	σ_2	σ_3
0.26	2	34	63	3	30.66	66.38	2.95	736.0	762.0	111.9	0.1208	0.1289	0.0217
0.26	2	39	58	3	36.42	60.71	2.87	794.8	814.3	109.2	0.1336	0.1389	0.0204
0.26	2	41	56	3	38.97	58.19	2.84	806.5	832.9	109.9	0.1367	0.1426	0.0201
0.26	2	46	51	3	45.54	51.61	2.85	842.6	845.6	111.9	0.1423	0.1449	0.0196
.	.	.	.	.	.	.	.	.	.	.	.	.	.
.	.	.	.	.	.	.	.	.	.	.	.	.	.
.	.	.	.	.	.	.	.	.	.	.	.	.	.
0.75	6	42	55	3	41.25	51.88	6.87	236.2	238.4	147.3	0.0369	0.0428	0.0131
0.75	6	44	53	3	42.95	50.19	6.86	235.5	234.4	152.0	0.0378	0.0417	0.0134
0.75	6	45	52	3	43.70	49.43	6.87	232.3	238.4	150.2	0.0386	0.0416	0.0132

and $T_{j,l}$ are the transaction times of future j in the lth run.

These three figures, $\bar{p}_j$ ($j = 1, 2, 3$) are shown in the first three columns of the right panel of Table 2.[4] The next three columns, Vol_j ($j = 1, 2, 3$) are the average of the trading volume over the 50 runs, and likewise for the price volatility.

$$\sigma_j = \frac{\sum_{i=1}^{50} \sigma_{j,l}}{50}, \quad j = 1, 2, 3; \quad l = 1, 2, ..., 50, \tag{12}$$

where $\sigma_{j,l}$ is the standard deviation of the price of the jth future in the lth run. Table 2, therefore, provides us the basic input (the left panel) and output (the right panel) correspondence which allows us to address further the effect of the two key parameters, s and r, on the prediction accuracy.

Based on Table 2, we shall start with a simple linear regression.

$$Y = f(s, r) + \epsilon = \beta_0 + \beta_1 s + \beta_2 r + \epsilon. \tag{13}$$

The dependent variable Y is the prediction accuracy based on the chosen error functions. In this paper, we shall use $\bar{p}_j$ as the key predictor of v_j and consider the following four error measures frequently used in the literature.

---

[4] We assume that the non-arbitrage condition is always satisfied, i.e.,

$$\sum_{j=1}^{3} \bar{p}_{j,l} \times 100 = 100, \forall l \tag{10}$$

However, if the above equality is violated, then we shall rescale our mean price as follows,

$$\bar{p}_{j,l}^{adj} = \frac{\bar{p}_{j,l}}{\sum_{j=1}^{3} \bar{p}_{j,l}} \times 100, \tag{11}$$

and use the re-scaled price $\bar{p}_{j,l}^{adj}$ to replace $\bar{p}_{j,l}$ in Eq. (8).

1. Mean Absolute Percentage Error (MAPE)

$$Y_1 = MAPE = \frac{\sum_{j=1}^{m} |\bar{p}_j - v_j| /v_j}{m} \tag{14}$$

2. Root Mean Square Error (RMSE):

$$Y_2 = RMSE = \sqrt{\frac{\sum_{j=1}^{m} (\bar{p}_j - v_i)^2}{m}} \tag{15}$$

3. Mean Square Error (MSE)

$$Y_3 = MSE = \frac{\sum_{j=1}^{m} (\bar{p}_j - v_j)^2}{m} \tag{16}$$

4. Euclidian Distance (ED)

$$Y_4 = ED = \sqrt{\sum_{j=1}^{m} (\bar{p}_j - v_j)^2} \tag{17}$$

The results of the prediction errors over these four error measures are provided in Table 3. Again, this is a simplified modification by only showing the first few and the last few rows. A complete table has 1,000 rows. This table then serves as the basis for running the linear regression (13).

The first regression result is shown in Table 4 (the upper panel). There we find that both s and r have a negative effect on the prediction accuracy, i.e., $\beta_1 > 0$ and $\beta_2 > 0$, and the result is consistent regardless of the measure being employed. This result is somewhat counter intuitive, since one might initially have thought that increasing either the toleration capacity (s) or the exploration capacity (r) can make individual agents more informative, which in turn may help the information aggregation in the later stage. Nevertheless, this is not the case which we have here, but why? One possible explanation is that when both s and r become larger, depending on the v_j, agents are not just better informed, but also more homogeneous in their expectations and reservation prices, which may cause transactions more difficult to happen and make the market less liquid. One such famous example is Tirole's zero-trading theorem [8], i.e., in an extreme case where agents are all perfectly informed, there will be no trade in the market; in other words, the market can predict nothing at all in this situation.

3.3 Homogeneity Effect

To see this homogeneity effect, Fig. 5 shows the average trading volume under different vote shares with respect to these two capacities. Three features immediately stand out.

First, there are hump-shaped curves in each sub-diagram with respect to a given exploration capacity (the left panel) or with respect to a given toleration

Table 3. Prediction accuracy

s	r	v_1	v_2	v_3	MAPE	RMSE	MSE	ED
0.26	2	34	63	3	0.0558	2.7434	7.5260	4.7516
0.26	2	39	58	3	0.0522	2.1605	4.6678	3.7421
0.26	2	41	56	3	0.0472	1.7278	2.9853	2.9926
0.26	2	46	51	3	0.0238	0.4468	0.1996	0.7739
.	.	.	.	.	.	.	.	.
.	.	.	.	.	.	.	.	.
.	.	.	.	.	.	.	.	.
0.75	6	42	55	3	0.4544	2.9006	8.4134	5.0239
0.75	6	44	53	3	0.4551	2.8261	7.9870	4.8950
0.75	6	45	52	3	0.4557	2.7824	7.7415	4.8192

capacity (the right panel) indicating that the trading volume increases when competition between the major political parties is keen, i.e., the share of the vote of the two major candidates is close.

Second, however, the hump-shaped curve has a tendency to shift down with the *increase* in each of the two capacities. Since the higher the capacities, the more homogeneous is the information received by the agent, the pattern of the shifting-down hump-shared curves indicates that the trading volume goes down with the degree of homogeneity.

Third, the curvature of the hump-shaped curve also decreases with the incr-ease in the toleration capacity (the left panel) or the increase in the exploration capacity (the right panel). For example, when these capacities are higher, such as up to 70 % (for s) or up to 6 (for r), the hump is flattened out. This indicates that the effect of the uncertainty, measured by the closeness of the two major candidates in their share of the vote, no longer affects the trading volume when voters are homogeneously well-informed. This is not surprising: when voters are homogeneously well-informed, market uncertainty perceived by voters is reduced and hence even a neck-to-neck competition has little effect on the trading volume. To sum up, our analysis above shows that, in addition to the vote share or market uncertainty, the two capacities also affect the trading volume, and they affect it in a downward direction.

The same analysis is further carried out for the price volatility. Figure 6 shows the effect of the two capacities on the average price volatility (Eq. 12). Qualitatively speaking, the result is the same. All three features with regard to the effect of the two capacities remain for the case of the price volatilities. The trading volume (the thickness of the market) with the price volatility is the indicator of a functioning market where information is aggregated and revealed. However, when the degree of homogeneity of traders is high, these functions are adversely affected.

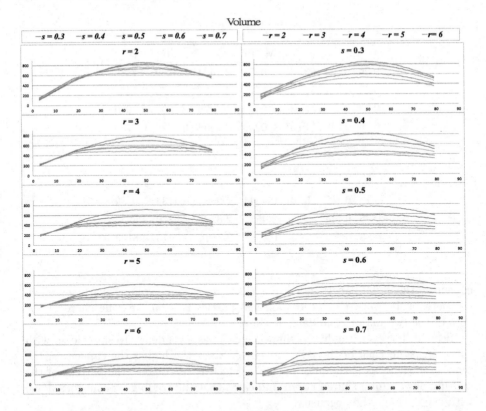

Fig. 5. Trading volume, exploration capacity, and toleration capacity. The five sub-diagrams in the left panel are drawn in the way by fixing the exploration capacity (r) and examining the effect of the toleration capacity (s) on the trading volume. To see the difference, different values of s are colored differently. The five sub-diagams in the right panel are drawn in the way by fixing the toleration capacity (s) and then examining the effect of the exploration capacity on the trading volume. Again, to see the difference, different values of r are colored differently.

3.4   Conditional Regression

Given the homogeneity effect, it would be desirable to control some market characteristics while running the regression against s and r. Therefore, we propose a second linear regression which takes into account the market characteristics. Two usual market characteristics considered in the literature are the trading volume (Vol) and the price volatility (σ). Following this convention, we propose the second linear regression (18).

$$Y = \beta_0 + \beta_1 s + \beta_2 r + \sum_{i=3}^{5} \beta_i Vol_{i-2} + \sum_{i=6}^{8} \beta_i \sigma_{i-5} + \epsilon, \tag{18}$$

where Vol_i ($i = 1, 2, 3$) is the trading volume of the ith futures, and σ_i ($i = 1, 2, 3$) is the price volatility of the corresponding futures.

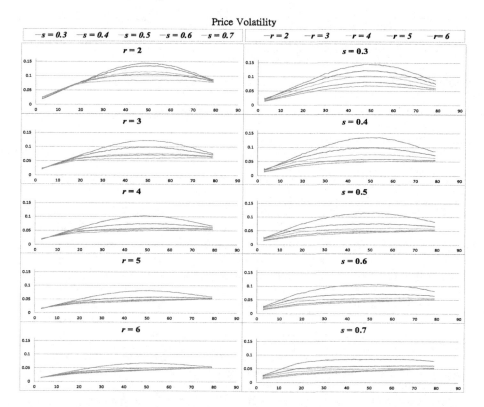

Fig. 6. Price volatility, exploration capacity, and toleration capacity. The five sub-diagrams in the left panel are drawn in the way by fixing the exploration capacity (r) and examining the effect of the toleration capacity (s) on the price volatility. To see the difference, different values of s are colored differently. The five sub-diagrams in the right panel are drawn in the way by fixing the toleration capacity (s) and then examining the effect of the exploration capacity on the price volatility. Again, to see the difference, different values of r are colored differently.

Since, as we have seen in Sect. 3.3, the trading volume and the price volatility have already been "polluted" by the two capacities (Figs. 5 and 6), in economet-rics, this is what is familiarly known as an *endogeneity problem*. To take care of the endogeneity problem, what we do here is then, first, to run the two auxiliary regressions, one on the trading volume and one on the price volatility, against the two capacities, then, second, to take the residuals as the "cleaned" (filtered) trading volume and volatility. We then use them as independent variables in the market performance regression (18).

The regression results of regression (18) are shown in the lower panel of Table 4. The results show that the inclusion of the market characteristics can improve the coefficient of determination (R^2). This result is not difficult to under-stand. Given the geographical complexity and variability of the two-dimensional lattice, controlling both s and r does not automatically imply the control of the

Table 4. Regression results with market characteristics

Regression results without market characteristics

	β_0	β_1	β_2							$\bar{R}^2$
MAPE	−0.034	0.0032	0.073							0.4
	0.0776	0.0000	0.0000							
RMSE	0.2987	0.0312	0.4177							0.27
	0.0826	0.0000	0.0000							
MSE	−7.086	0.2525	2.2298							0.21
	0.0000	0.0000	0.0000							
ED	0.5174	0.054	0.7235							0.27
	0.0826	0.0000	0.0000							

Regression results with market characteristics

	β_0	β_1	β_2	β_3	β_4	β_5	β_6	β_7	β_8	$\bar{R}^2$
MAPE	2.668	−0.013	−0.171	0.001	−0.002	0.003	−3.066	4.566	7.222	0.98
	0.000	0.000	0.000	0.000	0.000	0.000	0.000	0.000	0.000	
RMSE	17.724	−0.078	−1.304	0.035	−0.040	0.012	−171.418	179.218	88.613	0.81
	0.000	0.000	0.000	0.000	0.000	0.000	0.000	0.000	0.000	
MSE	114.085	−0.526	−10.081	0.309	−0.351	0.061	−1473.720	1649.300	790.791	0.78
	0.000	0.000	0.000	0.000	0.000	0.000	0.000	0.000	0.000	
ED	30.700	−0.136	−2.259	0.061	−0.069	0.021	−296.905	310.415	153.482	0.81
	0.000	0.000	0.000	0.000	0.000	0.000	0.000	0.000	0.000	

The two panels above show the regression results of regression Eqs. (13) and (18), respectively. The former does not include the market characteristics as the independent variables, whereas the latter does. The two regressions were run using different dependent variables (performance criteria). The first column gives the dependent variable used in the respective regression. The results for each regression and each dependent variable are given in the following columns in two rows. The first row gives the estimate of the corresponding coefficient ($\hat{\beta}_i$), and the second row gives the p-value of the respective estimate. The adjusted coefficient of determination, $\bar{R}^2$, is given in the last column.

geographical and other resultant specifications on which the market performance also depends. It has already been shown in regression (13) that s and r can only have limited explanatory power. For most performance criteria, $\bar{R}^2$ is not even up to 30 % (see Table 4, the upper panel). Therefore, once after incorporating these specificities through other variables, such as the trading volume and the price volatility, a large proportion of the unexplained behavior has now been incorporated (see the significant increase in $\bar{R}^2$ from the lower panel of the same table). We find that after controlling the market characteristics the two capacities can indeed help enhance prediction accuracy. After incorporating the trading volume and the price volatility, β_1 and β_2 are both negative for all four accuracy criteria. In other words, conditional on the same trading volume and the price volatility, the higher the toleration capacity or the higher the exploration capacity, the better that the prediction market can predict.

4   Concluding Remarks

In this article, we address the issue of whether the better informed agent can help prediction markets in a spatial context. The better informed agents are characterized by their larger toleration capacity (sociability) and exploration capacity. The result is that under unconditional regression neither of them shows this enhancement, whereas, after controlling some market characteristics, the conditional regression shows their significance. Hence, in this sense, our paper shows that the quality of individuals does have a positive effect on information aggregation and on the formation of the wisdom of crowds.

The work can be extended in several directions. First, the network used here is a spatial network. In this digital age, given the significance of social groups in social media, it would be desirable to include a social network as part of the framework, and to study the effect of social network topologies. Second, the behavioral setting of the traders is very simple, i.e., the device of zero intelligence. It would be interesting to consider other behavioral settings involving cognition or learning, such as reinforcement learning or rule-based models. These extensions allow traders to base their decisions upon the information revealed in the order book. Third, the prediction market can be designed with other trading mechanisms, such as the call auction. It would be interesting to know whether these different trading mechanisms matter.

Acknowledgments. The authors are grateful to the two anonymous referee reports for their quite careful review of the papers. The paper has been revised by following many of the suggestions made in their painstakingly written reports. The remaining errors are, of course, solely the authors' responsibilities. The NSC grant NSC 101-2410-H-004-010-MY2 is also gratefully acknowledged.

References

1. Chen, S.-H.: Varieties of agents in agent-based computational economics: a historical and an interdisciplinary perspective. J. Econ. Dyn. Control **36**(1), 1–25 (2012)
2. Chen, S.-H., Tung, C.-Y., Tai, C.-C., Chie, B.-T., Chou, T.-C., Wang, S.-G.: Prediction markets: a study on the Taiwan experience. In: Williams, L. (ed.) Prediction Markets: Theory and Applications, pp. 137–156. Routledge, London (2011). (Chapter 11)
3. Hayek, F.: The uses of knowledge in society. Am. Econ. Rev. **35**(4), 519–530 (1945)
4. Gode, D., Sunder, S.: Allocative efficiency of markets with zero intelligence traders: market as a partial substitute for individual rationality. J. Polit. Econ. **101**, 119–137 (1993)
5. Othman, A.: Zero-intelligence agents in prediction markets. In: Padgham, L., Parkes, D., Muller, J., Parsons, S. (eds.) Proceedings of 7th International Conference on Autonomous Agents and Multiagent Systems (AAMAS 2008), 12–16 May 2008, Estoril, Portugal, pp. 879–886 (2008)
6. Schelling, T.: Dynamic models of segregation. J. Math. Sociol. **1**, 143–186 (1971)
7. Smith, V.: Markets as economizers of information: experimental examination of the "Hayek Hypothesis". Econ. Inq. **20**(2), 165–179 (1982)

8. Tirole, J.: On the possibility of trade under rational expectations. Econometrica **50**, 1163–1182 (1982)
9. Yu, T., Chen, S.-H.: Agent-based model of the political election prediction market. In: Sabater, J., Sichman, J., Villatoror, D. (eds.) Proceedings of Twelfth International Workshop on Multi-agent-based Simulation, Taipei, Taiwan, 2 May 2011, pp. 117–128 (2011)

Agent Based Exploration of Urban Economic Dynamics Under the Rent-Gap Hypotheses

Stefano Picascia[1]($^{(\boxtimes)}$), Bruce Edmonds[1], and Alison Heppenstall[2]

[1] Centre for Policy Modelling, MMU, All Saints Campus, Manchester M15 6BH, UK
{stefano,bruce}@cfpm.org
[2] School of Geography, University of Leeds, Leeds LS2 9JT, UK
a.j.heppenstall@leeds.ac.uk

Abstract. We present a stylised agent-based model of housing investment based on the rent gap theory proposed by the late Neil Smith. We couple Smith's supply-side approach to investment, with individual-level residential mobility within a city. The model explores the impact of varying levels of capital flowing in the city and reproduces certain theorised and observed dynamics emerging from the cyclic nature of investment: the tendency of capital to spatially concentrate generating intra-urban inequalities, the occasional formation of persistent pockets of disinvestment and phenomena such as gentrification.

1 Introduction

The model presented in this paper is an attempt at approaching urban dynamics integrating structural, supra-individual factors that are sometimes overlooked by modellers in favour of a purely bottom-up vision of cities and their evolution. The tools of complexity science have proven particularly well suited to explore urban dynamics as bottom-up phenomena, as seminal research from Schelling [16] onwards [2], testifies. However the focus on bottom-up generative modelling, centred on individual or household-level agents as the main actors, which is prevalent in most models of residential mobility [11], has the risk of underestimating the broader economic processes that impact the urban form and constrain individual behaviour. A traditional line of research in human geography that has seen recent revival [9,19] sees the socio-spatial phenomena that shape contemporary cities - suburban sprawl, income segregation, gentrification - as consequences of the varying influx of capital towards urban systems, as opposed to strictly originating from individual-based residential choices. In this work we encode one of the most prominent structuralist theories of housing investment, the rent-gap theory, and couple it with considerations about residential location and cultural transmission, to balance top-down and bottom-up dynamics. The purpose is to build a simple abstract model that integrates the two visions and is capable of reproducing some of the urban dynamics that shape our cities and highlight the structural factors that may be contributing to their emergence.

© Springer International Publishing Switzerland 2015
F. Grimaldo and E. Norling (Eds.): MABS 2014, LNAI 9002, pp. 213–227, 2015.
DOI: 10.1007/978-3-319-14627-0_15

The model represents a city composed of three layers: (a) the city's infrastructure; (b) human agents that move through it, interact and influence each other; (c) economic forces that impact on both components, in the form of capital seeking to profit from housing renovation. The model was conceived and designed to investigate two aspects of the relationship between the three components: (1) the economic and spatial dynamics emerging from the interaction between investment/disinvestment cycles and residential mobility patterns; (2) the impact of such dynamics on the city's cultural fabric - specifically the conditions of emergence and dissolution of pockets of culturally peculiar areas within a city. Due to space constraints this paper will focus only on the first issue, referring to a future article for an extensive joint treatment of the two aspects.

In the next section we briefly discuss the rent-gap hypothesis of housing investment, which informs the economic layer of the model, in Sect. 3 we describe our model of housing investment/residential mobility and cultural exchange. Section 4 presents the outcomes of the model: we will discuss the emerging effects of the spatial distribution of investments and analyse the phenomenon of inner cities decline and subsequent gentrification (Sect. 4.1).

2   The "Rent-Gap Theory" and Its Computational Implementations

The theoretical framework that inspires our representation of the economic forces operating in the city is the *rent-gap theory* (RGT): a supply-side approach to housing investment proposed by the late Neil Smith [18], specifically for the study of the phenomenon of gentrification. In Smith's terms the rent-gap is

> the difference between the actual economic return from the rights to use the land that is captured given the present land use and the maximum economic return that can be captured if the land is put to its highest and best use

The gap between *actual* and *potential* economic return is due to progressive decline in maintenance which properties undergo, together with changes in technologies which render dwellings obsolete. Restoration or rebuilding increases the economic return that a portion of land or a dwelling generates, bringing it to the maximum possible. The locations with the highest difference between *actual* and *potential* economic return will be the ones more likely to attract investment capital and be put to "highest and best use". According to Smith this simple principle explains the sudden inflow of capital towards neglected inner city areas, and the subsequent change of socio-economic composition experienced by such areas, a phenomenon witnessed by US cities since the late 1970s. Although the rent gap theory was proposed to explain a specific phenomenon, gentrification, in our view it can serve as a good conceptualisation of general housing investment behaviour, suitable for a broad exploration and not incompatible with other approaches, including standard economic theory, as pointed out in [4]. A lengthy dispute on the validity of the rent-gap approach took place in the '90s [5]. The critics pointed out that the notion of "potential economic return under the best use" is a shading concept, difficult to quantify, and therefore the prediction capabilities of the theory are hampered. Such criticism is far from unjustified, as we will show in Sect. 4.1. Nonetheless, the rent-gap theory proved particularly appealing for computational modelling, where the problem of identifying the *highest and best use* has been addressed by employing the notion of *neighbourhood effect*. Here, the highest possible revenue achievable by a given property after redevelopment is bounded by the average (or maximum, in some implementations) price charged in the vicinity of the redeveloped property, so that, irrespective of the state of the property, the maximum obtainable rent or sale price is practically determined by the overall state of the neighbourhood. This intuition embeds the principle that the state of the surroundings strongly affects a property and builds into the model the *"location! location! location!"* mantra that is familiar to property investors. Such interpretation was proposed by [13] in his abstract, pure cellular automation model of gentrification - the very first computational model to implement a variant of the RGT. Subsequent work [7,8] concentrated on the supply side of an abstract housing market implementing the RGT with a finer-grained set of agents (property units, owner-occupiers, landlords, tenants and developers) and investment capital modelled as an exogenous factor. The authors tested different levels of capital and observed variations in the average price of properties and the share of under maintained properties in the city. This model is to date the most complete implementation of the mechanics of the RGT, although it lacks any consideration of the demand-side of the housing market.

3   The Model

The model proposed here implements an entire city, with multiple pre-defined districts. Such an implementation allows exploration of the spatial dynamics emerging from capital circulation at a more fine-grained level and to implement some demand-side dynamics, such as district-level cultural allure. The entities represented in the model are: (a) individual locations (residential properties), defined by their value and repair state; (b) individual agents that represent households, characterised by an income, mobility propensity and cultural configuration; (c) economic forces, represented in the form of exogenous "capital" level, aiming at profiting from redevelopment/restoration of residential locations. Each of the three aspects is described in detail in the following subsections.

3.1   City Structure and Economic Dynamics

We represent a city as a 21×21 square grid of 441 residential locations (Fig. 1a) characterised by a value V and a maintenance level, or repair state, r, grouped in 9 districts (Fig. 1b). r is initially set at random in the 0–1 range and V is set at $V = r + 0.15$. Dwellings progressively decay in their condition by a factor $d = 0.0012$ assuming that, if unmaintained, a location goes from 1 to 0 (becomes inhabitable) in 70 years (1 simulation step = 1 month). In order to match the

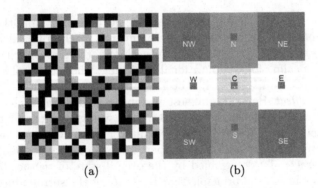

(a)   (b)

Fig. 1. The city is composed of 441 residential locations, each with a maintenance level and an economic value, divided in nine neighbourhoods. The colour shade of locations represents maintenance state from white (best condition) to black (worst). Depicted in (a) is the typical model initialization with random values assigned. The nine neighbourhoods (C, N, NW, NE, E, W, S, SE, SW) have a local centre (b). The district boundaries are "soft", they do not constrain the agents' behaviour. Only when an *allure* emerges (see Sect. 3.2) is a district represented as a recognisable entity in the agents' residential decision process (Color figure online).

theoretical assumption of a decline in property price over time, we set the value of the dwelling as decreasing by a depreciation factor of 0.02/year. We also assume that in case of prolonged emptiness of the dwelling (>6 steps) both decay and depreciation factors are increased by 20 %.

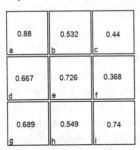

Fig. 2. Example of price gap formation. The numbers represent locations' value

The model represents investment in housing renovation/redevelopment as the fundamental economic force operating in the city. This is implemented by the "Capital" parameter, K, which represents the maximum number of locations that can be redeveloped in the current economic climate, expressed as a fraction of the total number of residential locations of the city, similarly to the approach proposed in [7]. A value of $K = 0.02$, as an example, would mean that every 12 steps $441 * 0.02 = 8$ locations are invested upon and redeveloped in the city. A high level of K represents a large inflow of investment in the housing market which results in more locations being redeveloped and gaining value. The selection of the locations where the investment lands is carried out deterministically, based on the value-gap of a location with the neighbouring properties, in accordance with the RGT discussed in Sect. 2. The relevant value gaps are determined in two ways, both in accordance with the *neighbourhood effect*, the principle that the amount of rent or the sale value attainable by a given location is always bounded by the characteristics and the desirability of the area where the property is located. We either set the new value nV of a redeveloped property p at the neighbourhood average, plus 15 % (representing a premium for a newly restored property) as in Eq. 1, or at the neighbourhood maximum (Eq. 2). As an example, the price-gap for location e in Fig. 2, is 0 if Eq. 1 is used $(1.15*[(0.88+0.532+0.44+0.667+0.368+0.74+0.549+0.689)/8] < 0.726)$, and 0.154 ($0.88 - 0.726 = 0.154$) if computed with Eq. 2 (assuming that we are considering the Moore neighbourhood - the eight locations surrounding the central location e - instead of the whole district for comparison). Therefore, the method based on local maximum will generate a higher number of locations with a positive price-gap, that based on the average will have less, generating, as we will see, more concentration. We choose to test two alternative, but equally plausible, methods because they give rise to somewhat different outcomes, as shown in Sect. 4.1. In order to model the possible varieties of neighbourhood effect, we also consider a vicinity to be either the Moore neighbourhood of a location or the entire district that the location falls in, *whichever is bearing the highest values* and therefore grants the highest return for an investment.

$$nV_p = 1.15 * max\,(avg(V_{moore}), avg(V_{district})) \tag{1}$$

$$nV_p = max\,(max(V_{moore}), max(V_{district})) \tag{2}$$

The value gap for location p will be $G_p = nV_p - (V_p + C)$, or 0 if $G_p < 0$. Here C is the cost of removing the present resident if the location is occupied. Once a location is selected for investment its value is set at nV_p and its repair state is set at $r = 0.95$. Table 1 summarises the variables associated with location.

Table 1. Location variables

Name	Type/range	Description
r	Float, {0,1}	Maintenance state
V	Float, {0,1}	Value
G	Float, {0,1}	Value-gap: difference with neighbourhood value
d	Integer	Distance from the centre of town
te	Integer	Time empty
o	Boolean	Occupied?

3.2   Agent Model: Cultural Exchange and Residential Mobility

Agents in the model represent individuals or households. They are endowed with an income level, i a mobility propensity m and a numeric string that represents their cultural configuration (Table 2). The agent's income level is set at random, normalised to the interval {0,1} and represents the highest price that the agent is able to pay for the right of residing in a property. The model,

Table 2. Agent variables

Name	Type/range	Description
m	Float, {0,1}	Mobility propensity
c	List t=10,v=4	Culture: memetic code
i	Float, {0,1}	Income level
d	Float, {0,1}	Cognitive dissonance level
th	Integer	Time here: steps spent in the current location

ultimately, implements a pure rental market. The agent's culture is modelled as a n-dimensional multi-value string of *traits*, inspired by Robert Axelrod's classic agent-based model of cultural interaction described in [1] and originally applied to the urban context in [3]. The string represents an individual's "memetic code", or "cultural code": an array of t cultural traits, each of which can assume v variations, giving rise to v^t possible individual combinations. In our model each trait is susceptible to change under the influence of other agents. Cultural influence is localised: agents that have been neighbours for more than 6 consecutive steps are likely to interact and exchange traits, thus rendering the respective cultural strings more similar. At the same time a cultural "cognitive dissonance" effect is at work, implementing a concept proposed by [14,15] under the label of *spatial cognitive dissonance*: this is, roughly, the frustration of being surrounded by too many culturally distant agents. Similarity between two agents is the proportion of traits they share:

$$sim_{ab} = \frac{\sum_{i=1}^{t} xor(index(i, agent_a),\ index(i, agent_b))}{t} \qquad (3)$$

Agents who spend more than six months surrounded by neighbours with few common traits ($sim < 0.3$) increase their mobility propensity each subsequent time step. The mobility propensity attribute represents the probability that an agent will abandon the currently occupied location in the subsequent time step. This parameter is set at a low level in the beginning of the simulation, drawn from a Poisson distribution centred at $m = 0.0016$, meaning that, on average, agents have a 2% chance of moving each year. Mobility propensity is affected by the conditions of the currently occupied dwelling and the aforementioned cognitive dissonance level. One agent's m is increased as follows: $m_{t+1} = 1.5m_t$ in the following circumstances:

- After 6 months in a dwelling with $r < 0.15$ (excessive time is spent in a dwelling in excessively bad condition)
- the cultural dissonance level exceeds a threshold for a period of 6 continuous steps.

A special circumstance is when the price of the dwelling currently occupied exceeds the agent's income. In such case the agent is automatically put in "*seek new place*" mode. This represents an excessive rent increase, unsustainable by the agent. The process of finding a new location is bounded by the agent's income: a new dwelling has to be affordable ($V \leq i$), in relatively good condition, and as close as possible to the centre of the district which contains it. The selection process is represented in Fig. 3. If no affordable and free location is to be found, the agent is forced to leave the city. As Fig. 3 shows, in certain cases the residential choice process of an agent includes the cultural configuration of the district as a factor. A special district-level variable called *allure* is set when the degree of cultural uniformity within a district exceeds a threshold, thus making the area recognisable for some of the features of its inhabitants. We measure cultural uniformity, u, as the average distance between the x agents residing in a certain neighbourhood.

$$pairs = \frac{x(x-1)}{2}$$

$$u = \frac{\sum_{i=1}^{x} \sum_{j=1}^{x-1} sim(agent_i, agent_j)}{t * pairs}$$

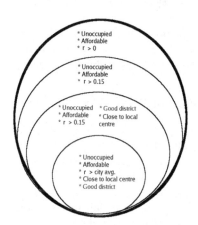

Fig. 3. The residential choice process. A dwelling has to be affordable, free and habitable ($r > 0$) for an agent to consider moving into it. If these requirements are met, other characteristics are considered. If any district has developed an allure, agents who are relocating consider whether it suits them, based on a homophily preference. When no dwelling meets the out most requirements the agent leaves the city.

The allure of a district is represented as a string of cultural features, similar to that of individuals, where each element of the string is the most common value for that trait in the district population. A district's allure is therefore an emergent feature of the model, which may or may not appear. This reflects the fact that not every neighbourhood has a special connotation visible to agents, but only those with a recognisable population do. The allure attribute can be thought of as the *reputation* of a neighbourhood in the eyes of agents. The attribute is sticky, after its emergence it is updated seldom and doesn't necessarily reflect the current composition of a district, representing the fact that reputation is a nearly permanent feature, difficult to eradicate or to replace [6], a characteristic that applies to places' as well as humans' reputation. Once a district's allure has emerged, agents include it in their residential decision under a homophily constraint: the agent will seek to move to a district with an allure similar to her culture string (Table 3).

4   Results and Discussion

We run the model for 1200 steps, representing a 100 years timespan, with the assumption of a constant value of K during the whole simulation time. We leave a systematic exploration of the parameter space to a later paper, here we focus our discussion on the parameter adjustments that

Table 3. District-level variables

Name	Type/range	Description
u	float,$\{0,1\}$	Cultural uniformity
a	list	Allure (cultural makeup)

produce some observed urban dynamics. In the next paragraph we will focus on the spatial distribution of investments that different levels of K and the two systems of computing the rent-gap give rise to, then we will show how the spatial dynamics of capital valorization can determine the familiar phenomena of inner city decay and gentrification. In this model, as in the real world, capital has a dual role: a sufficient amount of capital is needed to ensure that a good proportion of properties in the city is maintained and habitable, but the nomadic nature of capital, which travels across the city in pursuit of the highest profit, generates shocks - in the form of abrupt spikes in prices and cycles of under-maintenance - which affect the ability of (especially least well off, who have limited choice) agents to stay in, or move to, the spot of choice. From this duality arise, ultimately, all the dynamics that we see occurring in the model.

4.1   Uneven Development: Spatial Dynamics of Capital and Pockets of Disinvestment

The first noteworthy dynamic produced by the model has to do with the distribution of the redeveloped locations in the city throughout the simulation. All simulation runs start with a random distribution of prices and maintenance conditions across the city: the situation at $t = 0$ is similar to that represented in Fig. 1. We observe that, regardless of the price-gap computation mechanism, the model shows a tendency of capital to first concentrate spatially, and subsequently moving "in bulk" across the city, in pursuit of the widest gaps between actual and potential prices. The level of capital determines the speed and the scope of the process, that can involve only certain areas or the entire city. Figures 4, 5 and 6 represent the spatial evolution of maintenance conditions and the corresponding price dynamics for different levels of capital and for the two gap-setting mechanisms that we considered. As Fig. 4 shows, after an initial period during which the locations attracting investment are scattered throughout the city, strong clustering emerges, visible as wide white areas representing areas of high maintenance and high price. This happens because the locations receiving investment increase their value and, when a large enough number of locations is increasing value in a small area, the rent-gaps of neighbouring locations widen, making them more likely to attract further investment themselves, thus generating a feedback loop. However, as capital is limited, if investments

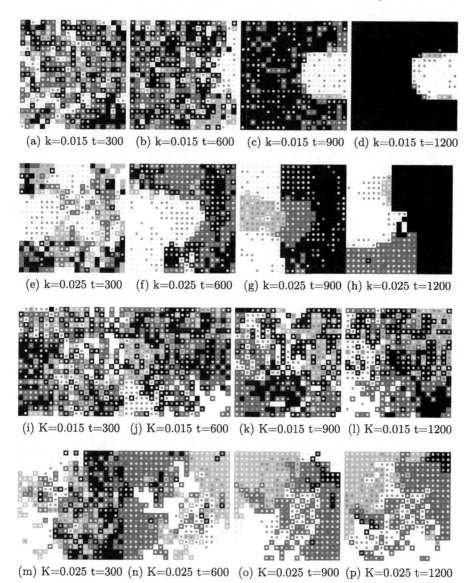

Fig. 4. Evolution of maintenance condition for different levels of K and price-gap setting mechanism. (a–h) is based on average, (i–p) on maximum local prices. The circles represent agents, colour represents income in 4 shades: dark green, light green, dark violet, light violet in decreasing order (Color figure online).

start to concentrate in an area, inevitably other areas experience neglect, and a phase of decline starts elsewhere in the city. The decline ends when the price-gaps become "competitive" again, which happens mostly when all the gaps are closed in the previously "successful" area, and provided that enough capital is available. If so, investment moves away to settle in another area, generating the typical development cycles shown in Figs. 5 and 6, matching Neil Smith's assertion that "urban development in capitalist economies tends to involve a cyclical process of investment, disinvestment and reinvestment". The overall effect is that

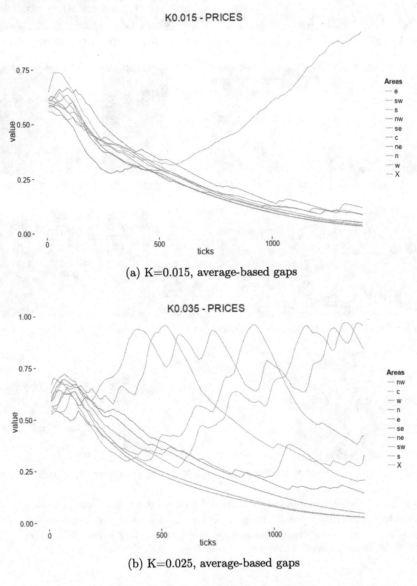

(a) K=0.015, average-based gaps

(b) K=0.025, average-based gaps

Fig. 5. Price dynamics by district for different levels of capital under average based gap-setting mechanism. The tendency towards concentration and the cyclic trend of investment, disinvestment and reinvestment are evident. In the case of average-based gap setting, higher levels of capital correspond to more districts being involved in the cycles.

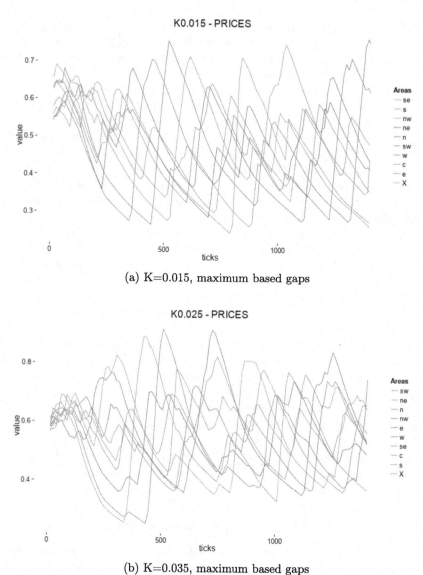

(a) K=0.015, maximum based gaps

(b) K=0.035, maximum based gaps

Fig. 6. Price dynamics by district for different levels of capital under maximum based gap-setting mechanism. When using maximum-based gaps, all the districts participate in the economic cycles even at lower levels of capital. Here higher capital corresponds to wider oscillations and higher prices

of white areas "moving" across the city from neighbourhoods with narrow price gaps to those with wider price gaps. The dynamics produced by the model are a powerful intra-urban depiction of what David Harvey calls the *spatial fix*, or "the need of capital to try and displace systemic pressures onto other geographical areas" [10]: when investment becomes unprofitable in an area, because the existing rent gaps do not grant enough yield any more, capital has to move to a new area. This mechanism is ultimately the source of unevenness in the development of different areas in the same city.

Utilising the neighbourhood maximum, instead of average, in the gaps-setting mechanism (i.e. using Eq. 2 in Sect. 3.1) generates a more fluid movement of capital that flows in the whole city even at low levels (Fig. 6), while the average has a constricting effect, due to the lower number of location developing a price gap, that concentrates the gaps - and therefore the profitable locations - in a limited area. In this case, for low level of capital only a limited set of districts are able to generate price-gaps wide enough to attract investment, and few districts participate in the economic cycles, while some others fall in permanent disrepair.

The fact that the model produces substantially different outcomes when using local maximum or local average as the price-gap setting mechanism - a difference not so fundamental, after all - seems to support the criticism that the RGT is too vaguely defined. It is also true that a clear-cut distinction between mean and maximum based price gaps is largely arbitrary. The two mechanisms could be at work at the same time in different areas of a city, for example responding to different demand levels: in popular, desirable areas an investor could charge the maximum local price for a restored property, whereas in areas of lower demand only the average could be successfully achieved. On the other hand, the model seems to disprove the argument of one of the fiercest critics of the rent-gap theory, Steven Bourassa. He pointed out that the existence of neighbourhoods which seem to never experience disinvestment contradicts the theory of the cyclical process of investment [4]. However the model shows that, in certain cases, a district can constantly achieve the highest rent-gaps within itself, and thus receive constant investment at the expense of the rest of the city, as is the case shown in Fig. 5a. Also, for higher levels of capital, the emerging cyclical process of investment generates oscillations of different magnitude in different areas, so that some areas never reach a substantial level of disinvestment.

4.2   Decay and Gentrification of the Inner City Core

One of the dynamics that have affected many cities in the Anglo-Saxon world for most of the 20th century is the slow decay of the inner core to the advantage of a sprawling and wealthy periphery. The "doughnut" cities have most of the wealth concentrated in the suburbs and an inner core in disrepair and populated by a low income, often predominantly immigrant, population. This tendency seems to have been reversed in the last decades, with the rapid gentrification of inner city areas. Most explanations of this phenomenon focus on the change of the social composition of cities and a consequent change of preferences in the younger population that now favours "city living" [12]. Another explanation sees this movement as supply, rather then demand, driven. It's the position that Neil Smith advanced in his 1979 paper, titled in the most self-explanatory fashion, "gentrification: a back to the city movement by capital, not people" [17]. Figure 7c illustrates the emergence of this dynamic in the model: in this instance

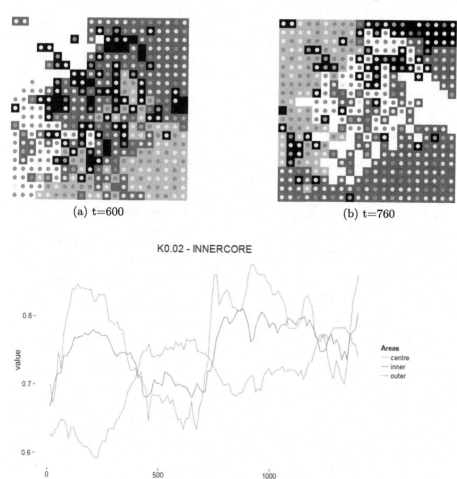

(a) t=600   (b) t=760

(c) Income levels of residents of the central, semicentral and peripheral areas

Fig. 7. Decay and gentrification of the inner city (K = 0.02, max-based price gaps). In (a) the "doughnut" is formed and visible: the centre of the city is in bad repair state and populated by middle-low income agents. In (b) capital *moves back to the city* centre. The decline of incomes in the central area is steady for the first 500 ticks (red line in (c)), with the corresponding rise of wealthy agents in the periphery. The process of gentrification lasts less than 100 ticks, then a new cycle starts (Color figure online).

agents have a preference towards living near the core of the city, nonetheless the trajectories of capital make the best housing available at the periphery of the city for a substantial amount of time, and therefore the wealthy agents concentrate in the suburbs. When investing in the centre becomes profitable again, the reverse movement materializes and the inner city gentrifies. While the historic emergence of the doughnut effect took place in a phase of urban expansion, not implemented in this model which only considers a fixed urban area with immutable boundaries, the model suggests that a cyclical "doughnut effect" can emerge purely as a consequence of capital movements, without having to rely on demand-side explanations.

5   Conclusion and Future Work

The model presented here falls squarely in the near end of the continuum between abstract/pedagogic and realistic models. The main aim has been to implement in code the assumptions of a particular socioeconomic theory, the RGT, and employ the model to clarify and visualise certain mechanics that geographers had described in theory.

In related ongoing work we look at further implications of the original theory: some non immediately obvious consequences of capital circulation, i.e. those that affect the cultural look and feel of a city. The idea upon which this work is conceived is that the city is the product of agents of different nature and the stress on bottom-up emergence of phenomena should not over-represent the role of individuals and households. A good model of urban dynamics should include agents of different magnitude and account for the mutation of the micro-level *scenario*, or context, that often derives from processes unfolding independently, at the macro-level. The model shown here also serves as a basis for the development of a more realistic model, currently in the works: one that integrates a wider set of agents, the entire geography of an actual city as well as the income distribution of its residents and the maintenance state of its dwellings. The aim will be to test and validate theoretical predictions against actual data and, possibly, to highlight new implications and extend the theory.

References

1. Axelrod, R.: The dissemination of culture: a model with local convergence and global polarization. J. Conflict Resolut. **41**(2), 203–226 (1997)
2. Batty, M.: Cities and Complexity: Understanding Cities with Cellular Automata, Agent-Based Models, and Fractals. The MIT Press, Cambridge (2007)
3. Benenson, I.: Multi-agent simulations of residential dynamics in the city. Comput. Environ. Urban Syst. **22**(1), 25–42 (1998)
4. Bourassa, S.: The rent gap debunked. Urban Stud. **30**(10), 1731–1744 (1993)
5. Bourassa, S., Badcock, B.: On "An Australian view of the rent gap hypothesis" by Badcock. Ann. Assoc. Am. Geogr. **80**(3), 458–461 (1990). CR - Copyright & #169; Association of September 1990
6. Conte, R., Paolucci, M.: Reputation in Artificial Societies Social Beliefs for Social Order. Kluwer Academic Pub, Boston (2002)
7. Diappi, L., Bolchi, P.: Gentrification waves in the inner-city of Milan - a multi agent/cellular automata model based on Smith's rent gap theory. In: Van Leeuwen, J.P., Timmermans, H.J.P. (eds.) Innovations in Design & Decision Support Systems in Architecture and Urban Planning, pp. 187–201. Springer, Dordrecht (2006)

8. Diappi, L., Bolchi, P.: Smith's rent gap theory and local real estate dynamics: a multi-agent model. Comput. Environ. Urban Syst. **32**(1), 6–18 (2008)

9. Harvey, D.: Rebel Cities: From the Right to the City to the Urban Revolution. Verso Books, New York (2012)

10. Harvey, D.: Globalization and the spatial fix. Geogr. Rev. **2**, 23–30 (2001)

11. Huang, Q., Parker, D.C., Filatova, T., Sun, S.: A review of urban residential choice models using agent-based modeling. Environ. Plann. B Plann. Des. **40**, 1–29 (2014)

12. Ley, D.: The New Middle Class and the Remaking of the Central City. Oxford University Press, Oxford (1996)

13. O'Sullivan, D.: Toward micro-scale spatial modeling of gentrification. J. Geogr. Syst. **4**(3), 251–274 (2002)

14. Portugali, J.: Toward a cognitive approach to urban dynamics. Environ. Plann. B Plann. Des. **31**(4), 589–613 (2004)

15. Portugali, J.: Revisiting cognitive dissonance and memes-derived urban simulation models. In: Portugali, J. (ed.) Complexity, Cognition and the City. Understanding Complex Systems, pp. 315–334. Springer, Heidelberg (2011)

16. Schelling, T.C.: Dynamic models of segregation. J. Math. Sociol. **1**(2), 143–186 (1971)

17. Smith, N.: Toward a theory of gentrification a back to the city movement by capital, not people. J. Am. Plann. Assoc. **45**(4), 538–548 (1979)

18. Smith, N.: Gentrification and the rent gap. Ann. Assoc. Am. Geogr. **77**(3), 462–465 (1987)

19. Smith, N.: The New Urban Frontier: Gentrification and the Revanchist City. Routledge, London (1996)

Emergent Collective Behaviors in a Multi-agent Reinforcement Learning Pedestrian Simulation: A Case Study

Francisco Martinez-Gil[1]([⊠]), Miguel Lozano[1], and Fernando Fernández[2]

[1] Departament d'Informàtica, Universitat de València, Av. de la Universidad S/n,
46100 Burjassot, Valencia, Spain
{Francisco.Martinez-Gil,Miguel.Lozano}@uv.es
[2] Department of Computer Science, Universidad Carlos III, Av. de la Universidad 30,
28911 Leganés, Madrid, Spain
ffernand@inf.uc3m.es

Abstract. In this work, a Multi-agent Reinforcement Learning framework is used to generate simulations of virtual pedestrians groups. The aim is to study the influence of two different learning approaches in the quality of generated simulations. The case of study consists on the simulation of the crossing of two groups of embodied virtual agents inside a narrow corridor. This scenario is a classic experiment inside the pedestrian modeling area, because a collective behavior, specifically the lanes formation, emerges with real pedestrians. The paper studies the influence of different learning algorithms, function approximation approaches, and knowledge transfer mechanisms on performance of learned pedestrian behaviors. Specifically, two different RL-based schemas are analyzed. The first one, Iterative Vector Quantization with Q-Learning (ITVQQL), improves iteratively a state-space generalizer based on vector quantization. The second scheme, named TS, uses tile coding as the generalization method with the Sarsa(λ) algorithm. Knowledge transfer approach is based on the use of Probabilistic Policy Reuse to incorporate previously acquired knowledge in current learning processes; additionally, value function transfer is also used in the ITVQQL schema to transfer the value function between consecutive iterations. Results demonstrate empirically that our RL framework generates individual behaviors capable of emerging the expected collective behavior as occurred in real pedestrians. This collective behavior appears independently of the learning algorithm and the generalization method used, but depends extremely on whether knowledge transfer was applied or not. In addition, the use of transfer techniques has a remarkable influence in the final performance (measured in number of times that the task was solved) of the learned behaviors.

Keywords: Pedestrians simulation · Transfer learning · Policy Reuse · Vector Quantization · Tile coding

© Springer International Publishing Switzerland 2015
F. Grimaldo and E. Norling (Eds.): MABS 2014, LNAI 9002, pp. 228–238, 2015.
DOI: 10.1007/978-3-319-14627-0_16

1   Introduction

The use of Reinforcement Learning (RL) techniques in graphics, animation and simulation tools is gathering increasing attention. Its use has mainly focused on selecting adequate frames from a collection of pre-computed movements or poses to generate interactive animations [1] or to create video textures [2]. The novelty of our framework consists on using RL to control directly the characters of a simulation. Thus, the embodied agents learn to navigate inside a virtual environment to simulate pedestrians groups. Different areas, such as architecture, civil engineering and game development, can benefit from simulation of pedestrians groups, in order to check the capacities of facilities in a building, to prevent accidents, or to give realism in urban scenarios. In our framework [3], each embodied agent learns autonomously to control its velocity to reach a goal.

It is said that an emergent phenomena have occurred in a collective when it can not be explained by the extrapolation of individual behaviors or properties of the members [4]. In the macroscopic world, emergent phenomena can be found in complex systems where autonomous individuals interact with each other such as in crowd simulation or in collective movements of animals. In these cases, new organization can emerge on a global scale derived from interactions on a local scale [5]. In real human pedestrians, several collective behaviors have been described to appear in specific group situations such as lane formations in corridors [6,7] or roundabout traffic at intersections [8]. This characteristic makes pedestrian simulations specially difficult. In pedestrian modeling and simulation, the capability to reproduce collective behaviors is an indicator of the quality of the model. Several pedestrians models have been successful in emerging collective pedestrian behaviors such as the social forces model and its variants [9], agent-based models [10] and animal-based approaches [11]. Therefore, it is important to know whether the use of different configurations in the RL framework is critic for generating these collective behaviors. This work has the following motivations:

1. To demonstrate empirically that collective behaviors emerge with different configurations of learning processes, specifically with different RL algorithms.
2. To study the influence of state space generalization methods and transfer knowledge techniques in the performance of learned pedestrian behaviors.

We will use a well-known pedestrian simulation scenario. The narrow-corridor scenario is a problem of pedestrian dynamics where two groups of pedestrians inside a narrow corridor have to cross in order to reach to the opposite side. This scenario is specially suitable to study the emergence of collective behaviors, specifically the lanes formation [6].

2   The Multi-agent RL Framework

RL uses optimization techniques to learn from a reward signal a sequential decision-based controller. In RL, problems are modeled as Markov Decision Processes (MDP) [12]. The goal is to find an optimal *policy* $\pi^* : S \rightarrow A$, that is, a mapping between states and actions, that provides the maximum discounted expected reward in each state of the space state. The discounted expected reward is defined in Eq. 1 where γ parameter sets the influence of future rewards and r_t is the immediate reward in time t and it can take a value between 0 and 1.

$$V(s) = E\{\sum_{t=0}^{\infty} \gamma^t r_t\} \tag{1}$$

Different families of RL algorithms solve this optimization problem. In our framework, we will use two Temporal Difference (TD) algorithms: Sarsa(λ) [13] and Q-learning [14] which are two well-known algorithms that have been used in this domain previously giving good results [3,15]. Both algorithms calculate an optimal *value function* $Q^* : S \times A \to \Re$ that represents the value of taking action a in state s. Each reward obtained after carrying out an action is used to update function Q. The update equation characterizes the learning algorithm. At step $t + 1$, when a tuple of experience $(s_t, a_t, r_{t+1}, s_{t+1})$ has been collected, the update equation for Q-learning algorithm is:

$$Q_{t+1}(s_t, a_t) = Q_t(s_t, a_t) + \alpha[r_{t+1} + \gamma \max_{a'} Q_t(s_{t+1}, a') - Q_t(s_t, a_t)] \tag{2}$$

where α is the learning rate. On the other hand, Sarsa(λ) algorithm uses the same policy that is being learned π to select action a' in the update rule:

$$Q_{t+1}(s_t, a_t) = Q_t(s_t, a_t) + \alpha[r_{t+1} + \gamma Q_t(s_{t+1}, \pi(s_{t+1})) - Q_t(s_t, a_t)] \tag{3}$$

Sarsa(λ) algorithm uses the immediate reward at step $t+1$ to update not only state-action pair (s_t, a_t) but also other past state-action pairs $(s_{t-1}, a_{t-1}), (s_{t-2}, a_{t-2}) \cdots$ The weighted update is defined by parameter λ which can take a value between 0 and 1.

In the learning process, the agent has to balance the selection of actions to explore new regions of the policies space and the selection of actions to get better rewards. The balance between exploration and exploitation is a characteristic of the problem domain and is critic to find a good solution policy. In this work we use a ϵ-greedy policy with a soft-exponential decay from an initial rate of exploration defined by the parameter ϵ. One RL process per agent is carried out simultaneously and independently so that each agent perceives the rest of the agents as a part of the environment.

The virtual 3D environment consists on a narrow corridor of 15 m long and 2 m wide (see the Fig. 1). Inside, two groups of embodied agents are initially placed at the ends of the corridor. The goal of each agent is to reach the opposite end of the corridor. The agents are represented by a cube surrounded by a circle with radius 0.3 m that represents the collision bounding area. The framework uses Open Dynamics Engine (ODE) calibrated with values of real pedestrians [15] to simulate interactions at the physical level. ODE module models the collisions, taking into account friction forces between agents and between agents and the floor.

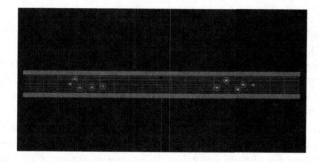

Fig. 1. The virtual scenario. Agents are represented as squares surrounded by a circle. The triangles represent the goals.

The state for each agent is described by the features shown in the table of Fig. 2 (left). The agent's sensorization is displayed in this figure at right. The chosen features have been used previously in pedestrian models and they are considered relevant for the kinematic description of the pedestrian [16]. The agent's actions modify its velocity vector. This variations have also been used to control the trajectories in pedestrian models [17]. In an agent's decision, actions are taken in pairs, which modify speed (increasing or reducing) and orientation of the velocity vector (clockwise or counterclockwise). There are eight different ratios plus the 'no operation' option for both speed and orientation, resulting in 81 possible combined actions. The maximum number of actions per episode allowed (steps) is 70. When the agents have learned the task they use about 30 actions per episode.

Sag	Speed of agent.
Av	Angle of the velocity vector relative to the reference line.
$Dgoal$	Distance to the goal.
$Srel_i$	Relative scalar velocity of i-th nearest neighbor.
Dag_i	Distance to i-th nearest neighbor.
Aag_i	Angle of position of i-th nearest neighbor relative to the reference line.
Dob_j	Distance to the j-th nearest static object (walls).
Aob_j	Angle of the position of j-th nearest static object relative to the reference line.

S = Sag, Av, Dgoal, Srel1, Dag1,...

Fig. 2. Left: List of the state space features. Right: Agent's reference system for the sensing. The reference line joins the agent with its goal.

In real-valued state spaces, the use of a generalization method is necessary. We compared two methods in our scenario: Vector Quantization (VQ) [18] and tile coding [13].

VQ is an aggregation method that uses a finite set of vectors (named codewords) as a code book to describe the state space. A metric maps each real state with the nearest vector of the code book (in our case, the euclidean distance is used because of the geometric nature of the features of the state space). The codewords are calculated using Generalized Lloyd Algorithm clustering method (GLA)[19]. Data for clustering are gathered from sensings of the agents inside virtual environment and each agent builds its own quantizer. Code book is used as the entry of a tabular value function where the value of each entry in terms of accumulated reward is calculated through the agent's interaction with the environment. The number of codewords has been empirically selected to 8192. VQ has been demonstrated to be an accurate method for state space generalization and transfer learning in other RL problems [20].

Tile coding is a specific case of linear function approximation with binary, sparse features. The value function for each state-action pair is represented as a lineal combination of the parameters as:

$$V_t(s) = \sum_{i=1}^{n} \theta_t(i)\phi_s(i) \tag{4}$$

Where the $\phi_s(i)$ features have binary values. Whatever the number of dimensions of the space is, it is divided in partitions named tilings. Each element of a specific tiling is a tile and there is only one active tile per tiling; therefore the total number of active binary features is always the same that the number of tilings. This value was determined empirically to 64 in this domain. Each tiling covers all the space and two neighbor points in the space activate similar sequences of tiles. Although the number of tiles should be exponential with the number of dimensions, in practice a hash function maps tiles into a finite memory structure. This technique works because learned policies use only a small region of the total space state.

3   Learning Schemas

Two different basic schemas that combine a type of space generalization method with a TD algorithm have been designed:

1. Iterative Vector Quantization with Q-Learning (ITVQQL). VQ generalization method is combined with Q-learning algorithm in an iterative schema that carries out several learning processes over the same task. The learned value function V_i (learned in the learning process l_i that uses the code book VQ_i) is used to collect policy-biased sensorization data to calculate a new VQ_{i+1} that represents the state space more accurately than VQ_i. Then, a new learning process l_{i+1} is carried out using VQ_{i+1} for learning a new value

function V_{i+1}. Additionally, two knowledge transfer methods are used in this schema:

(a) First, the learned value function of iteration l_i is transferred to initialize the new value function of iteration l_{i+1}. The values of this value function are loaded with values of the most similar codeword entry of the old value function. The similarity between codewords of different VQs is given by euclidean distance. This transfer can be considered a simple case of transfer of an inter-task value function between different representations of the state space, named *complexification* in [21]. This transfer is not a mere initialization because VQ code books of two consecutive iterations are different.

(b) Second, we have used Probabilistic Policy Reuse (PPR) [22] to incorporate domain knowledge. In PPR, a policy (π_0) is used as a bias in the exploration-exploitation trade-off. Specifically, policy π_0 is used with a probability ψ that decays exponentially in the number of episodes while an ϵ-greedy exploratory policy is used with probability $1 - \psi$. In our problem, policy π_0 always suggests the use of an action that drives the agent towards one side of the corridor[1]. It is important to note that PPR is used as a way of exploring efficiently the space of policies to find a solution. If the agent does not find useful to follow policy π_0 in a state, it will learn a better policy because the exploratory policy is active along all the learning process. The probability function for the selection of different policies is displayed in Eq. 5.

$$\begin{cases} \psi & \text{choose the } \pi_0 \text{ policy} \\ (1 - \psi)\epsilon & \text{choose an aleatory action} \\ (1 - \psi)(1 - \epsilon) & \text{choose the greedy policy} \end{cases} \tag{5}$$

2. Tile coding with Sarsa(λ) (TS). In this approach, each agent carries out a single learning process using tile coding and Sarsa(λ) algorithm. The parameters of tile coding cannot be adjusted easily using the knowledge acquired by previous learned policies. Therefore, the iterative process carried out in the first approach is not justified here. Besides, a complexification process is not possible in this schema because of the use of a linear function approximator to represent the value function. However, the PPR transfer method described above is also applied in this case.

4   Experiments and Results

Six case studies have been designed combining two basic schemas (ITVQQL and TS) with the transfer methods in order to determine the influence of each transfer method separately. Table 1 shows the characteristics of each one with its corresponding label.

---

[1] Specifically, the policy π_0 choose randomly from the set of actions that turns the agent's velocity vector towards the right side of the corridor.

Table 1. The case studies considered in this work with their characteristics.

Schema	Cases	Algorithm	Generaliz. method	Transfer value func.	PPR
ITVQQL	IT-ALL	Q-Learning	VQ	Yes	Yes
	IT-NOPR	Q-Learning	VQ	Yes	No
	IT-NOVF	Q-Learning	VQ	No	Yes
	IT-NOTHING	Q-Learning	VQ	No	No
TS	TS-ALL	Sarsa(λ)	Tile coding	No	Yes
	TS-NOTHING	Sarsa(λ)	Tile coding	No	No

Figure 3 shows the performance (mean percentage of times that an agent reach its goal independently of the rest of agents) obtained at the end of each learning process. At the first iteration, the IT-NOVF curve has a similar value to the IT-ALL curve because in that iteration both experiments have the same configuration (there is no value transfer). A similar situation occurs with the IT-NOPR and IT-NOTHING curves. The gap between the IT-NOPR curve and the curves that use PPR, indicates that the bias provided by the policy π_0 through PPR is very useful for the learning process. Observing all the iterations, the IT-ALL curve attains the highest values. This iterative schema converges in the third iteration. For the IT-NOPR curve, the iterative schema is useful from iteration 1 to 7. This fact shows that the transfer of the value function needs more iterations when used alone than when used in combination with PPR. The low values obtained with IT-NOTHING respect those observed in the rest

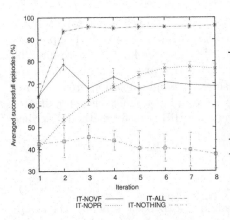

Number of agents	8
α	From 0.3 to 0.15
γ	0.9
Initial value of ϵ	1.0
Iterations	8
Episodes per iteration	50000
Reward Goal reached	100
Number of codewords	8192

Fig. 3. Left: Averaged performance for the ITVQQL schema. Performance is measured as the number of times that an agent reach its goal independently of the rest of agents. Each point is the average performance of all the agents at the end of each iteration of the learning process. Means are over the 8 agents. Right: The common configuration for the case studies derived of the ITVQQL schema.

of cases reveals the benefits of using transfer techniques. In the IT-NOTHING experiment, the iterative schema is not useful, possibly because the learning process is not long enough to generate better VQs between consecutive iterations.

In Fig. 4, the results of the TS approach are reported. Two curves that represent data collected from a single learning process, using PPR (TS-ALL) or not (TS-NOTHING) are represented. The initial gap between both curves is typical in a knowledge transfer process. In the TS-ALL curve, the beneficial effect of PPR is clear throughout the process with higher performance with respect to the TS-NOTHING case.

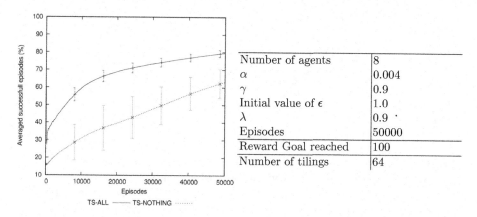

Number of agents	8
α	0.004
γ	0.9
Initial value of ϵ	1.0
λ	0.9 ·
Episodes	50000
Reward Goal reached	100
Number of tilings	64

Fig. 4. Left: Averaged performance for TS schema. Each curve is the average performance of all agents throughout a single learning process. Means are over the 8 agents. Right: Common configuration for the case studies derived of TS schema. The performance has the same meaning of Fig. 3.

The analysis of the simulation performance is displayed in Table 2. Now the performance measures the percentage of correct simulations, that is, the simulations in which all the agents reach the corresponding goal. The results for the IT-ALL and TS-ALL cases show that the performance is similar for the two schemas when using knowledge transfer. On the contrary, when no transfer techniques are used, the performance of TS-NOTHING is significantly higher than IT-NOTHING. These results indicate that the TS schema is more efficient, in terms of learning capabilities, than ITVQQL in this problem.

The IT-NOPR and TS-NOTHING cases, that do not use PPR, have lower performance with respect to IT-ALL and TS-ALL cases (30 and 68 *vs.* 81 and 80). The percentages are relevant enough to indicate that the emergent collective phenomena depends on whether the additional information is provided by the PPR transfer method. From this data, we can also conclude that the influence of the use of PPR is higher in the ITVQQL schema than in the TS approach.

The low value for IT-NOVF with respect to the other cases that include transfer of value function (IT-ALL and IT-NOPR) indicates that the use of this kind of knowledge transfer has a strong influence in the performance of the ITVQQL schema. For the IT-NOTHING case, a value performance of 0 is obtained. This reveals that the crossing problem is not solved correctly, and in simulation, lane formation can not be clearly observed.

Table 2. Analysis of performance in simulation. Mean of the percentage of episodes that end successfully from a series of 100 episodes. In a successful episode, all agents reach the corresponding goal. The mean of ten series is displayed.

Schema	Label	Performance in simulation
ITVQQL	IT-ALL	81 ± 4
	IT-NOPR	30 ± 4
	IT-NOVF	8 ± 2
	IT-NOTHING	0
TS	TS-ALL	80 ± 3
	TS-NOTHING	68 ± 4

Four moments of a simulation for the IT-ALL case are showed in Fig. 5. The emergent lane formation is visualized. The agents are placed at random positions at both ends of the corridor (one group in each end) at the beginning of the simulation. Note that the agents have learned to anticipate to the crossing forming lanes before reaching the center of the corridor (image B). The TS approach shows similar lane pattern generation. Videos for both approaches can be seen in the URL http://www.uv.es/agentes/RL, selecting the crossing experiments.

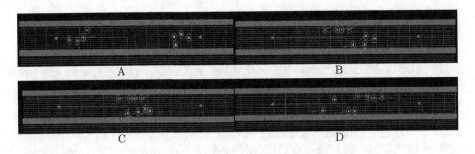

Fig. 5. Stills of four steps of a simulation with the IT-ALL case of study. Time follows the alphabetic sequence.

The final 3D simulation, that is also similar with both approaches, is showed in Fig. 6. In this sequence, data from the TS-ALL case have been used.

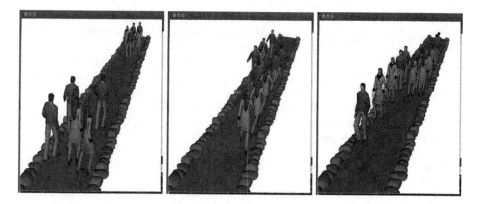

Fig. 6. Stills of three moments of a simulation with virtual pedestrians using data from the TS-ALL case of study. The agents are initially placed in random positions on thesides of the corridor.

5 Conclusions and Future Work

From the results of the experiments we can derive the following conclusions:

- Lane formation is an emergent collective behavior that appears independently of the learning/generalization approach used. However, it requires a learning bias in the exploration process, which is provided through the PPR method.
- The ITVQQL and TS schemas show similar performance results in simulation when the knowledge transfer techniques are active. However, the ITVQQL schema is computationally more expensive than TS because it has to carry out several learning processes (iterations).
- The use of knowledge transfer techniques improves the performance of both schemas. Specifically, the transfer of value function technique is important in the TRVQQL schema. However, TS is more efficient than ITVQQL when knowledge transfer techniques are not used in this problem domain.

The emergence of collective behaviors independently of the learning algorithm and generalization method suggest that our framework is robust, in term of its configuration, to address pedestrian simulation problems. A future work will be carried out in this direction, comparing the performance of different learning configurations in other pedestrian scenarios where collective behaviors should emerge.

Acknowledgments. This work has been supported by University of Valencia under project UV-INV-PRECOMP13-115032.

References

1. Treuille, A., Lee, Y., Popović, Z.: Near-optimal character animation with continuous control. ACM Trans. Graph. **26**(3), 7:1–7:7 (2007). (SIGGRAPH 2007)

2. Schödl, A., Essa, I.: Machine learning for video-based rendering. In: Leen, T.K., Dietterich, T.G., Tresp, V. (eds.) Advances in Neural Information Processing Systems, pp. 1002–1008. MIT Press, Cambridge (2000)
3. Martinez-Gil, F., Lozano, M., Fernández, F.: Multi-agent reinforcement learning for simulating pedestrian navigation. In: Vrancx, P., Knudson, M., Grześ, M. (eds.) ALA 2011. LNCS, vol. 7113, pp. 54–69. Springer, Heidelberg (2012)
4. Anderson, P.: More is different. Science 177, 393 (1972)
5. Charlotte, K.: Self-organization and Evolution of Social Systems. Cambridge University Press, Cambridge (2005)
6. Helbing, D., Buzna, L., Johansson, A., Werner, T.: Self-organized pedestrian crowd dynamics: experiments, simulations, and design solutions. Transp. Sci. 39(1), 1–24 (2005)
7. Moussaïd, M., Guillot, E.G., Moreau, M., Fehrenbach, J., Chabiron, O., Lemercier, S., Pettré, J., Appert-Roland, C., Degond, P., Theraulaz, G.: Traffic instabilities in self-organized pedestrian crowds. PLoS Comput. Biol. 8(3), e1002442 (2012)
8. Helbing, D., Molnár, P., Farkas, I., Bolay, K.: Self-organizing pedestrian movement. Environ. Plann. Part B Plann. Des. 28, 361–383 (2001)
9. Helbing, D., Molnár, P.: Social force model for pedestrian dynamics. Phys. Rev. E 51, 4282–4286 (1995)
10. O'Sullivan, D., Haklay, M.: Agent-based models and individualism: is the world agent-based? Environ. Plann. A 32, 1409–1425 (2000)
11. Shiwakoti, N., Sarvi, M., Rose, G., Burd, M.: Animal dynamics based approach for modeling pedestrian crowd egress under panic conditions. Transp. Res. Part B Methodol. 45(9), 1433–1449 (2011)
12. Kaelbling, L.P., Littman, M.L., Moore, A.W.: Reinforcement learning: a survey. J. Artif. Intell. Res. 4, 237–285 (1996)
13. Sutton, R.S., Barto, A.G.: Reinforcement Learning: An Introduction. MIT Press, Cambridge (1998)
14. Watkins, C., Dayan, P.: Q-learning. Mach. Learn. 8, 279–292 (1992)
15. Martinez-Gil, F., Lozano, M., Fernández, F.: Calibrating a motion model based on reinforcement learning for pedestrian simulation. In: Kallmann, M., Bekris, K. (eds.) MIG 2012. LNCS, vol. 7660, pp. 302–313. Springer, Heidelberg (2012)
16. Robin, T., Antonioni, G., Bierlaire, M., Cruz, J.: Specification, estimation and validation of a pedestrian walking behavior model. Transp. Res. 43, 36–56 (2009)
17. Bierlaire, M., Robin, T.: Pedestrians choices. In: Timmermans, H. (ed.) Pedestrian Behavior Models, pp. 1–26. Emerald, Bradford (2009)
18. Gray, R.M.: Vector quantization. IEEE ASSP Mag. 1(2), 4–29 (1984)
19. Linde, Y., Buzo, A., Gray, R.: An algorithm for vector quantizer design. IEEE Trans. Commun. 28(1), 84–95 (1980)
20. Fernández, F., Borrajo, D.: Two steps reinforcement learning. Int. J. Intell. Syst. 23(2), 213–245 (2008)
21. Taylor, M., Stone, P.: Representation transfer in reinforcement learning. In: AAAI 2007 Fall Symposium on Computational Approacher to Representation Change during Learning and Development (2007)
22. Fernández, F., García, J., Veloso, M.: Probabilistic policy reuse for inter-task transfer learning. Robot. Auton. Syst. 58(7), 866–871 (2010)

Cognitive Modeling of Behavioral Experiments in Network Science Using ACT-R Architecture

Oscar J. Romero[✉] and Christian Lebiere[✉]

Cargenie Mellon University, 5000 Forbes, 15213 Pittsburgh, USA
oscarr@andrew.cmu.edu, cl@cmu.edu
http://fms.psy.cmu.edu/

Abstract. The Network Science has dedicated a considerable amount of effort to the study of many distributed collective decision-making processes which must balance diverse individual preferences with an expectation for collective unity. Several works have reported their results about behavioral experiments on biased voting in networks individuals, however we will focus on the results reported on [1] on which were run 81 experiments, on which participated 36 human subjects arranged in a virtual network who were financially motivated in a heterogeneous manner and whose goal was to reach global consensus to one of two opposing choices. Multiple experiments were performed using diverse topological network configurations, different schemes of financial incentives that created opposing tensions between personal preferences, and finally different ratios of both inter and intra-connectivity among the network nodes. The corresponding analysis of the results demonstrated that changing those features of the experiments produced different kind of social behavioral patterns as a result. Thus, the purpose of this work is manifold: on the one hand, it aims to describe the possible structures that underlie the decision-making process of these experiments through the modeling of symbolic cognitive prototypes supported by a robust and complex cognitive architecture so-called ACT-R and, on the other hand, by applying modifications in the ACT-R parameters to find those subtle aspects that can either influence both the performance and speed of convergence of the experiments or cause the total inability to reach a global consensus in a reasonable amount of time.

Keywords: Cognitive modeling · Social behavior · Network science · Multi-agent systems · Cognitive architecture ACT-R · Coloring problem

1 Introduction

Most studies in the field of network science focus on the analysis of both individual and global behaviors in the absence of incentives [2–4], however, in order to observe the complex interactions that all elements of the network can show when opposing incentives schemes are present, some scenarios in which individual preferences are present but subordinate to achieving unanimous global consensus are

© Springer International Publishing Switzerland 2015
F. Grimaldo and E. Norling (Eds.): MABS 2014, LNAI 9002, pp. 239–251, 2015.
DOI: 10.1007/978-3-319-14627-0_17

proposed. A real example of such phenomenon appears in decision-making and voting processes in politics, business and many other fields.

Due to the main objective of our work is to design a cognitive model of the experiments done by [1], we focused on both the methodological aspects and the behavioral results obtained in each experiment in order to recreate these behaviors through cognitive models that were then executed in the ACT- R cognitive architecture.

In Sect. 2, the methodological fundamentals that were considered for the execution of the human experiments will be explained. In Sect. 3 the basic design principles and modules of the ACT -R architecture will be introduced. In Sect. 4 the computational cognitive modeling that reflects the results obtained in the experiments with humans will be presented and the design aspects that were taken into account for the implementation of the multi-agent system that supported the interaction among nodes (cognitive agents) will be detailed. Section 5 will analyze and discuss the results and finally, in Sect. 6 the conclusions obtained from this research will be presented.

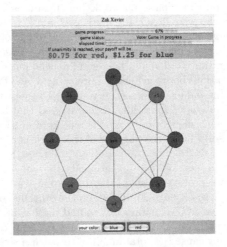

Fig. 1. Each subject sees only a local ("ego network") view of the global 36-vertex network, showing their own vertex at the center and their immediate neighbors surrounding. Edges between connected neighbors are also shown, as are integers denoting how many unseen neighbors each neighbor has. Vertex colors are the current color choices of the corresponding subjects, which can be changed at any time using the buttons at the bottom. The subjects payoffs for the experiment are shown (in this case $0.75 for global red consensus, $1.25 for blue), and simple bars show the elapsed time in the experiment and the "game progress" a simple global quantity measuring the fraction of edges in the network with the same color on each end. This progress bar is primarily intended to make subjects aware that there is activity elsewhere in the network to promote attention, and is uninformative regarding the current majority choice. This figure has been taken from [1] (Colour figure online)

2   Consensus Problem

The aim of the original experiment with humans in [1] was a typical problem from the graph coloring category which used a 36-vertex network. Every single node was only able to see a portion of the network: their closest neighbors as shown in Fig. 1.

Three different network configurations were used for the experiments: Preferential Attachment, Erdos-Renyi model and Minority Power model. Preferential Attachment model (PA) is an stochastic process in which additional nodes are added continuously to the system and are distributed among the network as an increasing function of the number of neighbors that every node already has. One of the most known scale-free networks of PA is the Barabási model [5]. Erdos-Renyi model (ER) generates random graphs, including one that sets an edge between each pair of nodes with equal probability, independently of the other edges [6], and Minority Power model (MP) is a principle mainly derivated from politics and voting models, which says that a minority of persons could attract members from the other parties, in order to do anything at all. In the following, the parameters of the experiments are described:

- Number of experiments (81): 27 with PA, 27 with ER and 27 with MP.
- Vertices (36): Initially, half of vertices (18) were randomly selected and said that red color receives the highest incentive whereas the remaining 18 were said the opposite. The exception to this rule is the MP model, on which a minority of the vertices with the highest number of neighbors were then assigned incentives preferring red global consensus to blue, whereas the remaining majority were assigned the opposite. The size of the chosen minority was varied (6, 9, or 14).
- Edge count (101 ± 1): All of the networks had 36 vertices and nearly identical edge counts. Only the arrangement of connectivity varied.
- Connectivity (inter or intra): It controls whether local neighborhoods were comprised primarily of individuals with aligned incentives (high cohesion → 1:2 inter:intra ratio), competing incentives (low cohesion → 2:1 inter:intra ratio), or approximately balanced incentives (1:1 inter:intra ratio)
- Financial incentive ($0.25–$2.25): It specifies the incentive for reaching a consensus on blue or red color which was arbitrary assigned to every node. "Strong symmetric incentive": $1.50 vs. $0.50; "Weak symmentric incentive": $1.25 vs. $0.75; and "Asymmetric incentive": $2.25 vs. $0.25.

3   Cognitive Architecture

The cognitive model was developed using the ACT-R cognitive architecture [7], [8]. Cognitive architectures are computational representations of invariant cognitive mechanisms specified by unified theories of cognition. ACT-R is a modular architecture, reflecting neural constraints, composed of asynchronous modules coordinated through a central procedural system as depicted in Fig. 2.

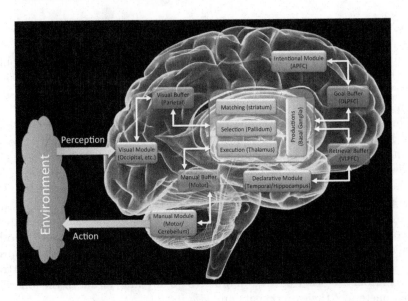

Fig. 2. ACT-R Cognitive Architecture

The procedural system is in charge of behavior selection and more generally the synchronization of the flow of information between the other modules. It is implemented as a production system where competing production rules are selected based on their utilities, learning through a reinforcement mechanism from the rewards and costs associated with their actions. The production system conditions are matched against limited-capacity buffers that control the interaction with the other modules by enabling a single command (e.g., retrieval of information, focus of visual attention) to be given at a time to a given module, and a single result to be returned (e.g., chunk retrieved from memory, visual item encoded). A declarative memory module holds both short-term information, such as the details of the current situation, as well as long-term knowledge, such as the procedural rules to follow. Access to memory is controlled by an activation calculus that determines the availability of chunks of information according to their history of use such as recency, frequency, and degree of semantic match. Learning mechanisms control both the automatic acquisition of symbolic structures such as production rules and declarative chunks, and the tuning of their subsymbolic parameters (utility and activation) to the structure of the environment. The perceptual-motor modules reflect human factor limitations such as attentional bottlenecks. Individual differences can be represented both in terms of differences in procedural skills and declarative knowledge, as well as in terms of architectural parameters controlling basic cognitive processes such as spreading of activation.

4   Cognitive Modeling

In the following, the computational cognitive mechanisms used for simulating the results of the social experiments obtained in [1] will be described. These mechanisms will be detailed in 4 subsections as follows:

4.1   Symbolic Productions

As mentioned before, the procedural system uses production rules which interact with different kind of buffers (retrieval, imaginal, declarative, visual, motor, and others) in order to carry the reasoning and inference process out according to the information that every node of the network (from now, the terms 'cognitive agent' and 'node' are equivalent) senses from its environment and acts over it. We have implemented several strategies to model the social experiments, and every one of these has a set of different productions as described below:

Follow-the-majority scenario: In this scenario, every cognitive agent senses the environment through the features in its visual buffer: (1) which color is the majority in the neighborhood (blue or red); (2) which is the current higher payoff for changing to either blue or red; and (3) whether or not is the majority color increasing through the time. As response, the cognitive agent can perform an action changing its color to either "blue" or "red". Thus, there are 4 variables (3 inputs and 1 output) and they are binary, so we have $2^4 = 16$ possible states which were reflected as productions. An example is shown in Fig. 3.

```
(p majority-red-payoff-red-majority-decrease-then-red
   =visual-location>
     isa visual-location
     !eval! (equal =increasing-majority false)
     !eval! (>= =red-color =blue-color)
     !eval! (> =payoff-red =payoff-blue)
  ==>
   +vocal>
     isa speak
     string "red")
```

Fig. 3. Production that change to red when: the majority color is red, the higher payoff is given when choosing red color and the amount of nodes of the dominant color is decreasing over time (Colour figure online)

Follow-the-most-influential scenario: In this scenario, some opposing productions compete against the others to obtain the global control over the decision-making process that performs the agent. Some productions follow the majority, some others follow that agent which is the most influential over the neighborhood (that is, that node which has more unseen connections, keeps its color for more time and when it changes its color there are a considerable amount of seen connected agents that do the same), as shown in Fig. 4; some other productions just keep the same color no matter if the environmental conditions are not favorable for that, that is, the stubborn productions. The productions are depicted in Fig. 5:

```
(p increasing-then-change-to-majority
    =visual-location>
      isa visual-location
      !eval!  (eq =increasing true)
==>
    +vocal>
      isa speak
      string "change-to-majority")
```

(a) if the dominant color is increasing then change to the dominant color

```
(p decreasing-same-majority-then-change-influential
    =visual-location>
      isa visual-location
      !eval!  (eq =decreasing true)
      !eval!  (eq =current-color =majority-color)
==>
    +vocal>
      isa speak
      string "change-to-influential")
```

(b) if current color is the same as the majority and its amount is decreasing then change to the most influential agent

```
(p increasing-then-keep-color
    =visual-location>
      isa visual-location
      !eval!  (eq =increasing true)
==>
    +vocal>
      isa speak
      string "keep-color")
```

(c) if global consensus is increasing then keep the same color

```
(p decreasing-different-majority-then-change-majority
    =visual-location>
      isa visual-location
      !eval!  (eq =decreasing true)
      !eval!  (not (eq =current-color =majority-color))
==>
    +vocal>
      isa speak
      string "change-to-majority")
```

(d) if current color is not the same as majority and its amount is decreasing then change to majority

Fig. 4. Productions related to the color changes in the cognitive agent's neighborhood

```
(p stuck-then-change-to-influential
    =visual-location>
      isa visual-location
      !eval!  (eq =increasing false)
==>
    +vocal>
      isa speak
      string "change-to-influential")
```

(a) if global consensus is stuck then choose stochastically the color of an influential cognitive agent in the neighborhood

```
(p stuck-then-change-another-majority
    =visual-location>
      isa visual-location
      !eval!  (eq =increasing false)
==>
    +vocal>
      isa speak
      string "change-another-majority")
```

(b) if global consensus is stuck then choose stochastically the color of another majority in the neighborhood

```
(p stable
    =visual-location>
      isa visual-location
      !eval!  (eq =increasing true)
==>
    +vocal>
      isa speak
      string "keep-color")
```

(c) if the global consensus is increasing then keeps the same current color

```
(p stubborn
    =visual-location>
      isa visual-location
      !eval!  (eq =decreasing true)
      !eval!  (not (eq =current-color =majority-color))
==>
    +vocal>
      isa speak
      string "keep-color")
```

(d) if current color is not the same as majority and this is decreasing then keeps the same color

Fig. 5. Productions related to the cognitive agent's internal motivations

As you can infer from Figs. 4 and 5, all the productions generate opposing tensions and a continuous competence for being the production to be fired. For example, "increasing-then-change-majority" production senses the same information as "increasing-then-keep-color" production but they trigger different actions: the first one will change its color in order to follow the majority and the second one will keep its current color if the majority is increasing (whichever its color is). Similar antagonisms are observed in the rest of productions. Due to the fact that multiple productions may match the same sensory input or that sometimes there is not a production which has a perfect match with the sensory input, a selection process based on production utilities and partial matching is required.

It is important to remark that both scenarios have another meaningful difference related to the production selection process: *follow-the-majority* scenario is completely deterministic, thus it calculates the number of seen/unseen nodes, the global consensus and the majority using always the highest number, whereas in the *follow-the-most-influential* scenario uses a stochastic selection process based on the Boltzman equation [8] as shown in Eq. 1.

$$P_i = \frac{e^{\frac{M_i}{t}}}{\sum_j e^{\frac{M_j}{t}}} \tag{1}$$

P_i is the probability that cognitive agent i follows agent j according to the function M, which can be either the majority or the most influential agent. t is the temperature which determines the randomness of the process and it is set at 0.35 for convenience.

4.2 Reinforcement Learning

The reinforcement model of ACT-R supports the utility learning mechanism of the architecture. The utilities of productions can be learned as the model runs based on rewards that are received from the environment. The utility of every production is updated according to a simple integrator model. If $U_i(n-1)$ is the utility of a production i after its $n-1st$ application and $R_i(n)$ is the reward the production receives for its nth application, then its utility $U_i(n)$ after its nth application will be as in Eq. 2 (typically, the learning rate α is set at 0.2).

$$U_i(n) = U_i(n-1) + \alpha[R_i(n) - U_i(n-1)] \tag{2}$$

In our experiments, cognitive agents were requested to maximize their expected total reward over a given number of trials and learn about the structure of the environment by taking into account the reward associated with each choice. Due to the fact that we used two modeling scenarios for the productions, we proposed two different reinforcement algorithms for each one of these.

Follow-the-majority Reinforcement: the reward is equal to the *higher − payoff* $\times k$ (with k as a constant) when the unanimity is reached by all individuals. Otherwise, if the current color of a node is equal to the majority color (observed in its neighborhood) then the reward is equal to $payoff/60$. If the current color is equal to the global consensus color the node receives and extra reward of $payoff \times 0.5$. If the node change the color when the majority decreases or keep the same color when the majority increases then the reward increases $payoff \times 0.01$. Otherwise, the payoff increases $payoff/20$.

Follow-the-most-influential Reinforcement: if the current color of the node is equal to the observed majority, then the reward is equal to: $payoff/100$. An additional reward is received from the influence that node i has over its neighbors, so if color of node i is equal to neighbor j then node i receives and increment of $k_1 = 5$. An additional reward comes from the validation whether the current number of nodes in consensus is higher than the previous number of nodes in consensus, in that case the reward would increment $payoff/60$ Otherwise would decrease $payoff/20$.

4.3   Multi-agent Approach

The experiments were run over a multi-agent platform on which multiple cognitive models interact through perception and action processes as shown on Fig.6

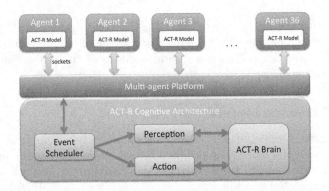

Fig. 6. Multiple cognitive models interact with the ACT-R architecture through a multi-agent platform. Socket channels make easier the communication between layers and an event scheduler is in charge of triggering the events of perception and action for every cognitive agent. Even though all the models share the same cognitive architecture (ACT-R), each one has its own separate set of productions, declarative memories, partial matching selection process and buffer contents; which are carried out through a multithreading approach.

5   Experimentation

The purpose of the experiments is manifold: firstly it aims to evaluate both the performance and convergence speed to reach a global consensus, secondly it expects to get close similar results between the cognitive simulation and the real

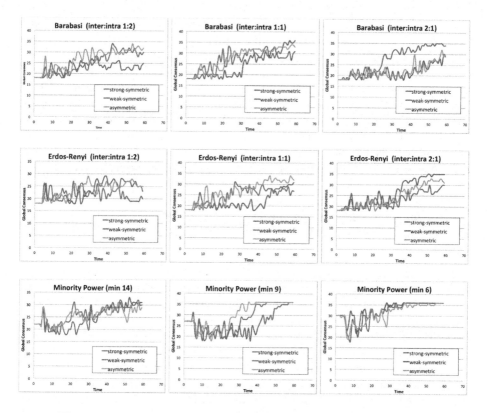

Fig. 7. Visualization of the collective dynamics for all 27 experiments

experiments with humans, thirdly it seeks to find meaningful variances regarding to the different network configurations and, finally, it aims to evaluate the differences between the different scenarios and modeling strategies proposed.

Results According to the Network Configuration: each one of the 27 experiments (3 network models × 3 intra-inter connectivity topologies × 3 incentive schemes) were run 100 times and the results were averaged using the harmonic mean value: 2700 experiments in total. The results are shown in Fig. 7.

A general remark about the results is that we had to include opposing and competing productions (such as making the wrong decision, following the minority, or being stubborn and never change the original color selection) in order to produce interesting convergence curves within the 60 seconds that lasted every experiment, otherwise the convergence was promptly reached and no meaningful differences were observed between all network configurations. In addition to that, only the results from the 'follow-the-most-influential' strategy are shown in Fig. 7 because of their similarity with the original experiments with humans.

From Fig. 7 we can remark some issues: In the Babarási experiments, the network configuration with a strong-symmetric incentive and a 2:1 inter-intra connectivity had the quickest and most stable (that is, the one that had the least fluctuations) curve of convergence. In a similar manner, both the Erdos-Renyi and the Minority Power experiments evidenced a quickest and most stable unanimous consensus whit a network configuration composed of a weak-symmetric incentive scheme and a 2:1 inter-intra connectivity. From left to right we can observe that Cohesion experiments (Babarási and Erdos-Renyi) gradually increase the degree of convergence when the number of inter-connections are augmented and symmetric incentives are kept. Asymmetric incentives worked better with both 1:2 and 1:1 inter-intra connectivity topologies. On the other hand, Minority Power experiments reached an unanimous consensus quicker than the Cohesion experiments. Specifically, an asymmetric incentive scheme seemed to work better when the minority was smaller (9 and 6 cognitive agents) in which case the majority was quickly influenced by the well-connected minority (at $\cong$ 30 s) despite of the fact that appreciable fluctuations were present at the early seconds.

Comparison Between Agent-Based vs. Human-Based Experiments: Table 1 summarizes the similarities and differences between both kind of experiments. Agent-based experiments were divided into 2 strategies: follow-the-majority (strategy-1) and follow-the-most-influential (strategy-2). Rather than looking for the perfect accuracy of the obtained results between human and agent-based experiments, the most pertinent question concerns whether the results are proportional and whether they are significantly different from each others. From Table 1 is possible to infer, for example, that in human-based experiments, the Minority consensus (88.89) got a proportional increment of success of 16.67 % over the Babarási consensus (74.07) and 54.16 % over the Erdos-Renyi consensus (40.74), whereas for the strategy-1 this proportional increment was 19.34 % and 24.19 % and for strategy-2 was 17.73 % and 53.3 % (the latter strategy was very close to the results of the human-based experiments). In general, Strategy-2 (*follow-the-most-influential*) obtained more similar results in relation to the human-based experiments than Strategy-1, suggesting that the more an agent supports its decision on the most influential agent in the local neighborhood instead of the local majority, the quicker the network reach an unanimous consensus and the more similar the results are in comparison with human-based experiments.

In order to estimate whether there is a significant difference between the results, we have performed an analysis of the variance of the three groups (the human-based and the two agent-based experiments) through an Anova test. Starting from defining as the null hypothesis: *"h_0: all the three groups of experiments are equal and do not reflect meaningful differences"*, we executed an Anova single factor test ($P < 0.01$) which analyzed both between and within group variances. As result, we got that $F < F_{crit}$ ($0.25 < 2.38$) for the variance analysis between human-based experiments and strategy-2 experiments, which means that null hypothesis may not be rejected and implying that strategy-2 does model in a more similar way the global and individual behaviors observed in the

Table 1. Comparison between agent-based vs. human-based experiments. St-1 means Strategy-1, PI is the Proportional Increment (%) of the highest value marked with an ∗ in relation to the other two values on the left column.

Feature	Human	PI %	St-1	PI %	St-2	PI %
Global Consensus all exp.(% succ.)	67.90	–	58.89	–	63.15	–
Averaged Convergence (sec.)	43.90	–	55.60	–	32.26	–
Standard Deviation	9.60	–	2.76	–	2.81	–
Mean Square Error	–	–	16.12	–	4.90	–
Consensus Babarási (% succ.)	74.07	16.67	55.56	19.34	56.67	17.73
Consensus Erdos-Renyi (% succ.)	40.74	54.16	52.22	24.19	32.17	53.30
Consensus Minority (% succ.)	88.89	∗	68.89	∗	68.89	∗
2:1 inter:intra (% success)	77.78	∗	64.44	∗	70.00	∗
1:1 inter:intra (% success)	44.44	42.86	56.67	12.05	42.23	39.67
1:2 inter:intra (% success)	50.00	35.71	55.56	13.78	62.22	11.11
Weak-symmetric (% success)	70.37	13.93	61.11	-1.85	60.00	8.48
Strong-symmetric (% success)	51.85	36.58	55.56	7.4	48.89	25.42
Asymmetric (% success)	81.76	∗	60.00	∗	65.56	∗

social experiment. On the other hand, we got that $F > F_{crit}$ (1.31 > 0.98) for the variance analysis between human-based experiments and strategy-1 experiments, reflecting that there is a significant difference between the experiments and therefore strategy-1 does not properly model the social behavior experiment.

6   Conclusions and Future Work

According to the results discussed on Sect. 5, the agent-based strategy that follow-the-most-influential agent in the local neighborhood seems to simulate better the results obtained by the social experiments with humans. However, there are some issues that are worth being discussed: The strategy-2 (following-the-most-influential-agent – that agent who has more seen and unseen connections with other agents) turns out to be a key differentiator compared to strategy-1 (follow-the-majority) because the former plays with the uncertainty of what color decisions are operating behind these unseen connections instead of just following the current state of the local neighborhood which in most of the cases comes up either in arbitrary fluctuations or in local sub-networks that do not want to change their preferred color.

Nevertheless, it is important to remark that strategy-2 used a stochastic selection process instead of a deterministic one as in strategy-1. The stochastic approach avoids both falling in recurrent states on which different parts do not come to an unanimous agreement and forming sub-regions with different color choices. Due the stochastic nature of the selection process, agents can follow sometimes the most influential agent, sometimes the local majority or sometimes just becoming in a stubborn agent. However, because of the stochastic process uses a temperature factor that controls the randomness during the experiment execution, better decisions are more likely to be made instead of bad or non-conciliator decisions.

We have chosen these two main strategies because they were the strongest ones identified in the social experiments with humans. Humans used another kind of strategies, of course, but they were irrelevant for the cognitive modeling work because they mostly rely on exogeneous conditions such as boredom because of the way the experiments were carried out, changes in temperature in the room, misunderstandings about the purpose of the experiment and so on.

Regarding to production utilities, they play an important role because they reflect which decisions may favor a global consensus in the future by adjusting their current relevance through a learning process, which will determine which productions will be more likely to trigger in future situations. In spite of the fact that strategy-2 got similar results in comparison with the human-based experiments, the results could be improved by modifying the reinforcement functions of the utility learning process in order to better reflect how the stubbornness of some agents may affect both the convergence towards an unanimous consensus and the global performance. Stubbornness was a key factor for the simulation because it reflected natural social phenomena such as the indecision of some humans, the conflicting interests or simply the absence of attention of some humans who miss the dynamics behind the scenes during the experiment execution and then kept always the same preferred color.

Along these lines, stubbornness should be consider as a key aspect that reflect a natural aspect of human decision-making that should be considered in depth when carrying out cognitive modeling. It might be worth mentioning that cognitive architectures provide a principled framework to model individual differences in both knowledge and capacity, and that a population of individual agents with variations in capacity might provide some results that are fundamentally different from any that can be generated with a uniform population, i.e., the network aspect of the domain provides some non-linear dynamics that the typical averaging in cognitive experiments doesn't address. As a final remark, modeling social behaviors is an complex task which should have into account some other aspects of human decision-making such as mood states, intentions, expectations, game strategies and so and so forth. Modeling these aspects probably would improve the accuracy of our experiments.

Acknowledgments. This work was conducted through collaborative participation in the Robotics Consortium, Agreement W911NF-10-2-0016.

References

1. Kearn, M., Judd, S., Tan, J., Wortman, J.: Behavioral experiments on biased voting in networks. Nat. Acad. Sci. **106**(5), 1347–1352 (2009)
2. Kleinberg, J.: Cascading behavior in networks: algorithmic and economic issues. Algorithmic Game Theory **24**, 613–632 (2007)
3. Granovetter, M.: Threshold models of collective behavior. Am. J. Sociol. **83**, 1420–1443 (1978)

4. Schelling, T.: Micromótives and Macrobehavior. Norton, New York (1978)
5. Barabási, A.: Emergence of scaling in random networks. Science **286**, 509–512 (1999)
6. Bollabass, B.: Random Graphs. Cambridge University Press, Cambridge (2001)
7. Anderson, J.R., Lebiere, C.: The Atomic Components of Thought. Lawrence Erlbaum Associates, Mahwah (1998)
8. Anderson, J.R., Bothell, D., Byrne, M.D., Douglass, S., Lebiere, C., Qin, Y.: An integrated theory of the mind. Psychol. Rev. **111**(4), 1036–1060 (2004)

Author Index

Printed in the United States
By Bookmasters